DELIVERANCE FROM WITCHCRAFT

To: My beloved daughter, Teda my dear
son-in-law, Ivor and my
precious grandchildren.
May you all be led by
GOD'S HOLY SPIRIT OF TRUTH
TO

DELIVERANCE FROM WITCHCRAFT

TO FAMILIES IN EVERY
NATION !!!!! ♡ ♡ ♡ ♡♡

FROM:

The Woman called Moses

Mom, mother in law
Nanna

03-08-2019

Library of Congress Control Number:		2018906664
ISBN:	Hardcover	978-1-9845-3088-2
	Softcover	978-1-9845-3087-5
	eBook	978-1-9845-3086-8

Print information available on the last page.

Rev. date: 06/08/2018

To order additional copies of this book, contact:
Xlibris
1-888-795-4274
www.Xlibris.com
Orders@Xlibris.com
770949

Because of the multitude of the whoredoms
Of the well-favored harlot,
The mistress of witchcrafts,
That sells nations through her whoredoms
And families through her witchcrafts.
Behold I am against thee, saith the Lord of Hosts;
And I will discover your skirts upon your face,
And I will show the nations your nakedness,
And the kingdoms your shame.

—Nahum 3:4–5 (King James Version)

FOREWORD

The title of this text was given to me on Sunday, January 22, 2017, during a sermon that was being preached at church. The sermon was entitled "Being Double-Crossed." In the middle of the preaching, when the entire sanctuary was charged with the awesome presence of God, the Holy Spirit dropped into my spirit and impregnated me with the title of this book, *Deliverance from Witchcraft*, in seed form. The pastor was preaching a series entitled Favor in the Famine, and he based his preaching on the biblical character Joseph. Long before I met this pastor, I was experiencing some extremely painful situations in my personal life years ago in my native country. In my "innocence," I was a victim of a situation, but I remembered standing in my kitchen, in the house my heavenly Father had blessed me with, and comforting myself with this thought: "Joseph was thrown into the pit and imprisoned through no fault of his own."

However, in retrospect, God had been preparing my spiritual womb to birth the book during this season in my life by allowing this pastor to water the seeds the Holy Spirit had deposited in me over the years. Every message the man of God preached from December 25, 2016, to the month of January 2017 caused the seeds of his greatness that were residing in me to be watered and begin springing up. God used my now-deceased spiritual father, who was from my native country, to start sowing seeds of greatness in me, and for this, I am extremely grateful. However, for this season in my life, he has divinely selected this other preacher to water the seeds that were sown in me.

When I received the name of the book, I knew the time had come for me to step into my labor room and produce my loaves and fish, which I knew would be blessed by Almighty God, my deliverer, and would be used to feed multitudes in every nation of the earth, throughout all generations. I am glad my heavenly Father has caused me to sit under the ministry of this prolific author to prepare me to give birth to my first book. I call my present home the birthing place, a spiritual hospital where whoever enters will be healed and delivered from the spirit of witchcraft, because I believe the same God who delivered me from that demonic spirit is no respecter of persons and is willing to do the same for whosoever surrenders wholeheartedly to the will of his holy Word.

Like the Virgin Mary did when she had a visitation from the Holy Spirit, I said yes to *Deliverance from Witchcraft* with my whole heart and soul and mind and strength. This script is my "virgin" book being downloaded from the portals of heaven as I faithfully waited to hear what the Holy Spirit would say. I finally came to the realization that he was skillfully putting together all the broken bits and pieces of my life from childhood to adulthood. Over the years, I have come to the realization of the importance of totally surrendering to my heavenly Father's will for every new season of my life.

Furthermore, during my time of seeking God early on Thursday, January 26, 2017, the Holy Spirit of truth revealed through God's holy Word in Nahum 3:4–5 that "the mistress of witchcrafts sells nations through her whoredoms and families through her witchcrafts." But he also revealed the intention, purpose, and plans of his Holiness. Almighty, omniscient, omnipresent, omnipotent God is Creator of the universe and all that dwell here. Almighty God's intention, based on verse 5 of the mentioned text, was, still is, and will always be to expose this spirit of whoredoms and reveal the nakedness and shameful acts of the enemy. Through this heightened awareness of the plots, schemes, and wicked devices of the enemy, Almighty God made a way of escape for me through the precious blood of Jesus.

Almighty God delivered me from this spirit of whoredoms, and my prayer is that the Alpha and the Omega, who is the same God, the beginning and the end, will deliver families, nations, and all generations—past, present, and future—from this spirit of witchcraft. I invite people of every creed, race, and tongue from every nation to embark with me on this journey as we explore together the true meaning of witchcraft from the perspective of God's holy Word and also as I tell my story of deliverance from manipulation, which is the spirit of witchcraft.

Almighty God loves us and is concerned about what happens to us as individuals, to our families, and to our nations. So let it be done in accordance with his holy Word, as he promised in Isaiah 61:11 that he would cause righteousness and praise to spring forth before all nations.

Acknowledgments

I would like to honor my deceased parents for all they did to provide for me and prepare me for my life's journey.

I would like to acknowledge my present husband for watchfully praying over my soul while I spent countless hours laboring over *Deliverance from Witchcraft*.

I would like to thank all my children for loving me and encouraging me to move forward in spite of my imperfections, especially my eldest daughter and my son-in-law for their prayer support over the years.

I would also like to thank all the true friends and families from my native country who've walked with me on life's journey for over twenty-five years and witnessed many of my struggles. I would also like to thank all those who were part of my first listening audience for taking the time to help me review parts of my manuscript.

I would like to thank everyone from the different churches, every pastor, missionary, elder, apostle, prophet, evangelist, teacher, and minister in the body of Christ who prayed with me, encouraged, and inspired me as we labored on the mission field over the past years.

ENDORSEMENTS

"Deliverance from Witchcraft" is a book needed today to tear down this spirit with many faces. I thank God for giving The Woman called Moses the desire to take on this enemy and bring it down. During the years I have known The Woman called Moses, she had been a woman of her word, a woman of God and a woman with great character and strength. Through this book that The Woman called Moses was bold enough to write, it will bring to reality that witchcraft not only exists, but is present today in various forms. It is truly a spirit that The Woman called Moses desires to make all readers aware so they are fully prepared to defeat the powers of darkness.

Through the testimonies shared, the Word of God and The Holy Spirit's guide, any reader can be delivered and healed from this tormenting spirit. I personally have grown and received healing and deliverance as The Woman called Moses has shared her experiences and covered me in prayer as she pleaded The Blood of Jesus over my life. May everyone experience true deliverance as they walk this journey out with The Woman called Moses, and then apply the Word of God to their personal lives. This is a book that everyone should have.

Elder Tamara Horn Williams-
Saved by Grace Ministries

The Woman called Moses has written a must- read primer for anyone who wants to understand Biblical Principles on "Deliverance from witchcraft." Read this book; it will empower and enlighten you!

Pastor Paula Smith-
Pastor & Founder Of Holy Arm Ministries
and Holy Arm International Church

"With today's issues, trials and tribulations that seem to be rapidly occurring in our lives, we are often faced with situations and struggles where we know neither the root cause nor the source. Many times there are unforeseen spiritual forces that have been released and assigned to work against us to keep us from fulfilling our God given purpose and destiny. The Woman called Moses in her timely new book, **'Deliverance from witchcraft'** is not only going to expose the enemy and his tactics, but is also going to give you, insight and revelation and inspire you to get the deliverance and breakthrough that you have been waiting for! Be free!

Elder Carolyn Jesse Johnson

CONTENTS

Section 1 The Veil of Darkness

Chapter 1   Natural and Spiritual Darkness..............................1
Chapter 2   God's Provision for the Sin of Ignorance.................6
Chapter 3   The Faces and Disguises of Witchcraft................13
Chapter 4   The Spirit of Divination.....................................19
Chapter 5   Observer of Times, Enchanter, Charmer.............27
Chapter 6   Witch, Wizard, Consulter of
             Familiar Spirits, Necromancer 34
Chapter 7   Sex Trafficking..38
Chapter 8   God Warns through Dreams and Visions.............44
Chapter 9   Pit Prayers of Desperation for Deliverance.............56

Section 2 Living in the Kingdom of Darkness

Chapter 1   Humble Beginnings 63
Chapter 2   The Family Religion: Religious Teachings
             at Home and School.......................................69
Chapter 3   The Picture-Perfect Family.............................77
Chapter 4   Celebrating Christmas in the Dark...................85
Chapter 5   Spirit of Rebellion: Tips for parents 89
Chapter 6   Transition Due to Emotional Turmoil 95
Chapter 7   For Better or for Worse 103
Chapter 8   The Headless Family......................................111
Chapter 9   Seeing God as Our Heavenly Father.................121

Section 3   Translated from the Kingdom of Darkness

Chapter 1   Translation from One Kingdom to Another 131
Chapter 2   Born-Again Experience 139
Chapter 3   Learning and Indoctrination 145
Chapter 4   On Christ the Solid Rock 150
Chapter 5   Mysterious Happenings at My Parents' Home 154
Chapter 6   Jesus My Best Friend in My New Home 160
Chapter 7   Deliverance and an Almost
            Near-Fatal Car Crash 166
Chapter 8   God Reveals Himself as the Great I Am 172
Chapter 9   The Righteous Judge Appears 181

Section 4   Empowered to Overcome Darkness Within

Chapter 1   Transition 189
Chapter 2   First Call to Ministry 195
Chapter 3   Following Jesus through the Wilderness 203
Chapter 4   God Reveals Himself as the Lord of Hosts 208
Chapter 5   The Blood of Jesus Works 215
Chapter 6   Introduction to the Prophetic Ministry 224
Chapter 7   Witnessing Spiritual Deliverance 230
Chapter 8   Jesus, King of Kings and Lord of Lords 236

SECTION 1

THE VEIL OF DARKNESS

In the beginning God created the heaven and the earth.
And the earth was without form and void; and
darkness *was upon the* face *of the deep.*
And the spirit of God moved *upon the* face *of the waters.*
And God said, Let there be light: and there was light.
—Genesis 1:1–3

CHAPTER 1

Natural and Spiritual Darkness

Have you ever been scared of the dark as a child? It's a frightening experience for some children to be alone in bed in a darkened room. In times past, the mother would light a candle and whisper a prayer, tuck the child under the covers, sit by the bedside until the child fell asleep, then blow the candle out with a soft smile on her face. In modern times of electricity, she would just plug in "the lesser light," the night-light, and that would be comforting to the child who's afraid of the dark. If a child woke up screaming in the middle of the night because of a bad dream, daddy, if there was one around, would rush into the room and flick the switch so the greater light from the light bulb would flood the room. I keep a light on in my bathroom area not because I'm afraid but because my eyes will hurt if I have to peer into darkness to see my way. When the light is on, I focus on it, and that enables me to walk through the dark until I get to the light. I pray that you stay focused on the light of God's Word as we examine the veil of darkness.

The omniscient God, the one and only true and ever-living God whose heart is overflowing with loving kindness, mercy, and grace for lost humanity, doesn't want us to live in the dark. In the beginning of time, when there was darkness, his solution was to create light for humanity to see. Genesis 1:16 clearly states that God, in his infinite wisdom, created two great lights: the greater one to rule by day and the lesser one to rule by night. Man has always imitated Almighty God, the Creator of the heavens and earth and everything therein. God moved by his Holy Spirit and created light in the heavens with the intent of dispelling darkness. I believe God's creation inspired man in his quest to dispel darkness on the earth and create light.

According to the article "History of Lighting," from the website www.historyoflighting.net, "there is evidence that the earliest candles were made from whale fat in China during the Quin Dynasty, some 200 years B.C. In India, about the same time, they were made from wax that was a residue of boiling cinnamon." The same website acquaints us with the transition from candles to gas and kerosene lamps, to electric lamps, then to the discovery of the first commercially used electric light discovered in the 1870s by Joseph Swann and Thomas Edison ("History of Electric Lamps and Lighting"). Now we simply flick the switch and pay the electric bill. Some of us pay without a hassle, while others reap the penalty of being disconnected by the electrical service provider. The consequence for late payment is increased charges on the electric bill. Ultimately, nonpayment of the bill will result in us living in darkness.

The truth is that no human being wants to live in darkness in the twenty-first century. Consequently, we in the Western world all find ways of being connected to the light. Unfortunately, according to the *Washington Post*'s website, www.washingtonpost.com, in 2012, nearly 25% of the population of all developing countries had no electricity, and around the world, 1.3 billion people lacked access to electricity ("Living in the Dark"). The following statistics were published on the website on November 6, 2015, and updated on November 10, 2015:

Asia—Nearly 2 out of 10 people do not have electricity; 622 million of 3.6 billion do not have electricity.

Sub-Saharan Africa—About 7 out of 10 people do not have access to electricity; 622.6 million of 1.1 billion people in Africa do not have electricity.

We are so grateful to Almighty God, our Creator, that he set the greater lights in the heavens to give light to the earth—the greater light to rule the day and the lesser light to rule the night (Genesis 1:14–18). The text continues that God saw he had done a good thing then, and it's still a good thing now because people in countries without electricity can see through the light of God's creation. Scientists are even now tapping into God's creation of the greater light to produce electricity through solar technology. In the beginning, there was indeed a veil of darkness over the earth, and God did more than create lights to enable humanity to see clearly. God set the lights in place so we know beyond the shadow of a doubt that both the greater and lesser lights will be in operation every day and night. If we choose not to pay our electric bill, we'll suffer the consequence of living in the dark, and sadly, this would affect every area of our life and the lives of those around us. Our heavenly Father, on the other hand, is so full of mercy, compassion, and love that *he makes the sun rise on the evil and on the good, and sends rain on the just and the unjust.* Our Father wants all humanity to live in the light, benefit from the light, and ultimately become light to shine for him (Matthew 5:45–46).

Have you ever arrived home after sunset, walked into your house, flicked on the light, and asked your family member, "Why are you sitting in the dark?" and the immediate response would be "I can see!"? Darkness can creep up on us; we get used to it, so we train our natural eyes to continue reading or doing whatever we were doing in the dark. Have you ever turned the light on in someone's bedroom before the natural sunlight arose and gotten the response "Turn the light off, it's too bright!" Or have you ever tried to drive toward the east and encountered the blazing glory of God's rising sun? It's so blinding that you have to grope for a pair of sunglasses to protect your eyes from God's greater light. How can something that's so powerfully good cause discomfort at the same time? It's one of God's heavenly mysteries. But the universal truth prevails, and light will always penetrate darkness to cause us to see clearly to transact our daily affairs. God, in his infinite wisdom, lifted the veil of darkness over my life gradually, as I was a victim of witchcraft and unaware of it. God counseled me in his holy Word through preachers and teachers with the help of his Holy Spirit. So take my hand and walk with me, because what he has done for me he will do for you and for others as we journey together and lift this veil of darkness step-by-step. You may be living in your midnight hour, which may have lasted for years, but we know beyond the shadow of a doubt that just as Almighty God set the sun to shine in the heavens, he has predestined his light to penetrate your darkness.

There's natural darkness and natural light, and there's also spiritual darkness and spiritual light. Omniscient God, who created the greater and lesser lights, is a spirit, and he wants his spiritual light to penetrate the veil of spiritual darkness over our lives. He wants us to see everything from his heavenly perspective. I was living under a cloud of darkness for years, but I was unaware of it; however, before time collided with eternity, our almighty, omniscient God had a plan to transition me to the light. Have you ever heard or used either of the idiomatic expressions "ignorance is bliss" and "what you don't know won't hurt you"? Well, as a young child, I was ignorant, unschooled, unlearned, and not taught about sexual abuse, and it caused me years of heartache, not bliss. Additionally, I really didn't know there were evil people in the world who would plan to control and manipulate you and cause you to fall into traps through deceptions and lies. My deceased father worked hard until his retirement and sacrificed to build a house for his family. However, there are some people who will connive and try to steal the inheritance others have labored for, through unorthodox secret methods. But the all-knowing, only wise God whom I serve is "a God of gods, the Lord of kings, and a revealer of secrets" (Daniel 2:47).

God revealed the secret plans the devil had to destroy my life and leave my innocent children orphaned and homeless. I am and will be ever so grateful that the Most High God rules and reigns in the affairs of this world. I don't know the origin of the saying "God doesn't like ugly," but I agree with it wholeheartedly. Somehow, in my state of ignorance and innocence, God protected me and delivered me from the spirit of witchcraft, and with all my heart, I want him to do the same for you. Firstly, I must warn you that the events of my story may sound like a modern-day soap opera, but trust me, I'll give you the PG version, not the rated-R version. God, through all the changes and seasons of my life, allowed his light to shine and penetrate the darkness around me and within me, bit by bit, all for his glory.

Heaven alone knows why we do the things we do habitually. We have all done things in ignorance, and it has been said that we are products of our childhood. Our ability to communicate through words and actions or, conversely, through lack of words and actions started as a baby and was developed in time. We learned language and behavior from our parents and from family members around us. We learned from authority figures at school and at church. But how can you tell if one of your authority figures at home, school, the neighborhood, or church is living under a dark cloud? Do we throw punches and temper tantrums at God for allowing terrible things to happen to us? If we are not protected through family prayer and the power of God's Word, evil will surely grab hold of us and bring us under that veil of darkness. However, God, in his infinite mercy, can somehow take every crooked piece of our history and divinely connect and fit the pieces together with the connecting thread of his healing, cleansing blood.

In the Bible, which is God's holy Word, there are lots of accounts of the difference between good and evil, crooked and straight, and righteous and unrighteous acts. However, if people live under a cloud of spiritual darkness all their lives and don't know why they lead unproductive lives, please forgive their ignorance. Before we investigate what God says about witchcraft (which he hates, by the way), I would like to acquaint you with the fact that the almighty, omniscient God has made provision for the sins of ignorance in his holy Word. It's always his intent that we will turn from darkness to light and shine for his honor and glory.

Chapter 2

God's Provision for the Sin of Ignorance

Leviticus 4:1-3 (KJV)

As mentioned earlier, if we do things in ignorance, we will reap the consequences of making bad choices. But I invite you to explore the meaning of the word *ignorant* from the dictionary and then from God's holy Word. According to *Webster's New World Dictionary of the American Language*, the word *ignorant* means "lacking knowledge, education or experience, uninformed or unaware of."

Since Almighty God saw it fit to deliver me from being a victim to the spirit of witchcraft by revealing himself to me over a period of years, I've developed a habit of seeking him early, as he admonishes us from his holy Word. It has been said that the early bird catches the worm. Well, one morning, in my quest for truth and wisdom, my spiritual eyes were opened by the Holy Spirit of truth when he stopped me in my tracks at Leviticus 4:1–28. I stopped at the light of his holy Word and started to plead the blood of Jesus as my spiritual eyes popped open, and he gave me a deeper revelation of the true heart of Almighty God. I knew from John 3:16, "for God so loved the world that he gave His only begotten Son that whoever believes in Him should not perish but have everlasting life." But this scripture from the Old Testament made me more aware of the fact that God didn't want us to be separate from him because of the things we do. Even now I am still extremely amazed at the length and depth and breadth and height of God's infinite love for humanity.

In Leviticus 4:1–28, God made provision for all those who committed the sin of ignorance; they could atone for their sin with the ceremonial shedding of the blood of an animal, depending on the individual or individuals who acknowledged their guilt. Firstly, if an anointed priest sinned and did something that was contrary to God's commands, he had to bring "a young bullock without blemish unto the Lord for a sin offering" (verses 3–12). In the same manner, if the whole congregation sinned through ignorance and it was hidden from "the eyes of the assembly," when the sin became known, then the whole congregation had to offer "a young bullock for the sin, and bring him before the tabernacle of the congregation" (verses 13–21). If a ruler sinned through ignorance, was found guilty, and then came to an understanding of his sin, he had to bring a young male goat without blemish to offer up as a sin offering before the Lord, who is holy (verses 22–26). Lastly, in verses 27–35, this chapter states that "if any one of the common people sins through ignorance" and acknowledges guilt, he or she needs to bring "a female kid goat without blemish" as an offering for sin.

Even though the animals were different—a bullock without blemish for spiritual leaders and the congregation, and a kid goat for other leaders and civilians—there was a similarity in how the sin offering was to be done. The process was the same for each person who had sinned in ignorance. They were guilty but at first were unaware of their sin. God's hand of mercy was extended to the guilty ones until they were made aware of their sin, and then they acknowledged it and decided to bring their sin offering to God's chosen assembly and submit to God's leaders in the assembly. In each instance, the anointed priest had to obey the ceremonial law prescribed during that dispensation. He had to slay the animal, apply the blood on "the horns of the altar," and "pour out all the blood at the bottom of the altar." In addition to that, the anointed priest had to take all the fat and the inward parts of the animal and burn them on the altar of sacrifice. We are told in verse 31 that the priest should make atonement in this manner, and the sin would be forgiven. The individual or individuals would be at one with God again and begin to walk in the truth of his word with the intent of pleasing God and not themselves.

It is interesting to note that there were four categories namely the priests, the congregation, the rulers and the common people, so we realize it's possible for our modern-day spiritual leaders and church people to commit sins of ignorance. The same God of the Old Testament has made provision in the New Testament for forgiveness of sin by means of bloodshed. Hebrews 9:22 states, "And according to the law almost all things are purified with blood, and without shedding of blood there is no remission of sin." It further states in verse 28, "So Christ was offered once to bear the sins of many." The words of this scripture were the inspiration of our church hymn.

Nothing but the Blood

What can wash away my sin? Nothing but the blood of Jesus;
What can make me whole again? Nothing but the blood of Jesus.
Oh! Precious is that flow that makes me white as snow;
No other fount I know, nothing but the blood of Jesus.
For my pardon this I see, nothing but the blood of Jesus.
For my cleansing this my plea, nothing but the blood of Jesus.
Nothing can for sin atone, nothing but the blood of Jesus.
(*Baptist Hymnal*, 1975 edition, 158)

In the Old Testament, the blood of bullocks and goats and lambs were poured out on the altar of sacrifice to make atonement for sin. God wanted his church to be cleansed and free from sin, and he also wanted political leaders and civilians to be free from the sins of ignorance. He wanted people in the old dispensation to be close to him, and that's why he made provision for cleansing. God doesn't want humanity, which he created, to be separated from him, and one of his prophets from the former dispensation explains to us what causes us to become separate from our holy God.

> Behold the Lord's hand is not shortened, that it cannot save: nor his ear heavy that it cannot hear. But your iniquities have separated you from your God; and your sins have hidden his face from you, so that he will not hear. For your hands are defiled with blood, and your fingers with iniquity. Your lips have spoken lies; your tongue has muttered perversity. (Isaiah 59:1–3 NKJV)

God wants to hear and answer our prayers, but he wants us to repent and acknowledge all the things we have done or said in ignorance, unknowingly, especially when we reap the consequences of our thoughts, actions, and words. Almighty God, who knew we would sin ignorantly before we were born, has also made provision for his people to be cleansed, made whole, and become attuned to God's will and purpose on earth. During the former dispensation, God instructed the earthly anointed priests to kill and present the sacrificial blood of animals to be poured out on the altar of sacrifice. But for this dispensation, we see Jesus as the sacrificial Lamb of God, "slain from the foundation of the world" (Revelation 13:8 NKJV). We also see the picture of Jesus painted as our great high priest in Hebrews 4:14–16.

> Seeing then we have a great High Priest who has passed through the heavens, Jesus the Son of God, let us hold fast our confession. For we do not have a High Priest who cannot sympathize with our weaknesses but was in all points tempted as we are, yet without sin. Let us therefore come boldly to the throne of grace that we may obtain mercy and find grace to help in time of need.

I had to stop and smell the roses, and in the stillness of his holy silence, I waited as the Holy Spirit was breathing new light and life and wisdom from this scripture that I knew would impact my life forever. Like the proverbial early bird, I allowed this fresh revelation, which theologians call rhema, to worm its way and penetrate deeply into my mind. My spiritual womb had been opened when I received that fresh download from God's heavenly throne. The bridegroom seated at the right hand of the throne in majesty in the heavens (Hebrews 8:1) had impregnated his spiritual bride here on planet Earth. My spiritual eyes and ears had been opened, and consequently, in obedience, I started to taste the Word of God and put it in my mouth and mixed it by faith because I wanted it to remain with me (Psalm 34:8).

I was in the culinary school of the maestro himself as the Holy Spirit, such an excellent teacher, gave me a divine strategy when he brought to my remembrance Hebrews 4:2. My mouth became the mixing bowl, and my tongue became the whipping spoon as I put this Word in my mouth, mixing it repeatedly with the life blood of Jesus. He reminded me of the teaching technique of repetition I had used countless times in the classroom as an elementary school teacher. Like a broken record, I began to release these words into the atmosphere: "Almighty, omniscient God forgives us for sins of ignorance!" Something unexplainable began to happen! I believe my brain was being washed by the blood of Jesus, and this fresh school of thought was being implanted in my soul, replacing every vestige of shame, guilt, and regret of everything that had been done to me, as well as what I had done when I was a slave to sin. I had been arrested by the Holy Spirit of truth and emerged from my secret place impregnated by the awesome wonder of God's irresistible love. I wish you and everyone you know who was either a victim of witchcraft or trained to be a perpetrator of witchcraft could have the same experience in His Majesty's presence.

God always warns us beforehand about dangers we may encounter, because he wants his sons and daughters to be aware of possible dangers so we can avoid them. Sadly enough, there are some adults who had no one to warn them and teach them the difference between good, which is God's way, and evil, the devil's way. Consequently, we were manipulated and coerced into succumbing to things that were contrary to God's holy Word. I will forever be grateful to Almighty God for sending help from his heavenly sanctuary to make me aware of the fact that I had stumbled into the devil's woodyard on more than one occasion. Not only did he reveal it through his special agent, his Holy Spirit, and his holy Word, but he also made a way of escape for me as I cried out in my desperation.

Well, I studied the account of God's provision for sins of ignorance in Leviticus 4:1–25 in the Old Testament during that dispensation of time, and I started to fall in love all over again with the heart and mind of our heavenly Father, who does not change. I put two and two together as my gaze shifted to the New Testament.

But if we walk in the light as He is in the light, we have fellowship with one another, and the blood of Jesus Christ his son cleanses us from all sin. If we say we have no sin, we deceive ourselves and the truth is not in us. If we confess our sins, He is faithful and just to forgive us our sins and to cleanse us from all unrighteousness. (1 John 1:7–10)

So armed with this knowledge, as I compared scripture and married the Old and the New Testaments, I threw myself at the mercy of the high court of heaven, where the honorable, righteous Judge was presiding on his glorious throne, and my defense attorney was Jesus Christ, my Savior and Lord. I confessed I was a slave to sin and plea-bargained my life in reckless abandon with the Most High God, Creator of the universe. The only witness I called upon then and will always call upon after my confession was my High Priest, who paid the price of his precious blood for me and lost humanity on the cross of Calvary more than two thousand years ago. Just as a mother prepares bathwater for herself and her babies and young children to cleanse them when they become filthy, I have been preparing the bathwater of the blood of Jesus. If found guilty as we study the faces of witchcraft, I invite you to step into the bathwater of the blood of Jesus. Please allow me to present another reminder about the blood, taken from another hymn.

There Is a Fountain

1. There is a fountain filled with blood
drawn from Immanuel's veins;
And sinners plunged beneath the flood, lose all their guilty stains.

2. The dying thief rejoiced to see that fountain in his day,
And there may I though vile like he wash all my sins away.

3. Dear dying lamb, your precious blood shall never lose its power,
Till all the ransomed church of God be saved to sin no more.

4. Ever since by faith I saw the stream
your flowing wounds supply,
Redeeming love has been my theme and shall be till I die.

(William Cowper, 1771, *Baptist Hymnal*, 107)

CHAPTER 3

The Faces and Disguises of Witchcraft

As a child in the Caribbean, I used to watch the TV show called *Bewitched*, and it was entertaining at that time watching people disappear and appear with just a twinkle of Samantha's nose. When I arrived in the USA, I found out about Halloween, an American custom. Some people purchase costumes and dress up like witches, as it's customary when they celebrate Halloween, and they do it for fun. I'm not certain if they really understand who a witch is and what she does to make a living. According to *Webster's New World Dictionary of the American Language*, a *witch* is "a woman supposedly having supernatural power by a compact with evil spirits, a bewitching or fascinating woman or girl." Well, based on that explanation, we see that a witch can be a woman or a girl who has made a pact with evil spirits of the devil with the intent of bewitching or fascinating people.

Why would someone entertain the thought of bewitching or beguiling people? The answer can be found in Nahum 3:4: "Because of the multitude of the whoredoms of the well-favored harlot, the mistress of witchcrafts, which sells nations through her whoredom sand families through her witchcraft." This woman commits whoredoms; she is popular and is destroying nations and families for money. We know that a whore is a woman who sells her body in exchange for money, with the intent of pleasing men. She may be doing it to provide for her children and may not be aware that she is under the spell of witchcraft as, by her dress and behavior, she entices men. Some women have agents called pimps who not only provide customers for the woman committing the whoredom but control the woman; she becomes the pimp's slave and is a victim of witchcraft. Both the whore and her agent, the pimp, are destroying their families for money by making a pact with the devil through witchcraft. The devil hates families and will offer you money and fame in one hand with the intent of destroying your family with his other hand while you are enjoying his money for a season.

How does God feel about witchcraft? He tells us in the book of Nahum 3:5, "I am against you says the Lord of Hosts and I will discover your skirts upon your face and I will show the nations your nakedness and the kingdoms your shame." God is against witchcraft being committed in families and in nations. Some heads of nations sell their nation and make pacts with evil spirits for fortune and fame, and as a result, the innocent victims in nations suffer the consequences for what the head of the nation did in secret. The Lord of Hosts, who is the King of kings and the Lord of lords, will fight our battles for us if we choose Jesus Christ to be the head of our household. He will expose the evil plans of the enemy, who is seeking to destroy families and nations of the earth.

Let's come to the fountain of blood flowing from Calvary's cross and pray, "Heavenly Father, we thank you that you love us with an everlasting love and you sent Jesus to pay the price for our sins. By faith, we plead the cleansing blood of Jesus over our families and the families who are being victimized by witchcraft. We pray that you make a way of escape for every family in every nation from this wicked, devilish spirit of witchcraft. We pray for conviction and repentance for those who may have been performing acts of witchcraft as a result of the actions of their forefathers. We take authority in the spirit and break this generational curse in Jesus's name and release generation blessings over their lives from this day forward, in Jesus's name! Amen!" (prayer written by the Woman Called Moses).

The Word of our holy God explicitly states in Deuteronomy 18:10–12, "There shall not be found among you anyone that makes his son or daughter pass through fire, or that uses divination, or an observer of times, or an enchanter or a witch, or a charmer, or a consulter with familiar spirits, or a wizard or a necromancer. For all that do these things are an abomination unto the Lord." Before God took the chosen nation of Israel into the Promised Land, he warned them against adopting some of the practices the heathens were performing. Leviticus 20:4–6 explains that it was customary for the heathen "to give their seed to Molech" and "to go a-whoring after wizards and those who had familiar spirits." According to *Strong's Exhaustive Concordance of the Bible*, Molech was the chief deity of the Ammonites. Almighty God, Creator of all mankind, is concerned about what we do in our children's lives and about all ungodly influences they may be subjected to. God, the only righteous Judge, declared emphatically that anyone that was practicing such an abomination during that dispensation would be killed.

Sacrificing Children

And they caused their sons and daughters to pass through the fire, and used divination and enchantments, and sold themselves to do evil in the sight of the Lord, to provoke him to anger.
—2 Kings 17:17

I suspect there may be generations of children whose hearts and minds are filled with hatred and animosity concerning the things they were subjected to as children. Not only have they turned away and rebelled in disgust at the injustices they were subjected to as children, but some of them have actually become angry at God. This is especially so if their bodies were violated by a religious figure. A popular unanswered question to some has always been—and I believe will always be—"God, where were you when I was molested, raped, or abused as a child?" Another popular question asked, with hands thrown up in despair, would be "Why me, Lord?" This act of witchcraft done to children and families in every nation is such an atrocity that the Lord of Hosts, who fights our battles for us, says he is against this shameful spirit of witchcraft and will expose it.

I believe family prayer erects an umbrella of protection over family members. Jesus himself taught us to pray in Matthew 6:13: "Deliver us from evil." If there's no family prayer, there's no protection, and this is a spiritual door, an open invitation for the evil one to take a foothold in someone's life. Parents may do their very best in meeting all their children's physical needs and taking them to church, but if there is no family prayer at home or no open discussion about sexual matters, the devil will enter that situation. When I was touched inappropriately in the girls' bathroom at the age of nine years, I was in ignorance and told no one. A couple of years later, when I was touched inappropriately by another girl a little older than me, I kept this dark secret to myself. Thank God I didn't adopt the lesbian lifestyle, but the demonic door of promiscuity was opened during my teenage years, which resulted in date rape, as I was looking for love in all the wrong places. God knew and understood the history of my stolen innocence and created an opportunity for me to be rescued from the spiritual whoredom, manipulation, and control. This spirit of whoredom had invaded my life, but in God's perfect timing, he sent help from his heavenly sanctuary and rescued me from the clutches of the enemy.

In our dispensation of God's grace and mercy, the one and only true and living God is extending mercy to any parent or parents who used their innocent child or children to commit to this spirit of witchcraft for the purpose of material gain. Sometimes parents may not know what to do and may have even prayed about the situation. However, if they did not take action and report the child abuse to the proper authorities or child protective services, it would be considered neglect because they failed to take action. This apparent lack of godly counsel would affect their child or children, who would become pawns in the devil's devices to destroy their lives and families. Confession and forgiveness are now available to anyone who runs to the open arms of Calvary and receives cleansing from the blood of Jesus. After true conversion has taken place in that parent's soul, he or she would have to acknowledge their sin of neglect to the child or children and ask for their forgiveness. Healing can then take place in the heart of the child, who may still be angry or bitter at the parent because of that seed of unrighteousness that was planted as a child and that grew into a tree of bitterness.

On the other hand, there are parents who have become and are still victims of witchcraft unawares. They may be stuck in a way of life but have accepted it as their norm, knowing deep within that something's not right, and their faces may be filled with shame and guilt. They may be living in such a state of gloom and doom, void of understanding and never imagining that God has already made a way of escape through the healing, cleansing blood of Jesus. As a fisher of souls, my assignment is to throw out to you the lifeline of the blood of Jesus, praying that you allow the Holy Spirit of truth to arrest you and bring you out one step at a time. As we meditate on the power of the blood of Jesus, allow me to present another hymn to you. It may not be your family, but there are other families in our communities, our cities, and our nations whose lives have been affected by this demonic spirit of witchcraft. Since I've begun my assignment, the Holy Spirit of truth has had me ministering to other families affected by this spirit. At the same time, he's giving me a deeper awareness of how individual families may have been affected by this evil spirit of witchcraft. I am no longer a victim, and with my whole heart, I thank God for delivering me from the witchcraft that was in my personal life. God is no respecter of persons, and the same God who delivered me can deliver families, generations, and nations.

1. Out of my sorrow, bondage and night,
Jesus I come, Jesus I come;
Into thy freedom gladness and light, Jesus I come to thee;
Out of my sickness into thy health, out of
my want and into thy wealth,
Out of my sin and into thyself, Jesus I come to thee.

2. Out of my shameful failure and loss, Jesus I come, Jesus I come;
   Into the glorious gain of thy cross, Jesus I come to thee,
   Out of earth's sorrows into thy balm, out
   of life's storms and into thy calm,
   Out of distress to jubilant psalm, Jesus I come to thee.
   (*The Baptist Hymnal*, 178.)

We can all come to Jesus by faith, believing he has the power to absolve us from every kind of sickness and sin because he paid the price for our freedom by the shedding of his blood on Calvary. Let us continue pleading the blood of Jesus by faith over the innocent generations of children who were born into a family or nation, believing for their ultimate deliverance in God's perfect timing. Even though my innocence was stolen when I was pulled into the restroom and touched inappropriately by another nine-year-old, God had already set a plan in motion over two thousand years ago to redeem me to himself because he loves me unconditionally.

Another practice that is abominable from God's heavenly perspective, which was mentioned in Deuteronomy 18:10, was the use of divination. *Webster's New World Dictionary* describes divination as "the act or practice of trying to foretell the future or the unknown by occult means." Sadly enough, I was under the veil of darkness unknowingly and was subjected to the evil spirits around me, and when I was in college, some friends and I played with a makeshift Ouija board made from a piece of glass, trying to find out who we would marry. I remember it being mysterious and scary, and after a while, I left the Ouija board alone. I'd heard about it and decided to try it out for fun. I was a novice in the game, and I didn't know what I was doing; I'm so glad I didn't look for expert help. I didn't realize I had opened a door, and the evil spirits were covering me with a thicker veil of darkness, unknown to me at that time. As the years passed, this demonic activity affected my life more and more in mysterious ways, but I had no clue it was present in my life. It took me about twenty-seven years to become completely free from this demonic entity, and that is why I'm writing with a sense of urgency to expose the plans of the enemy.

CHAPTER 4

The Spirit of Divination

In Numbers 22–24 (KJV), there is a very interesting story about Balak, the king of Moab, and Balaam, the prophet of God. This is a detailed account of the spirit of divination in action. The Bible tells us Balak was afraid and distressed because the children of Israel, God's chosen people, were his neighbors and were increasing. In other words, he became jealous and wanted to stop their progress. So he decided to let his money talk for him. Balak sent his elders of Moab, loaded with rewards, to Balaam. He wanted Balaam, the servant of the living God, to curse the Israelites, who were God's chosen people. His intention was to persuade Balaam to curse the Israelites, which would enable him to overpower them, break down their defenses, and drive them out of the land. However, the almighty, omniscient God intervened and had a conversation with Balaam and gave his decision. "And God said unto Balaam, you shall not go with them, you shall not curse the people for they are blessed" (Numbers 22:12). God emphatically stated that the Israelites were blessed.

Now what do you think happened when Balaam relayed the message to the elders that God had refused to allow him to go with them or take their money? Balak, consumed by the evil forces of witchcraft and divination, apparently didn't fear God and was not at all perturbed by what God said. Balak was filled with the desire to control the Israelites and decided to send more influential men with promises, because he thought he could bribe Balaam with promises of grandeur. He told his men to remind Balaam, in case he didn't understand who he was, that it was Balak and that his father's name was Zippor. He encouraged Balaam and said he shouldn't let anything prevent him from coming to see Balak. This was his persuasive promise: "For I will promote thee unto very great honour and I will do whatsoever thou sayest unto me: come therefore I pray thee, curse me this people" (Numbers 22:17).

This seductive plan to promote and honor Balaam was extremely tempting, and he responded to Balak: "And Balaam answered and said unto the servants of Balak, if Balak would give me his house full of silver and gold, I cannot go beyond the word of the Lord my God, to do less or more" (Numbers 22:18). Sadly enough, I don't believe Balaam understood clearly what Almighty God had said the first time—that he shouldn't curse the nation of Israel, because they were blessed. He went to Balak, and God was angry with him. But through a series of events, Balaam learned the following lesson: "God is not a man that he should lie; neither the son of man that he should repent: hath he said, and shall he not do it? Or hath he spoken, and shall he not make it good? Behold I have received commandment to bless: and he has blessed: and I cannot reverse it" (Numbers 23:19–20).

In spite of Balaam's disobedience to God when he followed Balak, God was still merciful to Balaam and helped him understand that he meant what he said the very first time. Sadly, this enemy of doubt will keep coming to us, causing us to doubt the sincerity of the one and only true and living God. The voice of the enemy was silenced, and Balak learned that all his money, power, and influence were no match for the Lord God Almighty. "And when Balak saw that it pleased the Lord to bless Israel, he went not, as at other times, to seek for enchantments, but he set his face toward the wilderness" (Numbers 24:1). Even though Balak decided to desist from his plan to have someone else curse the children of Israel, because they were divinely protected by God, he still didn't decide to serve our living God.

In Acts 16, in the New Testament, there is an account of the spirit of divination in action. "And it came to pass, as we [Paul and Silas] went to prayer, a certain damsel possessed with a spirit of divination met us, which brought her masters much gain by soothsaying: The same followed Paul and us, and cried saying, These men are the servants of the most high God which show us the way of salvation." She did this for many days, and Paul was so grieved that he commanded that tormenting spirit to set her free in the name of Jesus Christ. The damsel received deliverance instantaneously. When the masters who had been controlling the damsel saw that they had lost their means of livelihood, they caught Paul and Silas and brought them before the city officials, namely the rulers and magistrates. These Roman officials falsely accused Paul and Silas, who were Jews, of causing great upheaval in the city. The accusers convinced the city magistrates that Paul and Silas were teaching customs that were contrary to their Roman beliefs, and consequently they couldn't receive or observe them.

The entire multitude and the magistrates were enraged and stripped Paul and Silas and commanded them to be beaten. After such a severe beating, they were given to the jailer, who had received strict orders to keep them locked away in the inner maximum security section of the prison. What a price Paul and Silas paid for their staunch and firm belief as they demonstrated that anyone can be delivered from demonic forces in the name of Jesus. They were naked, and I am sure that they were bleeding and wounded and that their feet were chained to the stocks. We don't know if they were hungry, but one thing is for certain: they were definitely hurting. The story continues that at midnight, Paul and Silas did the unexpected, as they had to develop a plan of action. These two hurting God-fearing men came to a unanimous decision. This decision had to have been made by the revelation of the Holy Spirit. They prayed to the almighty God, Creator of the universe, and sang praises to the Most High.

In the midst of their praises, Almighty God, with all power in his hand, bowed the heavens and came down and rocked the foundations of the prison. This terrific earthquake caused all the prison doors to open, and all the prisoners were loosed from their bands. In the midst of all this commotion going on around him, the jailer awoke and was about to kill himself because he thought the prisoners had escaped. Paul, however, shouted out to him in the midst of the darkness and reassured him they had not escaped. With fear and trembling, the jailer fell down at the feet of Paul and Silas, calling them sirs and asking them what he needed to do to get saved. *"And they said, Believe on the name of the Lord Jesus Christ, and you shall be saved and your house" (Acts 16:31 KJV)*. Consequently, the jailer took them into his house that same hour of the night. He washed their stripes and fed them. He and his entire household were baptized, and a family of believers was born into the kingdom of God through Jesus Christ because Paul and Silas were radical in their faith.

This damsel was possessed, which means "controlled by a demon (an evil spirit)" (*Webster's New World Dictionary*). She was being controlled by "a spirit of divination"; *divination* is "the act or practice of trying to foretell the future or the unknown by occult means" (*Webster's New World Dictionary*). Her masters were making a lot of money through her by the practice of *soothsaying*. According to *Strong's Concordance, soothsaying* is derived from the root word meaning "to divine," i.e., to utter spells (under pretense of foretelling) by soothsaying. This girl was being controlled by others who were influencing her for the purpose of making money. It reminds me of how I was being used unawares at the age of twenty-three as a pawn in someone else's greed for control and power. As the saying goes, "there's nothing new under the sun," and every life experience can be found in the Bible, the holy, unadulterated Word of God. At that time, I didn't know what was happening to me, but in retrospect, I see the hand of an almighty and majestic God who had a plan to not only rescue me but use me to expose the plans of the enemy, to enable other damsels to be set free from exploitation, manipulation, and control.

God used Paul, whose personal testimony is as follows and is recorded in his own words in Acts 26:9–15. Paul acknowledged that he had made a determination to do many things that were contrary to the name of Jesus of Nazareth. While in Jerusalem, he had shut up many saints in prison because he had received authority from the chief priests. He had also given verbal assent in support of those who were being put to death. He added that he had been extremely mad at them and had often punished them in every synagogue and had compelled them to commit blasphemy. He admitted to persecuting them until they fled into strange cities. He talked about when he was on his way to Damascus with sanctions of commission and authority from the chief priest. At midday, he saw a light in the heavenly realm that was brighter than the noonday sun. This light was shining around him and his entire entourage, who were journeying with him. In unison, they all fell to the ground, and a great voice asked him an extremely pertinent question. The voice spoke in Hebrew and called him by name and asked him why he was persecuting him. Saul, as this was his name before his conversion, inquired the name of the Lord, who had called his name and had knocked him off his feet. The majestic voice declared that he was Jesus, whom he had been persecuting. Saints, if you are being persecuted for your faith, just remember that your persecutors will have to answer to the Lord God Almighty.

Paul was influenced by the beliefs of his religious leaders, and being fully persuaded they were right, he submitted to their evil, wicked plans and punished and killed Christians. However, Almighty God, who is the Alpha and Omega and who knows the beginning and the end, already knew the plan and purpose he had predestined for Paul's life, even though at that time he was traveling on a path of destruction. On the road to Damascus, as Paul was commissioned by earthly authority, the Most High God delivered him from the antichrist as God penetrated the veil of darkness over his mind. His spiritual eyes were opened by a light from heaven (Acts 9:3), and he lost his natural sight for three days (Acts 9:9).

We see that Paul's account of his own behavior and divine encounter with Almighty God was the prelude to this damsel's deliverance from this spirit of divination. Paul was now operating under the influence of and totally submitted to God's heavenly authority. He had been snatched from the influential forces of darkness and was walking in the fullness of the light of God's holy Word on his way to prayer, accompanied by Silas (Acts 16:16–19). The damsel was uttering positive words and acknowledging them as "servants of the Most High God, which show us the way to salvation" (Acts 16:17), but Paul realized she wasn't genuine. After listening to her chant for three days, Paul, whose spiritual ear was now attuned to the Holy Spirit of truth, was grieved because she was being used in such an ungodly way. He addressed the evil spirit that was controlling her mind: "I command thee in the name of Jesus Christ to come out of her" (Acts 16:18). It was revealed in the same verse that it came out of her instantly. Our heavenly Father, the one and only true and living God, will always cause us to triumph and be victorious if we put our absolute faith and trust in him when we are tested.

The person under the influence of divination knows the correct influential words to say to entice you into their confidence, and Paul, who was influenced by the Holy Spirit of truth, recognized this evil spirit. Sadly, however, I encountered this spirit of divination in my life. I was a damsel, about twenty-two years old, recently graduated from college, and had left my home in anger and rebellion, not realizing that the enemy wanted to control me. My father, a hardworking man, had provided well for his family and built us a beautiful home when I was about nine years old; my mother was a homemaker who took care of her family's immediate needs. However, I had never heard the words *I love you* in our home. I was ignorant of the devil's devices and the "love" bait he uses. I stepped right into the devil's territory and fell prey to the spirit of divination when the magic wand with the words *I love you* was waved in my direction. When young girls are ignorant of the enemy's devices, they fall prey to anyone's enticing words, whether male or female. People of the world can sense where there is an unmet need, whether it is emotional, social, or physical, and entice innocent victims by meeting their needs. I would like every girl to know from the cradle that there's a real spiritual thief whose intent is to steal our destiny and hinder God's plan and purpose for our lives.

The same God that said *the use of divination* was an *abomination* in the Old Testament delivered Paul in the New Testament, because he, too, was being used as a pawn by those in authority to kill and destroy innocent lives. Almighty God had already made provision for the "sins of ignorance" by the shedding of animal blood during that dispensation. Now the same merciful God who can read the hearts of men somehow knew that, in his perfect timing, Paul would get the revelation of the power of the Blood of Jesus and receive the gift of God's redeeming grace, which brought conversion to his soul. Paul received his spiritual sight when the veil of darkness was lifted, and he realized he had been prey to this spirit of divination. He was a passionate man by nature, but now his passion was intertwined with God's purpose for his life. His new agenda to transact kingdom business can be found in Acts 26:15–18.

> I am Jesus whom you persecutest. But rise, and stand upon your feet: for I have appeared unto thee for this purpose, to make thee a minister and a witness both of these things thou hast seen, and of those things in the which I will appear unto thee; Delivering thee from the people, and from the Gentiles, unto whom now I send thee, To open their eyes, and to turn them from darkness to light, and from the power Satan unto God, that they may receive forgiveness of sins, and inheritance among them which are sanctified by faith that is in me.

When Paul surrendered to Jesus by the divine encounter he had on his journey to Damascus, his spiritual eyes were opened, and he was delivered from the power of Satan unto God. Paul opened up his heart to receive his purpose from God and, from that day, submitted himself to godly leadership and received fresh instructions about his function in the kingdom of God. God changed Saul's name to Paul when God visited him and converted his soul.

After Paul's conversion, he was able to understand clearly that Almighty God had a plan and a purpose for all his future endeavors. God revealed through his Holy Spirit of truth that he was calling Paul to minister and be a witness in his spiritual kingdom. God further outlined to Paul that he had a deliverance ministry. Paul learned that God was delivering him from people's opinions and was assigning him to the Gentiles. God's intention was for the Gentiles, representing unbelievers everywhere, to be turned from darkness to light and from the power of Satan unto God.

God wants us to confess and receive forgiveness for our sins and be washed by the precious blood of Jesus. The same God who delivered Paul also delivered me from the power of satanic influence, and now I'm free, as Jesus filled the void in my heart. The arms of Calvary are still open wide through this invitational hymn taken from *The Baptist Hymnal* (179).

Let Jesus Come into Your Heart

If you are tired of the load of your sin,
let Jesus come into your heart,
If you desire a new life to begin, let Jesus come into your heart.
If 'tis for purity now that you sigh, let Jesus come into your heart,
Fountains for cleansing are flowing nearby,
let Jesus come into your heart.
If there's a tempest your voice cannot still,
let Jesus come into your heart.
If there's a void this world never can fill,
let Jesus come into your heart.

(Chorus)
Just now your doubting give o'er, just now reject him no more,
Just now throw open the door, let Jesus come into your heart.

CHAPTER 5

Observer of Times, Enchanter, Charmer

According to *Strong's Concordance*, the term *observer of times* is derived from the primary root meaning "to cover; from 6051, to cloud over; figuratively to act covertly, i.e., to practice magic; enchanter, soothsayer, sorcerer" (Hebrew 6049, 90). The term *charmer (fascinate)* is from a primary root meaning "to join (literally or figuratively) specially (by means of spells) to fascinate: charm, be compact, couple together" (Hebrew 2266, 36). The term *enchanter* is from the primary root meaning "to cover; from 6051, to cloud over." The purpose of these methods of witchcraft is deception, with the intent of controlling the minds of individuals.

Acts 8:1–22 gives us an account of Simon the sorcerer's deliverance, and if God did it then, he can do it again. This was before Paul's conversion, during the period when the early Christian church was being prosecuted after Jesus's death, so the apostles were scattered. Philip went to Samaria and was preaching about Christ and his resurrection power. Signs and wonders and miracles took place; as Philip preached about Christ, people were delivered from unclean spirits, and the lame were healed. The story continues that a particular individual called Simon had bewitched the Samaritans. He had been practicing sorcery for quite a while, giving people a false impression that he was powerful and great. He had been bewitching them for so long that everyone in the city actually believed he was a man of great influence and possessed the power of God, and they really looked up to him.

> But there was a certain man, called Simon, which beforetime in the same city used sorcery, and bewitched the people of Samaria, giving out that himself was some great one: To whom they all gave heed, from the least to the greatest, saying, This man is the great power of God. And to him they had regard, because that of long time he had bewitched them with sorceries. (Acts 8:9–11)

The aforementioned verses tell us Simon had been using sorcery among the people for a long time and had influenced both great and small. He portrayed himself as a great person, and the people believed he was portraying the great power of God.

> But when they believed Philip preaching the things concerning the kingdom of God, and the name of Jesus Christ, they were baptized, both men and women. Then Simon himself believed also: and when he was baptized, he continued with Philip, and wondered, beholding the miracles and signs which were done. (Acts 8:12-13)

Can you imagine this? Simon the sorcerer had an encounter with the one and only true and living God and decided to humble himself, got baptized, and continued following Philip. However, Simon had to be totally delivered from his former way of thinking; his heart had been touched, but he still possessed a sorcerer's mind. The apostles Peter and John arrived from Jerusalem when they heard about the miracles taking place in Samaria. They laid their hands on those who had been baptized in the name of the Lord Jesus, and they received the gift of the Holy Ghost (Acts 8:14–17).

Simon was so impressed when he saw the manifestation of the power of the Holy Ghost that he offered them money. He had been operating with this evil spirit of sorcery and charging the people money for so long that he thought he could purchase the gift of the Holy Ghost. His actual words were "Give me also this power, that on whosoever I lay hands, he may receive the Holy Ghost" (Acts 8:19). He wanted God's power to advance his business.

> But Peter said unto him, Thy money perish with thee, because thou has thought that the gift of God may be purchased with money. Thou hast neither part nor lot in this manner: for thy heart is not right in the sight of God. Repent therefore of this thy wickedness, and pray God, if perhaps the thought of thy heart may be forgiven thee. For I perceive that thou art in the gall of bitterness, and in the bond of iniquity. (Acts 8:20–23)

Peter, who was operating with a holy boldness, declared to him that his heart was not *right with God* and that he needed to repent and change his way of thinking. He cautioned him that he had to seek God's forgiveness through prayer for deliverance from this wicked spirit of iniquity (Acts 8:21–23).

> Then answered Simon, and said, Pray you to the Lord for me, that none of these things which ye have spoken come upon me. (Acts 8:24)

Simon decided to go all the way and surrender his life totally to God after he heard the preaching of the gospel of truth. God can still deliver those who are practicing sorcery in ignorance as a way of life, and he sent Jesus to bring deliverance for victims of sorcery and witchcraft.

Sadly enough, not everyone who's practicing sorcery may want to be delivered from this evil spirit, but God still wants everyone to have the opportunity to know there's power in the name of Jesus to save and bring deliverance. In Acts 13:1–12, Paul and Barnabas were led by the Holy Ghost to the isle of Paphos, and they received an invitation from the deputy of the country, Sergius Paulus, who was a prudent man. However, a sorcerer, a Jew named Bar-Jesus who was also a false prophet, withstood them because he wanted to sway the deputy away from his faith. Then Paul, who was filled with the Holy Ghost, looked directly at him and arrested that spirit of sorcery. He openly confronted the sorcerer and declared he was a child of the devil and was full of mischief and was the enemy of righteousness. He pointed out that, since he refused to turn from his wicked ways, the hand of the Lord would be upon him and he would be blind for a season. The account continues that he was immediately shrouded by a mist of darkness and was groping blindly for someone to lead him by the hand. As a result, the deputy was astonished by the Lord's doctrine and became a believer.

Paul was on a mission that was initiated by the Holy Ghost after his deliverance when the glorious light from heaven, which was brighter than the noonday sun, penetrated the darkness of his soul. I believe that when he encountered the sorcerer, a false prophet attempting to hinder the Word of truth from being imparted to the deputy, he remembered his encounter with Jesus. He had been arrested by Jesus and realized he had been used by the devil to hinder the work of God, which was being done through the early church. Paul, in turn, wanted the sorcerer to understand the serious consequences of his actions and pronounced blindness upon him for a season by the hand of the Lord. The sorcerer was immediately struck with blindness, and when the deputy saw what had been done, he *believed and was astonished by the doctrine of the Lord.* We as followers of Christ need to take a stand for God as we confront the forces of darkness and declare the manifestation of God's righteous kingdom nationwide and worldwide. When we make kingdom declarations of God's holiness and righteousness in the nations, the mighty hand of God will penetrate the darkness and eradicate the deceptions and lies and every evil, false action of the enemy, bringing deliverance to innocent victims.

Some years ago, a former pastor led his family members and his congregation, comprising so many families and innocent children, to paths of destruction. He was persuasive and influenced so many victims to drink poison. The veil of darkness had been cast over his followers for so long that they believed what they perceived to be true. Darkness can creep up on us gradually, and our eyes can get accustomed to operating in the dark. Only God knows the entire truth of that matter, but I know that when someone is exposed to the whole truth of God's Word, that person will be able to take a stand of righteousness for the truth. Isaiah 5:20 cautions us, "Woe unto them that calls evil good and good evil; that put darkness for light, and light for darkness; that put bitter for sweet and sweet for bitter." It is imperative we become accountable and make an intentional decision to surround ourselves with people of integrity who are familiar with God's standard of holiness and righteousness. People we can submit our ideas, thoughts, and plans to, who really care about us, will confront us after prayerful consideration if we go contrary to God's holy Word.

That's why I take my assignment about exposing the deceptions and wicked devices of the devil seriously. We really need under-shepherds who would emulate the Good Shepherd in Psalm 23:3: "He restoreth my soul: he leadeth me in the paths of righteousness for his name's sake."

At this juncture, allow me to remind you of our foundation scripture from Nahum 3:4–5: "Because of the multitude of the whoredoms of the well-favored harlot, the mistress of witchcrafts that sells nations through her whoredoms and families through her witchcraft. I am against you says the Lord of Hosts. I will discover your skirts upon your face and I will show the nations your wickedness and the kingdoms your shame." Almighty God hates wickedness in all forms and fashions, and he said he would expose the spirit of wickedness that seeks to destroy families and that has sold out nations. Those of us who have been delivered from darkness and are living in the kingdom of God's marvelous light have a responsibility to work with God, being empowered by his Holy Spirit of truth, to expose this evil, wicked spirit and set the captives free.

After being a baby Christian in my native country for about ten years, God appeared to me in a dream and gave me a warning to give to the church authority where I was serving. God's righteous judgment still prevails. I will give more of the account in a later chapter, but I have been inspired to ask this question from God's holy Word, in Psalm 94:16: "Who will stand up for me against the evildoers? Or who will stand up for me against the workers of iniquity?" The psalmist was making a petition to God against evil and the workers of iniquity, but God's Word is so alive that I believe in my heart that God's Holy Spirit was directing that question to me. Like Paul, after my deliverance, God used me to pray for individuals I encountered who were being affected by that same spirit of witchcraft. I was able to recognize it and pray for the deliverance of innocent victims. Almighty God can do the same for you in whatever nation you are because he is the King of nations.

Some may be going contrary to the principles of God and are operating secretly in their lust for power, but it's clearly stated in Daniel 2:22, "He revealeth the deep and secret things: he knoweth and what is in the darkness, and the light dwells with him." Because I am fully persuaded that the Lord God Omnipotent reigns, I would like to encourage you to assist me in my God-ordained assignment to begin praying for Almighty God to get into the secret places where witchcraft is in operation and interrupt the evil occurrences in families and nations. Didn't Jesus himself teach us how to pray for deliverance from evil for ourselves and our loved ones in Matthew 6:13? Didn't John, the beloved disciple, reveal Jesus's purpose and mission in 1 John 3:8? "He that committeth sin is of the devil; for the devil sinneth from the beginning. For this purpose the Son of God was manifested, that he might destroy the works of the devil." If you are in the Caribbean, the United States of America, Europe, Asia, Australia, Africa, or in any of the islands of the sea, and you are willing to stand with me against works of iniquity in your family, city, or country, please write me and my prayer team, and we will be supporting you in prayer. We'll be interceding with you until Calvary's victory is established in your family and community.

CHAPTER 6

Witch, Wizard, Consulter of Familiar Spirits, Necromancer

According to *Strong's Concordance*, the term *witch* is taken from a primary root meaning "to whisper a spell, i.e., to enchant or practice magic: sorcerer, (use) witch (craft)." According to *Webster's Dictionary*, a witch is "a woman supposedly having supernatural power by a compact with evil spirits, a bewitching or fascinating woman or girl; (verb) to put a magic spell on, to charm or fascinate." A wizard, according to *Strong's Concordance* (3049), is "a knowing one, a conjurer," and *Webster's Dictionary* also describes a wizard as "a magician, a conjurer, a very skillful or clever person."

I read an article a while back that mentioned that a magician had hung himself by placing a rope around his neck, but his death was ruled as an accident. The magician—not intentionally, but accidentally—destroyed his own life. I learned in English classes in school that a witch is the female counterpart and a wizard is the male counterpart. However, I'm aware the meaning of the word *witch* may have different meanings depending on the cultural belief system of an individual or of groups of people. Jesus clearly outlines his purpose and the devil's devices in John 10:10: "The thief cometh not but for to steal, and to kill, and to destroy: I am come that they might have life, and that they might have it more abundantly."

When we follow Jesus Christ, who is Almighty God's representative here on earth, we can experience the fullness of everything our heavenly Father has in store for us. According to *Webster's Dictionary*, *necromancy* is "divination by alleged communication with the dead." God warned us from the beginning, in Deuteronomy 18:10–12, that none of the above practices should be found among humanity and, furthermore, that they are an abomination to him. You may know someone in your family, city, or nation that may be practicing witchcraft in ignorance. Let us study the account of the witch of Endor from God's holy Word, taken from 1 Samuel 28. However, before we do, I would like to remind you that Almighty God has already made provision to forgive us for sins of ignorance if we repent and turn from our wicked ways. God doesn't want us to destroy ourselves through foolish behavior and has placed signposts along our daily path, from Genesis to Revelation, to enable us to lead victorious lives in Christ. Let us reflect on the power and purpose of the blood of Jesus with the words of one of the foundational hymns of our faith, taken from *The Baptist Hymnal* (147):

1. Have you been to Jesus for the cleansing power? Are you
washed in the blood of the Lamb? Are you fully trusting in his
grace this hour? Are you washed in the blood of the Lamb?

(Chorus)
Are you washed in the blood, in the soul-cleansing blood
of the Lamb? Are your garments spotless? Are they white
as snow? Are you washed in the blood of the lamb?

The hymn then continues to ask more pertinent questions about our state of readiness when the bridegroom, who is Jesus Christ, returns for his bride, the church. It also questions if our souls will be ready to inhabit God's heavenly mansions and refers to white robes to signify our purity after being washed in the blood of Jesus. It asks us if we are walking daily by our Savior's side and resting securely in the power of Jesus's crucifixion. Our heavenly Father wants us to be part of the marriage feast he's preparing in heaven for the bride of Christ.

In the book of 1 Samuel 15:26, Almighty God, the righteous judge, used the prophet Samuel to declare these words to King Saul: "You have rejected the word of the Lord, and the Lord hath rejected thee from being king." Now in 1 Samuel 28:1–6, we have the account that the Philistines had gathered their armies to war against Israel and that Samuel was dead. However, before Samuel's death, "Saul had put away those that had familiar spirits and the wizards out of the land" (1 Samuel 28:3).

> And when Saul saw the host of the Philistines, he was afraid, and his heart greatly trembled. And when Saul inquired of the Lord, the Lord answered him not. . . . Then said Saul unto his servants, seek ye a woman that hath a familiar spirit, that I may go to her and inquire of her. And his servants said to him, behold there is a woman that hath a familiar spirit at Endor.

The story continues that Saul, the king, disguised himself by putting on other clothes and went with two men by night to seek advice from the witch of Endor. The woman reminded the man who had come to seek advice from her that Saul, the king, had cut off all those who had been operating under the influence of familiar spirits and wizards and sent them out of the land. The witch accused him of laying a snare for her, but Saul assured her she would not be punished for practicing divination. The rest of the chapter gives an account of how the woman, through her conjuring spirit, communicated with the spirit of Samuel, who had died.

Now the Bible doesn't tell us how the witch had the ability to "bring up Samuel's spirit from the underworld." But King Saul communicated to the spiritual entity that God had departed from him and wasn't answering him anymore, not by prophets or by dreams (1 Samuel 28:15). Through his communication with the spiritual entity the woman had conjured up, Saul heard once again the words of the judgment Almighty God had pronounced on his life.

> The Lord had departed from King Saul and had rent the kingdom and given it to King David because Saul

had not obeyed God's voice. The spirit furthermore declared that the following day Saul and his sons would be dead. (1 Samuel 28:17–19)

I believe this particular chapter is teaching us that if we do not seek God for his wisdom and truth and if we disobey the Most High God, Creator of the heavens and earth, we will seek out man's spiritual wisdom. This is contrary to the plan God has for our lives. God is showing necromancy in action through the witch of Endor to enable us to see the horrific lengths humanity would go to get a word for their future. God doesn't want us to put our trust and faith in another human being who will also die just like us. God is the eternal God who knows everything about our past, present, and future. He knows our beginning and our end. I'm so glad God sent his only begotten Son, Jesus, to earth to shed blood on Calvary to cleanse those of us who are truly sorry for our wrongdoings, called sin. Why not join me at the cross as we meditate on another one of the foundational hymns of our faith? This hymn reminds us about the cross and the fact that Jesus paid the price for the sinful nature of humanity. This hymn is thought-provoking and makes us ponder on the depth of God's love for humanity and comes to the conclusion that the only way we can repay Jesus is to give ourselves to him without reservation.

At the Cross

(Chorus)
At the cross, at the cross where I first saw the light,
and the burden of my heart rolled away.
It was there by faith I received my sight,
and now I am happy all the day.

2. Was it for crimes that I had done he groaned upon the tree?
Amazing pity, grace unknown, and love beyond degree.

CHAPTER 7

Sex Trafficking

Because of the multitude of the whoredoms of the well-favored harlot,
the mistress of witchcrafts, that sells nations through her whoredoms
and families through her witchcraft. I am against you says the Lord
of Hosts and I will discover your skirts upon your face and I will
show the nations your nakedness and the kingdoms your shame.
—Nahum 3:4–5

I bowed my head with a heart of submission and in deep humility at the cross, where I first saw the light of who Jesus is. I began to seek Almighty God at this crossroad of my text for fresh enlightenment, wisdom, and understanding. I thanked God for shedding the light of Jesus on my life and delivering me from being a victim of the spirit of witchcraft. That seed of wickedness that stole my innocence in the girls' restroom had blossomed in my life during my teenage years and early adulthood and had caused me to bear the fruit of unrighteousness. But when his majestic grace shined his spotlight in my heart and planted his holy Word of truth within me, my spiritual eyes popped open, and immediately I made a conscious decision to stop dancing with the devil.

As I was praying for God's mercy to be poured out on both victims and perpetrators of witchcraft, I heard the Holy Spirit communicate with my spirit about the issue of sex trafficking. The same God who delivered me from sexual sin can deliver those who are tired of listening to the thoughts and endless demands of the devil while dancing to the rhythm of his changing beats, which I know is costly. Let's meditate on the words of this ancient hymn before we step into the devil's arena to set the captives free. May I remind you of the title of this book, *Deliverance from Witchcraft?*

Jesus Paid It All

(Chorus)
Jesus paid it all, all to him I owe.
Sin had left a crimson stain; he washed it white as snow.

1. I hear the Savior say, "Thy strength indeed is small,
Child of weakness watch and pray, find in me thy all in all."

2. Lord, now indeed I find thy power and thine alone,
can change the leper's spots and melt the heart of stone.

I stand before God's throne of mercy and grace, pleading the precious blood of Jesus over both victims and perpetrators of witchcraft among people of every nation, kindred, and tongue, for great deliverance of souls who will be captivated by God's love and will surrender to his will at the cross of Calvary. I pray for the divine intervention of Almighty God and his interruption and exposure of this modern-day slave trade in all the dark places, wherever it's occurring in territorial waters, land, and air.

I heard a story about sex traffickers who were dressed in law enforcement uniforms. Some girls had given them all their documents with the expectation of getting jobs. They housed the girls in apartments close to the dock and sexually molested them several times daily. The girls were then put on rubber boats and transported across the Mediterranean Sea from Istanbul to the country of Athens.

The coast guard appeared in the territorial waters, and to avoid being caught, the sex traffickers threw the girls overboard into the sea. Sadly, only five of the sixty girls survived and were rescued from a brothel in Athens.

I began to think about these innocent victims who had been coerced into thinking they would have a better life. Each of these girls had some sort of family. Can you imagine the parents, sisters, brothers, children, grandparents, and other blood relatives waiting and maybe praying for their precious girls, the fifty-five who would never return home? These fifty-five girls all died in such a horrific manner, and these families would never have closure because there were no coffins to close after the final view; no hymns were sung. Their precious girls had not been placed in their local cemetery, so these families would probably be mourning and wondering all the way to their deathbeds about what had become of their loved ones.

I was able to glean the following information from the website PolarisProject.org. In an article, sex trafficking is described as a type of slavery that is being practiced throughout the USA and many parts of the world. "Sex traffickers use violence, threats, lies, debt bondage and other forms of coercion to compel adults and children to engage in commercial sex acts against their will." It is considered a federal crime here in the USA to induce anyone under the age of eighteen years to engage in any type of sexual activity.

People become pawns in the game of sex traffickers for many different reasons. Sometimes these victims may become romantically involved with an individual who would then begin to manipulate and use them in unexpected ways. Some may have been baited like fish with false promises of a job either in the modeling or dance industries. Sometimes these victims are forced to become active in this sex trade for money by parents or family members. The times of involvement may vary between days, weeks, or years. A prime target for these sex traffickers could be rebellious young people who are on the run as they try to evade parental authority. Other targeted groups could be victims of domestic violence or refugees of war-torn territories. The sex trade business can be operated from different venues, which may include phony massage businesses, truck stops, motels, hotels, or recognized brothel houses. Business transactions could be conducted via various social media channels or even newspaper advertisements.

Key Statistics

- Since 2007, the *National Human Trafficking Hotline,* operated by Polaris, has received reports of 22,191 sex trafficking cases inside the United States.
- In 2016, the *National Center for Missing and Exploited Children* estimated that one in six endangered runaways reported to them were likely sex trafficking victims.
- Globally, the International Labor Organization estimates that there are *4.5 million people trapped in forced sexual exploitation globally.*
- In a 2014 report, the *Urban Institute* found that the underground sex economy ranged from $39.9 million in Denver, Colorado, to $290 million in Atlanta, Georgia.

The following is an excerpt from an online article published on the website Untold Stories of the Silenced, written on December 4, 2015, by Taneem Saeed. The article is entitled "Human Trafficking in Sub Saharan Africa."

Trafficking and Children

Trafficking of children mainly occurs because of the market for children in labor and sex trade. Sex trafficking includes bride trafficking, child prostitution and child pornography. There is a demand for underage sex and vulnerable children are becoming victims when they are trying to earn money from the so called "sex tourists." Sometimes, there is also a supply of children from poor families due to a desire to support the family economically. Children are also often exploited during armed conflicts. They may be abducted and transported by rebels as well as governments. Children are perceived to be cheap and can be brain-washed into committing violent acts.

The article also reveals that one of the reasons for trafficking children is for the purpose of sacrificing them in religious rituals. Some of these rituals, sadly enough, include uncircumcised boys, as there is a belief that killing them enhances the practice of one's spells.

The excerpts from the above mentioned articles, which were found through the Google search engine, show the atrocity of not only sex trafficking but human trafficking as well. Undoubtedly, Almighty God is using these organizations and the writers of the articles to foster awareness about the manipulation and exploitation of individuals throughout the world. According to Nahum 3:4, it is indeed "the multitude of whoredoms of the well-favored harlot," and it can be noted that this practice is being committed worldwide. The Word of God clearly states that this is indeed an extremely profitable trade occurring nationwide and worldwide that is affecting families and tearing them apart. Almighty God loves families and is concerned about every single family in every nation of the whole earth. Almighty God declares emphatically that he's against such atrocity in the nations and will expose the wicked practices of whoredoms, which he equates with "the mistress of witchcrafts" (Nahum 3:4–5).

Genesis 19:24 says, "The Lord rained upon Sodom and upon Gomorrah brimstone and fire from the Lord out of heaven." Just before this destruction, the men of Sodom were pounding on Lot's door, commanding him to bring the two visitors out to them "that they may know them." Lot pleaded with them not to perform their wicked intent of having sexual intercourse with his male visitors, and he even offered to let them have his two virgin daughters instead (Genesis 19:5–9). God, our heavenly Father, hates wickedness and loves righteousness, and that's why he sent Jesus from heaven to earth to pay the price for all manner of sin through the shedding of his precious blood on Calvary.

God's plan of salvation to rescue individuals, families, communities, and nations was motivated by his love for us, his creation, as we can witness from the following scripture:

> For God so loved the world that He gave His only begotten Son, that whosoever believeth in Him should not perish, but have everlasting life. For God sent not His Son to condemn the world: but that the world through Him might be saved. (John 3:16–17)

Humanity is being destroyed by means of self-destructive behaviors. If we make a decision to drink poison, we destroy ourselves, and it's not God's fault if we choose to ignore the warning label on the bottle.

Conversely, we may drink poison in ignorance if the label has been removed from the container, and our lives would still be devastated. God wants us to know that the spirit of witchcraft is poison. He does not want to condemn us, and he has made a way of escape for us from these hellish practices. There are signposts in God's holy Word, from Genesis to Revelation, that reveal to us the wrong path that leads to destruction and the right way that leads to eternal life. God is full of love and compassion for humanity, which is his creation, and his mercies are new every day.

CHAPTER 8

God Warns through Dreams and Visions

In the book of Revelation, Almighty God, who is the Alpha and Omega, the beginning and the end, the Omniscient One, reveals through a series of visions to the apostle John, who is in a secluded place, God's ultimate plan of righteous judgment for creation. In Revelation 17–19, we have an account of God's righteous judgment of "the great whore," but because of God's richness in his love and grace and mercy, he also utters a warning to humanity.

> And I heard another voice from heaven, saying, "Come out of her my people, that ye be not partakers of her sins, and that you receive not of her plagues. For her sins have reached unto heaven, and God has remembered her iniquities." (Revelations 18:4)

The righteous Judge has already made a way of escape from spiritual death through the blood on Calvary's cross. God has always given us a choice between doing good or evil, and we will ultimately reap the fruit of whichever way we choose.

For the wages of sin is death, but the gift of God is eternal life through Jesus Christ our Lord. (Romans 6:23)

From the beginning, God also gave man the power of choice and consequence.

I call heaven and earth to record this day against you, that I have set before you, life and death, blessing and cursing: therefore choose life, that both you and your seed may live: That you may love the Lord your God, and that thou may obey His voice, and that you may cleave unto him: for he is your life, and the length of your days. (Deuteronomy 30:19–20)

Our heavenly Father always gives us choices because we are not puppets on a string. He doesn't want us to control others and make them puppets. In Nahum 3:4–5, Almighty God promised to expose to the nations the multitude of whoredoms committed by "the well favored harlot," otherwise known as "the mistress of witchcrafts." Her assignment is to sell nations and break up families through her witchcraft.

The Most High God, who is the Lord of Hosts, reveals to us his righteous judgment of "the great whore" in Revelation 17–19, and he also reveals to us her sphere of influence over the nations. The Holy Spirit of truth reveals to us, in the words of the apostle John, "I will show you the judgment of the great whore that sits upon many waters" (Revelation 17:1). The Holy Spirit of truth further reveals to John that the waters he had seen, where the whore sat, were multitudes of people from different nations who spoke different languages (Revelation 17:15). The name of this spiritual woman is written on her forehead: "MYSTERY, BABYLON THE GREAT, THE MOTHER OF HARLOTS AND ABOMINATIONS OF THE EARTH" (Revelation 17:5). The woman, as aforementioned, is "well favored," and the Holy Spirit of truth reveals her attire of wealth and opulence.

Her wardrobe consists of garments that display royal colors of purple and scarlet. She has decorated herself with all manner of precious stones and jewelry. Metaphorically speaking, she is drinking from a golden cup she holds in her hand. That cup is full of "abominations and filthiness of her fornication" (Revelation 17:4).

This spiritual entity is referred to as a woman, but evil spirits have no gender. She is referred to as a whore because of a whore's propensity to allure people of the opposite sex in exchange for currency. So this spirit of temptation is widespread in every nation, among people of different languages. Even today lonely men will sit in dens of iniquity, paying for drinks to intoxicate their bodies, and satisfy their lust by looking at women dancing on a pole, all because of the temptress called the mother of harlots. How many people, I wonder, have been tempted and persuaded to commit abominations in secret for the sake of money, position, and power? Instant gratification is the name of this pleasurable game of lust, but many of them don't realize the full significance of this cup, which was handed to them on a golden platter. I am certain many became addicted to this cup of abomination, and after partaking of the cup for a season, they looked into the cup they were partaking and saw their faces. I'm sure it must have been tormenting to look into the cup in their hands, to look at themselves and what they had become. In their minds, there was only one way out, and that was seemingly to drown their shame and guilt with more wine and more women, listening to the alluring voice of the temptress luring them deeper into the pit of destruction. But I am so glad that we are in the dispensation of the richness of God's grace and mercy and that he's giving humanity an opportunity to "repent, and be baptized in the name of Jesus Christ for the remission of our sins" (Acts 2:38).

About forty years ago, I made the decision to follow Jesus Christ as my Lord and Savior. After being abused and then used by the spirit of witchcraft in practicing sexual immorality, I cried out to God, and he delivered me. Let's meditate on another one of my favorite hymns.

Love Lifted Me

1. I was sinking deep in sin, far from the peaceful shore,
Very deeply stained with sin, sinking to rise no more.
But the master of the sea, heard my despairing cry,
From the waters lifted me, now safe am I.

(Chorus)
Love lifted me, love lifted me when nothing
else could help! Love lifted me.

The second verse describes how, when his love lifts us out of sin and a life of hopeless despair and sin, it causes us to cling to Jesus. It becomes so personal because you just want to live in his awesome presence and, with a heart full of gratitude, sing well-deserved praises to him. After coming to a full understanding of the depth of God's powerful and strong love for lost humanity, we need to serve our Savior lovingly because we now belong to him. The hymn also appeals to souls who are in the midst of life's dangers and perils to look to Jesus, who is the Author and Finisher of our faith. It encourages those who are surrounded by situations that may be causing emotional turmoil and distress in their souls to cry out in the midst of their despair, and God will intervene. Almighty God, our Creator, will throw out his lifeline of love through the blood of Jesus and bring salvation today to any desperate soul who may have lost their way.

Do we understand the power and passion of God's love for humanity? Can you hear his massive heartbeat of love? Do you feel the rhythm and pulse of his perfect timing for you as the arms of Calvary are extended toward you in mercy? God, through the Holy Spirit of truth, is appealing to those who are in darkness to come and be washed in Jesus's blood, clean of all the fleshy desires and manifestations of the spirit of witchcraft, so they can be completely free. It's such a wonderful thing to be free from the bondage of sin—no longer slaves to sin, no longer bound by bad and destructive habits.

It was revealed by The Holy Spirit through John the beloved apostle that *great men of the earth from all nations are being deceived by the sorceries of the mother of harlots* (Revelation 18:23), and it was further revealed by John that "the Lord our God who is a true and righteous judge will judge the great whore who corrupts the earth with her fornication" (Revelation 19:1–2). God dislikes corruption in any form or fashion, and he wants us to treat our fellow men in the right way; he doesn't like it when people of authority in different nations misuse their authority in deceptive ways.

Jeremiah 9:23–24 reveals to us the things that are important to God, and if our heart's desire is to please the Lord God Almighty, Creator of the heavens and the earth and all that dwell therein, this should be our road map for life.

> Thus says the Lord, let not the wise man glory in his wisdom, neither let the mighty man glory in his might, let not the rich man glory in his riches: But let him that glorieth, glory in this, that he understands and knows me, that I am the Lord which exercise loving-kindness, judgment and righteousness in the earth: for in these things I delight says the Lord.

Firstly, our heavenly Father is a God of love, and he commands us to love him with our whole heart and to love our neighbor as ourselves. Our heavenly Father also loves to exercise his righteous judgment on the earth. He wants us to do right; to love, not hate, one another; to walk in righteousness; to live right; to talk right; and to treat one another in the right way.

God declares his will again in Job 33:14–16.

> For God speaks once, yea twice, yet man perceives it not. In a dream, in a vision of the night, when deep slumber falls upon men, in slumbering upon the bed; then he openeth the ears of men, and sealeth their instruction.

Our heavenly Father, who is a spirit, loves us so much and wants us to overcome the fleshy desires to manipulate others through witchcraft for money and bribery, which causes breakdown in families.

God is speaking to humanity, but we do not perceive what he is saying. He is not only speaking once but twice, because he is a God who gives us the opportunity again and again to get things right and conduct our lives with appropriate behavior. Since these unrighteous acts are committed when we are awake, God gives us an opportunity to get things right when we are asleep, because he is a righteous Father. As a former classroom teacher, when I corrected my students' papers, it was with the intention of having them correct the mistakes on the paper, for them to learn right. I marked their papers and revealed their errors, not because I hated them, but because I wanted them to have excellent grades when they did their end-of-term examination.

The almighty, omniscient Father wants us all to make it into heaven one day to be with him.

> The lord is not slack concerning his promise, as some men count slackness; but is longsuffering to us-ward, not willing that any should perish, but that all should come to repentance. (2 Peter 3:9)

God gives us an opportunity to get it right, and while we're sleeping, the almighty, omniscient One, who has a perfect plan and purpose for our lives, opens our spiritual eyes through dreams and visions. In the nighttime, when there are no earthly distractions, he communes with our spirit and seals his blueprint and instructions for our individual lives.

Job 33 further reveals to us God's purpose for speaking to us through dreams and visions. In verses 18 and 24, we understand that God doesn't want us to go down to the pit of destruction, and he's warning us about the dangers ahead and the traps and snares the enemy has for our lives, families, communities, and nations. The almighty, omniscient God wants to make us aware of the wicked devices of the devil. God, in his merciful kindness, wants to keep our souls from going down to the pit of destruction.

Do you know of anyone who likes to be in a pit? There is no ladder in a pit. It's dark in a pit, and you can't see a way out. You feel trapped in a pit. *Webster's New World Dictionary* describes a pit as "a hole in the ground, an abyss, hell, any concealed danger, and trap." Have you ever fallen to the ground as a child and landed on your behind or on your hands and knees? Thank heavens you were able to get up. Now just imagine falling into a pit you can't get out of, and even though you have a desire to get out, you are powerless. But our heavenly Father has made a supernatural way for all of us to be rescued from the pits or traps of destruction where we have found ourselves intentionally or unintentionally.

From a report on USAToday.com, let us review the chilling modern-day rescue mission of thirty-three miners who were trapped more than two thousand feet underground for over two months (sixty-nine days) before being reunited with their families. According to the report, a mine collapsed in the Atacama Region of North Chile on August 5, 2010, trapping the miners deep underground. The rescue operation began on October 13, 2010, and ended 22 ½ hours later, as a worldwide audience monitored every development. It was stated that for seventeen days, no one had heard from the miners, who only had a three-day supply of emergency food. One can only imagine that, in the midst of this seemingly hopeless situation, they must have decided to ration their limited food supply. Somehow the emergency team of officials was able to detect exactly where the miners were trapped. The miners, however, had to pay close attention to the instructions they received that would enable the officials to facilitate their rescue. I am certain all these men wanted to emerge from that pit of darkness around them and were eager to see the light of day. I imagine they were reliving the last time they saw the smiling faces of their loved ones and were remembering the loving embraces of their wives, children, and other family members.

You may be feeling trapped like the miners because of the lifestyle that was passed on to you from your parents. Or perhaps you were a victim of circumstances and may have adopted an erroneous lifestyle and feel trapped because there seems to be no way out. Somehow you missed every attempt Almighty God has been using to get your attention, as you were not aware of how he speaks. God has been speaking through dreams and visions because he wants your spiritual ears to be open so he can imprint your life's instructions and seal it with his stamp of approval (Job 33:16).

Almighty God is a deliverer; he states in Job 33 that even on your deathbed, when you may be tormented by all your wrongdoings in the past, he would still send a messenger to give you a final opportunity to repent of all your wrongdoings before you step into your grave (Job 33:22–23). Please allow me the privilege of quoting the following text (Job 33:22–24) from the Amplified Bible.

> [God's voice may be heard] if there is for the hearer a messenger or an angel, an interpreter, one among a thousand to show to man what is right for him [how to be upright and in right standing with God], then [God] is gracious to him and says, Deliver him from going down into the pit of destruction: I have found a ransom (a price of redemption an atonement)! (Brackets in Amplified version)

God, our Creator who is always so graciously full of mercy, had a heart, even in the Old Testament, to rescue mankind from his foolish, sinful way of life. God's voice of love in the New Testament was proclaimed when Jesus was crucified on the cross and paid the ransom for our lost souls by shedding his precious blood.

For God's voice to be heard, there has to be a messenger. God's rescue mission is also captured through the words of this old foundational hymn.

Rescue the Perishing

1. Rescue the perishing, care for the dying,
Snatch them in pity from sin and the grave.
Weep o'er the erring one, lift up the fallen,
Tell them of Jesus, the mighty to save.

2. Though they are slighting him, still he is waiting,
Waiting the penitent child to receive.
Plead with them earnestly, plead with them gently.
He will forgive if they only believe.

The hymn proclaims that God understands that way down in the human heart, feelings of love have been crushed by the tempter of humanity, the devil. God knows that people's hearts have become cold and callous and that feelings of pure love can be restored by God's grace. The writer of the hymn is saying that if someone with a loving heart comes along and touches a broken heart, the broken heart would be awakened by kindness and would begin to vibrate in love once again. We are commanded to rescue the perishing because it is a heavenly mandate. The hymn advises us that God will provide the strength we need if we patiently seek out those who may be wandering aimlessly through life. We need to let as many lost souls know that Jesus, our Savior, made a way of escape for us from our sinful lifestyle, because he is the way, the truth, and the light.

The messenger declares God's desire to rescue those whose lives are wasting away, and elaborates that a ransom has been paid. According to *Webster's New World Dictionary*, a ransom is "the price paid or demanded to obtain the release of a captive." Well, Jesus himself gave a ransom for all (1 Timothy 2:6), and that means for all manner of sinners, including perpetrators of witchcraft. The ransom he paid was his shed blood on Calvary. That's the reason, as a spiritual mother in God's kingdom of truth, I have been preparing the bathwater of the blood of Jesus for us to thoroughly immerse ourselves in, by faith. Let's refresh our spirits by meditating on the previous blood songs.

There is a fountain filled with blood flowing from
Immanuel's veins and sinners plunged beneath that flood
lose all their guilty stains. (*Baptist Hymnal*, 107)

What can wash away my sins? Nothing but the
blood of Jesus. What can make me whole again?
Nothing but the blood of Jesus. (158)

Are you washed in the blood? In the soul-cleansing
blood of the lamb? Are your garments spotless? Are
they white as snow? Are you washed in the blood of the
lamb? Lay aside those garments that are stained with
sin and be washed in the blood of the lamb. (147)

The Amplified Bible continues to enlighten us, in Job 33:25–26,
about the sequence of events that will follow if we believe in the
ransom Jesus paid for us to be free from our sinful nature.

[Then the man's] flesh shall be restored; it becomes
fresher and more tender than a child's: he returns
to the days of his youth. He prays to God, and He
is favorable to him, so that he sees his face with joy:
for [God] restores to him his righteousness (his
uprightness and right standing with God—with its
joys). (brackets in original)

May I remind you of an excerpt from the aforementioned story
about the miners? "Once emergency officials were finally able to
communicate with the trapped miners, they relayed instructions in
how they had to aid their own escape." The emergency officials were
relentless in their pursuit to rescue the miners, who were trapped
about two thousand feet underground. Job is stating that when a
person on their deathbed receives and believes the words of the
messenger sent by God to rescue their soul, they receive a new lease
on life, and their life is renewed. That person who was separated from

God because of sin will be able to sense the awesome presence and power of God's love. It literally lifts your spirit when you realize you are loved by Almighty God unconditionally.

God sent his messenger, Jesus, about two thousand years ago to rescue us from our sinful path of destruction. He sent his messenger in the form of a preacher to share the good news about Jesus, and I responded to the message of repentance. I acknowledged that I needed to be rescued from sin, and I laid hold on the powerful cross of Jesus. I wanted to be free and responded to the messenger. Many others before me and after me have also responded in their desire to be free from bondage, and now it's your turn. God wants to hear from you. When you talk to him and acknowledge your sin, he will favor you. He will restore your health. You will come face-to-face with the reality of being in right standing with God, who wants you to walk in uprightness.

Now you've responded to God's love, repented in your heart, and received the joy of his forgiveness. What happens next? Does God expect anything from us? Let's continue in the Amplified Bible's account of Job 33:27–28.

> He looks upon other men and sings out to them.
> I have sinned and perverted that, which was right,
> and it did not profit me, or He did not requite me
> [according to my iniquity]! [God] has redeemed my
> life from going down to the pit [of destruction], and
> my life shall see the light. (brackets in original)

God wants us to be messengers and to continue telling the story of Jesus's redemption. He wants us to acknowledge to others that we were in the pit of destruction, that we turned to him, and that he rescued us and is keeping our soul alive so we can live in peace. Almighty God, who is the Creator of the heavens and earth and everything in it, is extending his assignment to you, for you to be part of his rescue mission to deliver the souls of men who have been captivated by sin.

You may be on your bed, afflicted with strong pain in your bones! God has been speaking once, yea twice, but you did not perceive that it was God (Job 33:14). God has been speaking to you through dreams and through visions all your life to seal your instructions, but your soul was sleeping and not taking heed. Even now, in the midst of your affliction, you have lost your appetite, but God is still speaking loudly and clearly as you lie in silence on your bed. Your flesh may be consumed or eaten away by cancer, and your bones that were not previously visible may now be sticking out; however, God is still trying to get your attention (Job 33:21). Your soul may be drawing close to the grave and your life to the destroyers, but God wants to give you an opportunity to understand what he wants to say to you.

I am one of God's messengers, sent to show you the right way, the way of deliverance, the way of restoration and healing for your soul (Job 33:23). By God's spirit, I am here with you. This book has not been placed in your hand by mistake. It's all part of God's design. If you are reading this book and know someone who may be on their deathbed as a result of the unrighteous works of their hands, please hasten to their bedside as God's messenger and show them the way to the path of righteousness. If you listen to the messenger, God will graciously deliver you from going down to the pit of the grave of hell because the ransom for your soul has been paid!

1 ⁵ This is the message which we have heard from Him and declare
to you, that God is light, and in Him is no darkness at all.

⁷ But if we walk in the light as He is in the light, we
have fellowship with one another, and the blood of
Jesus Christ His Son cleanses us from all sin.
⁸ If we say we have no sin, we deceive
ourselves, and the truth is not in us.
⁹ If we confess our sins He's faithful and just to forgive us
our sins, and to cleanse us from all unrighteousness.
(1 John 1:5, 7–9)

CHAPTER 9

Pit Prayers of Desperation for Deliverance

If your soul is in distress and you cry out to God, he will hear the prayers of your heart. I don't know how long it's going to take God to rescue you from your agonizing situation, but I can promise you he will rescue you in his perfect timing, in his perfect way. Here's a list of some of the "pit prayers" I prayed from God's Holy Bible.

> *Psalm 6:2–8.* Heavenly Father, I come to you asking for mercy. I acknowledge that I am weak, and my life is so full of troubles that my soul is being tormented by feelings of frustration. I'm pleading for your mercy, Lord, because I'm feeling weak and tired. I don't know how long it's going to take, but I ask for your mercy upon me. If I die, how will I be able to give you thanks? I feel so weary that all I can do is groan and water my pillow with my tears all night long when no one else is looking. I cry so long and hard that my bed is drenched with my tears. My eyes are all puffy and swollen because I'm grieving, because of the people who have been committing works of iniquity against me. Lord, I know that somehow you are hearing my

prayer and that you will somehow deliver me from those who are committing atrocities against me.

Psalm 25:15–18, 21. Heavenly Father, I am looking to you now and always because I know you will pull me out of the trap that has been set for me. I'm asking you to look upon my present condition with mercy and compassion, because I have no one else to turn to but you. My troubles seem to be increasing, and my heart is overwhelmed; I'm asking you to bring me out of all my distressing situations. Look upon my entire affliction and the pain I may have caused others, and please forgive all my sins, which are tormenting my soul.

Psalm 31:9–10. Lord, I'm pleading for your mercy because I am in deep trouble. I am full of grief and cry so much every day that it's affecting my physical body. I spend my life grieving because of my wrongdoings, and I'm getting weaker as I'm losing strength wallowing in my sins of iniquity as my life is wasting away.

Psalm 40:11–13. Almighty God, I'm asking you to surround me and continually preserve me with your loving kindness and your truth. Lord, please don't withhold your tender mercies from me; the works of iniquity I have performed have overtaken me, and I feel overwhelmed. I am so ashamed and laden with guilt because these shameful acts are numberless, more than the hairs on my head. My heart is failing with hopelessness, and I am not able to face you. I'm asking you, please, Lord, to help me speedily and deliver me because of your loving kindness and tender mercies.

Psalm 130:1–6. O God, I cry out to you from the depths of my soul. I'm asking you to hear me and be attentive to my prayer of supplication. Hear my desperate cry, O Lord. O Lord, if you decide to mark our iniquities, no man would be able to stand before you! You, O Lord, are able to forgive us when we make a decision to fear you, O Lord. I will hope in your Word, and I will watch because my soul is waiting in anticipation for you to shine your light, just like those who are waiting for daybreak to come.

Psalm 51:1–11. Lord, I'm pleading with you to blot out all my wrongdoings from your book of records. I know you are overflowing with loving kindness and tender mercies. Wash me thoroughly and cleanse my soul of the sin I've committed. I'm being haunted by the sin of (name the sin you have committed); I take full responsibility for what I have done, and I will no longer blame someone else for my evil and wicked actions. I have sinned against you, Lord, and have done this wickedness when I thought you weren't looking, but I'm aware now that you saw everything I was doing. You know the truth of my existence—that I was born into this sinful world because of Adam's sin of deception and lies against you. You want me to be open and honest with you from deep within my heart and not try to hide the wicked things I did in secret. Teach me wisdom from deep within my heart. Purge me and wash me and make me whiter than snow. You've broken my plans, and my selfish dreams and desires and well-orchestrated plans have been broken into pieces and dashed to the ground. I want to hear joy and gladness again all around me. Create within me a clean and pure heart that would allow me to have right motives. Please do not cast me away from the presence of your Holy Spirit, but let my spirit be renewed so I can be steadfast in my devotion to you.

Psalm 25:1–7, 11–12, 15–21. I lift my soul, my mind, my emotions, my will, my life, and my very being to you, Lord. I put my confidence and trust in you. Lord, please do not let me be ashamed. Don't let my enemies be triumphant against me. Don't let us be ashamed, Lord, because they're being treacherous for no apparent reason. Show me the right way, O Lord. Teach me the right things to do in accordance with your Word of truth. I'm waiting on your guidance all day long because you are the God of my salvation, and you will show me the way to enable me to make the right choices and decisions. Dear Lord, I ask you to remember how you have always been a God full of tender mercies and loving kindness. God, I appeal to you because you are a good God, and I'm asking you not to remember the sins I committed in my younger days. I'm asking for your mercy in spite of all the decisions I have made that were contrary to your holy Word, because I know you are a good God.

I ask you to pardon my countless works of iniquity, because now I know that, since I have decided to fear, honor, respect, and show reverence to your holy name, you will teach me your righteous ways, which would be better for me. I know you will hear me and look at my desolate situations. You will look at my pain and trouble, which are causing my heart to be overwhelmed with grief and sorrow. I feel so lonely and lost, and I'm asking you to forgive all my sins and rescue my distressed soul. Don't let me be ashamed because of my enemies who hate me in such a cruel way. I put my trust in you, as I know you will allow me to walk in integrity and uprightness before you because I am waiting for you to protect and preserve me.

Psalm 30:1–3, 10–12. Lord, my God, I lift a grateful heart unto you, because I was distressed when I thought about all those who hated me. I appealed to you, O Lord, in the midst of my calamity, and you responded. My spirit was lifted because you healed me emotionally. I was so downcast, but you brought me up out of that state of despair and hopelessness. I am alive because of you, because you didn't allow me to sink into a state of despondency. I will continually keep reaching out to you for help and mercy in the midst of life's challenges. Lord, my God, I can now strip myself of all my mourning apparel because you have clothed me with a garment of praise to enable me to dance, sing, and praise you forever.

These prayers of deliverance were inspired by the abovementioned Psalms and were all written by the Woman Called Moses.

SECTION 2

LIVING IN THE KINGDOM OF DARKNESS

He Knew You
Before you were born,
Your substance was seen in his mind's eye.
When you were still part,
Of the dust of the earth,
Your members were already written in his book!
Oh! What a marvel!
Before he formed you in the womb,
He knew you!
He fit your pieces together and set you apart,
To fulfill your life's destiny.
He could never forget you!
As your blueprint,
Is engraved,
On the walls of eternity!
—The Woman Called Moses

CHAPTER 1

Humble Beginnings

My series of deliverances has and will always be an extraordinary gift from God for his exceeding, abundant grace and mercy. The Ancient of Days, the omniscient God who inhabits eternity, saved me from my mother's womb. I was born in the Caribbean, the last of my mother's five children. Based on my mother's account, the doctor gave her some pills to abort me when I was lodged in the secret place in her womb. According to the doctor's report, she was having children too quickly, and they were concerned about her health!

I can almost sense the spiritual assignment my heavenly Father whispered to me through the awareness of his awesome presence in eternity. "I'm about to release you onto the stage of planet Earth to fulfill my plan and purpose. Many obstacles will be put in your way, but at the appointed time, when you begin to recognize my voice in the midst of all the other voices on planet earth, you will discover my blueprint for your life. You will not be aborted, because I will stretch forth my mighty right hand over your earthly father and compel him to intervene!" My earthly father received the revelation from God's heavenly throne, based on the mandate from my supernatural heavenly Father, and uttered this pronouncement to my earthly mother, who was carrying God's precious "jewel" (because that's the meaning of my real name). "You have a husband, so I say you are going to give birth to this baby!" And in accordance with God's master plan, my mother gave birth to this September jewel. My mother gave me her earthly story of my nativity, and every once in a while, I meditate on how my heavenly Father saved me from my mother's womb.

So I graciously stepped onto the stage of planet Earth, in accordance with Almighty God's clock. My heavenly Father delivered me from the womb through the process of my natural birth. Through his mighty right hand, he protected me from the womb, especially because he knew that "behold I was brought forth in iniquity and in sin my mother conceived me" (Psalm 51:5). This is the plight of every human being; because of Adam's sin, we are born with a sinful nature and the propensity to sin without being taught. Who teaches an innocent toddler to slap his baby sibling? Who teaches a child to be selfish and not want to share his toys with another child? Who teaches a child to steal cookies when parents are not looking and then lie, with the telltale crumbs in the corners of his mouth? Parents spend time correcting their children to restrict them from practicing these traits. At times, parents may ask themselves, "Did we switch babies at the hospital?" They may even accuse each other jokingly by stating, "He got that trait from your side of the family, certainly not from my side!"

I wasn't born, according to the proverbial saying, with a silver spoon in my mouth, but somehow, through the intricacies of God's divine master plan, I arrived on planet Earth without fanfare. My mother, the country girl, had relocated to the city and married my father. I realize now that since I was my mother's fifth child, I am and will forever be God's child of grace. I really believe my parents performed to the best of their ability with the opportunities afforded them on the stage of life. My father was a ledger keeper working with the city, and my mother was a homemaker. Now sixty-seven years later, I will forever be grateful to my heavenly Father for the parents he chose for me.

I didn't know what life was all about, and I don't have much recollection about my childhood. I remember that, in kindergarten school, the teacher covered my mouth with Scotch Tape; she called me a chatterbox and said I talked too much. I don't remember talking too much, but I remember the silencer that was placed over my mouth that caused me to stop speaking to be heard. I became silent, and maybe that's why I didn't say a word when I was touched inappropriately. I don't believe the average family in those days had open family discussions. Many years after, when I relocated and was working in a treatment facility for women and children, I was asked to teach parenting skills. As I was preparing parents for reunification with their children, this saying literally jumped off the page of the curriculum and made a deep impression in my heart: "When family talks, nobody walks."

This was a defining moment for me; it was as though someone had flipped a switch and allowed me to penetrate the dark corridors of my past. Things happen in families. There are both good days and bad days. It creates a positive atmosphere in the home when parents and children are able to sit together and discuss family matters when the going gets rough. I've heard the adage "What goes on in this house stays in this house." I believe that was how the older generation would place a cover on family secrets no one dared to tell. However, some of these secrets were able to escape into the neighborhood, as the gossipmongers were waiting to share the latest news on the block. Unfortunately, some people take delight in seeing families come to destruction. Thank God that I knew who my father was, that he was married to my mother, and that we lived in our home together.

I didn't know my family was disintegrating before my very eyes, because I was just a child. I didn't know it then, but it would take the changing of countless seasons before Almighty God would shine his light on my darkened soul. Everyone was busy playing their role in the game of life, and I was trying to play my role also. Now when I hear my adult contemporaries talk about getting a "whooping" when they were growing up, I realized I never did get one. I think I played my role pretty well, and I realized that initially I never did give my parents problems.

When I was about nine years old, we moved into our brand-new house in a new neighborhood. It was the very first house my father had built for his family. He was a hardworking man and rode a bicycle all his working days. But he built a two-storied house for his family, and folks thought we were rich. My father, who is now deceased, said it was the first loan he had ever taken which he used to build a home for his family. His parents had their own bedroom and bathroom downstairs, on the same floor with the kitchen and the dining and living rooms. Upstairs he had built a master bedroom, one bedroom for his girls, one for his boys, and a study room. My father was an avid reader and was big on education and decided to send me to the best girls' elementary school in the neighborhood.

It was shortly after we moved into our new house that I had my first lesson in what I now call sex education. I was touched inappropriately in the restroom at the new elementary school by a girl about my age. It happened so suddenly and it was just for a few seconds and that is all I remember. I had never had any type of sex education. I wasn't even thinking about boys at that time. But along came this girl who touched me, and I didn't even know what to make of it. I didn't know it at the time, but even though she didn't continue touching me, she had stolen my innocence.

She also used me for the first time in her game of theft. She knew where my classroom was, and one afternoon, before school was dismissed, she came into my classroom and got permission from my teacher to speak to me. She came to me and gave me a dime, asking me to keep it for her until school was dismissed. I kept it for her, and I still cannot believe I was so naive at that time. After school, I gave it to her, and she was happy. On my way home from school, I overheard that a dime had been stolen from one of the girls in another class; the teacher had searched the children, but the dime was never found. I almost froze in my tracks, and I quickly made my way home. I never had another encounter with this little thief again. Now I know who Jesus said the enemy was. He explicitly states in John 10:10, "The thief does not come except to steal, and to kill and to destroy. I have come that they may have life, and that they may have it more abundantly." The devil had launched his first attack on me.

Since leaving the Caribbean, I have learned the whole truth about sexual abuse from different reading materials. Sexual abuse includes but doesn't have to be actual penetration. Exposure is considered sexual abuse. Inappropriate touching of any part of the human anatomy is considered sexual abuse. During my studies as a lay counselor, I learned that even if you have a suspicion of sexual abuse, it must be reported so a thorough investigation can be made. I've learned that, in many instances, children are abused by someone they know, either a family member or a caretaker. Other grown adults have also acknowledged that they had been sexually abused as children but never told anyone. The times have changed, and parents can now educate their children about what is considered an unsafe touch. Most parents now teach their children how to establish healthy boundaries by saying the word *no* to anyone they feel may be invading their privacy.

Romans 1:24–28 outlines clearly what our Creator, our heavenly Father, states about same-sex relationships. God has given us the ability to make choices freely. However, these scriptures state that men and women choose to dishonor their bodies and satisfy the lust of their flesh through unclean, unmentionable sexual acts of misconduct. They choose to change the truth of God and turn it into a lie and change the natural use of women. In the beginning, God created Adam, the man, and Eve, the woman, and he blessed them and gave them their assignment to multiply and replenish the earth. However, men are leaving the natural use of women and burning in their fleshly lusts toward other men and reaping the consequences of their sinful actions. Since they refuse to keep their minds on God's way of creating wholesome and healthy relationships with members of the opposite sex, God gave them up to a reprobate mind. We really need to teach our children what the Bible says about sexual immorality.

As I travel through this journey of remembrance, reflecting on all the stages and changing scenes of my life, I am amazed at the majestic power of an omniscient God who created me. This amazement is due to the fact that he somehow knew how to fit all the broken pieces of my life's puzzle together to form his tapestry. I remain spellbound by how he was able to take my abuse; my shame; my hidden secrets; my disappointments; my hurts; my stupid decisions; my insecurities; my frustrations; my doubts and fears; my licentious lifestyle; my sins of ignorance; my rejections; the pieces of my broken heart; my fragmented mind, with all its negative emotions; the insanity around me; my being possessed by demons; and my wounded soul, and fit the pieces together and make me whole.

I don't know how my heavenly Father did it, because it is his nature to do supernatural things all the time. But I know now the reason he delivered me. He offered me his deep, unfathomable, priceless love when my soul was sinking deep in sin. I accepted his forgiveness when I came to Calvary's cross, and my spiritual eyes were open when he showered me with his healing, cleansing blood. He is able to do the same for others who come to him to be made whole. By his divine design, the day came when my spiritual eyes were open as I was arrested by the Holy Spirit of truth and shackled by the power of God's all-encompassing love.

Chapter 2

The Family Religion: Religious Teachings at Home and School

Family Religion

We are all born into families of different religious persuasions, the traditions of which are observed by our children. These beliefs may or may not become part of the child's heritage. My mother was an avid churchgoer and practiced her faith weekly by going to church and carrying me along. I remember my mother had a picture of the Sacred Heart on the wall. It was a picture of Jesus with his heart pierced and his hands outstretched. It seemed strange, but she and I never talked about the picture. I imagine it must have been difficult to share her religious beliefs. I believe my now-deceased father was an altar boy when he was young, but he only visited church on special occasions.

The practice of not going to church is a habit that can be passed on to children, who may become atheists and assume God doesn't exist. Or they may become agnostics, not certain if God is real or not and assuming that if he is real, he'll show up someday. Some children may be aware they need to have a spiritual experience and may start looking for God in other religions besides their parents' religion, as happened in my case. We don't know what thoughts may be circulating in children's heads, especially if they were never allowed to ask questions. Parents should be able to share the core of their religious persuasions in a real and tangible way; otherwise, going to church would become commonplace. They should discuss the importance of having a personal relationship with God. It is imperative that we transition from religious practices, like going to church only on special occasions, to having an active daily relationship with God.

Besides the required basics in our school curriculum, we were taught Bible history from a little book, but I don't remember much about Bible history. However, I remember the Ten Commandments, the Lord's Prayer, the "I believe" prayer, and the foundations of our faith. Even though these religious teachings and the church doctrines didn't teach me about salvation and the loving relationship with God, I thank God for these religious teachings. Many years later, I encountered some women who had never been taught the Lord's Prayer. They were never taught the first prayer Jesus taught his disciples when they asked him to teach them how to pray. They were, however, eager to learn how to pray. They asked me to make copies of the prayer for them, which I gladly did, but that was as much as I was allowed to share concerning religion. I pray that prayer every day with more understanding, and I thank God I knew that prayer by heart. I may not have always prayed it, but I knew it.

The Lord's Prayer (Matthew 6:9–13)

Our Father in heaven, hallowed be your name.
Your kingdom come your will be done on earth as it is in heaven.
Give us this day our daily bread.
And forgive us our debts, as we forgive our debtors.
And lead us not into temptation, but deliver us from the evil one.
For yours is the kingdom and the power
and the glory forever. Amen.

Another powerful prayer is the "I believe" prayer. I had learned it by heart and didn't understand how powerful this prayer was until I became born again years after I had left the church. I thank God for the nuns who taught me this prayer. So let's meditate on the words as we pray together. If we don't know what we believe and have no solid spiritual persuasions, we'll fall prey to beliefs that are contrary to God's holy Word.

Apostles' Creed

I believe in God the Father Almighty, Creator of heaven and earth,
And in Jesus Christ, his only son, our Lord,
Who was conceived by the Holy Ghost, born of the Virgin Mary,
Suffered under Pontius Pilate, was crucified, died, and was buried.
He descended into hell; on the third day,
he rose again from the dead.
He ascended into heaven and sits at the right
hand of God the Father Almighty.
From thence, he shall come to judge the quick and the dead.

The prayer continues by affirming belief in the Holy Ghost, the importance of communion and fellowship with the saints, and forgiveness of sins. It concludes with the belief of bodily resurrection and the fact of eternal life.

At the church I went to, most of the mass was in Latin, and the prayer books were also in Latin; however, during the mass, the priest would lead us in reciting the foundation of our faith in English.

The Foundation of Our Faith

Christ has died.
Christ is risen.
Christ is coming again.

I was taught the Ten Commandments at school. I believe God used the knowledge of his law to prick my conscience. When I was about the age of eleven, it happened again, but this time it awakened something in me. I was touched by a girl a little older than me. I visited this home with my father. While the men were talking, we were playing in another room, but we weren't playing dollhouse. Here came the inappropriate touching again, but this time it aroused feelings in me that I never knew existed. My father had been so intent in keeping me away from boys that he never imagined girls were beginning to get dangerous at that time. We played the touch game several times, but I thank God it somehow came to an end because I started to become interested in boys. My heart goes out to young girls who have been molested at an early age but were not able to escape and have become lesbians. At this point, I would like to encourage parents to talk to their children about inappropriate touching from either males or females. Our heavenly Father understands their plight and wants to set them free. I had already done my First Communion, and at age eleven, I performed the religious rite of Confirmation. We were prepared at school, but the ceremony was performed at the church.

I do not despise my Catholic upbringing, where I was taught the Ten Commandments (Exodus 20:1–17).

The Ten Commandments

And the Lord spoke all these words saying:
1. "I am the Lord your God, who brought you out of the land of Egypt and out of the house of bondage.
   You shall have no other God's before me.
2. You shall not make for yourself a carved image—any likeness of anything that is in the heaven above, or that is in the earth beneath, or that is in the water under the sea; you shall not bow down to them nor serve them. For I the Lord your God am a jealous God, visiting the iniquities of the

fathers upon the children to the third and fourth generations
of those who hate me, but showing mercy to thousands,
to those who love me and keep my commandments."
The third commandment teaches us we should not take the name of the Lord in vain, because we would have to give an account to God himself. The fourth commandment reminds us of the importance of keeping the Sabbath day a holy day. We are reminded by the fifth commandment that we should honor our father and mother if we want to live a long life on earth. The sixth commandment admonishes us not to kill. The seventh commandment is extremely explicit in the fact that we shouldn't commit adultery. We are admonished by the eighth commandment not to steal. The ninth commandment cautions us not to bear false witness against our neighbor. In the tenth commandment, we are warned about coveting our neighbor's wife or anything belonging to our neighbor. I honestly believe that if every family embraced this as part of their daily devotion with their children, we would have a new generation who would fear, revere, and honor God and be respectful of others.

Church Pilgrimages and Acts of Mercy

I always enjoyed the pilgrimages to Mount St. Benedict with my mother and the religious group from the Catholic church. This was a holy place, a monastery situated at the top of a hill where the priests resided. My mother would get up early and prepare lunch, since we would be gone all day. I never wondered why she never took either of her two sons on the pilgrimage. We would meet the bus at the church, and it would be an enjoyable time for me because our family never owned a car. We would drive many miles east away from the city until the driver got to the bottom of the hill and turned left. Everyone would be excited as they grabbed on to the backs of the seats in front of them as the driver would maneuver the bus along the narrow road until the monastery came in sight. The ladies would leave their baskets of food and belongings in the fellowship hall, and then we would all walk to the church for morning mass. After mass, we would have lunch and then return to the church for the evening session, called vespers. This I remember so well because the priests would sing in Latin for the duration of the time.

According to Wikipedia, "*vespers* is a sunset evening prayer service in the Orthodox, Western and Eastern Catholic, and Lutheran liturgies of the canonical hours. The word comes from the Greek *eottepa* ('hespera') and the Latin *vesper* meaning 'evening.' It is also referred to in the Anglican tradition as evening prayer or evensong. The term is also used in some Protestant denominations (such as the Presbyterian Church and the Seventh-day Adventists) to describe evening services." In recent times, I suddenly remembered the vespers as I was singing in the Holy Spirit in the heavenly language God has blessed me with. I smiled to myself as I thought about the Catholic priests singing in Latin, but I don't remember if they sang the translation in English. As a child, I sensed it was a solemn time of reverence but didn't know why. Now I treasure the special times when Almighty God, through his precious Holy Spirit, allows me to penetrate the heavens in an unknown tongue in such a miraculous way.

Our family Sunday special was stewed chicken, rice, macaroni cheese casserole, kallaloo with ochroes cooked in coconut milk, and sliced sweet potato. Mother always prepared just one extra meal for the poor. The Catholic men from the St. Vincent De Paul Society would come every Sunday around lunchtime and collect that extra meal. They collected lunches from other Catholic families in the neighborhood for distribution to the poor. We never knew who those families were, but the poor were fed. My mother's ministry to the poor in such a simple manner inspired me to distribute more than one extra lunch, sometimes five, every Sunday during a particular season in my life after I became born again.

My present husband and I have a ministry to the poor in our neighborhood. We do a chapel service every fourth Sunday in a safe haven God has opened for the homeless population. These souls are fed daily, three times a day, both spiritual food and natural food.

I mention this because my husband and I both have something in common. We talk about how our mothers fed the poor while we were children and how what we learned as children influenced our adult life and put us both on common ground.

I became actively involved in the Legion of Mary. I enjoyed visiting the poorhouse for the elderly. We also visited the homes for physically and mentally handicapped children, which I enjoyed. These facilities were run by the nuns, and I remembered helping them do pattern exercises on the limbs of the children. The seeds for my life's calling and destiny were sown in my heart from childhood as a Roman Catholic while I was living in darkness. My heavenly Father saw to that because years later, when I was an adult, these were the areas of ministry that were dear to my heart.

Years later, I became a teacher at an elementary school in a depressed area where the children sang hymns every morning at assembly and recited prayers. Prayers were also said before meals, after meals, and upon closing at 3:00 p.m. After teaching there for about seventeen years, I retired on the grounds of marriage. After my retirement, I visited an area I never knew existed, where there was abject poverty. By the grace of God, I was able to provide furniture, teaching materials, books, and apparatus for the children. Of course, we were free to teach these children how to pray, and impact their lives with spiritual truth. Sadly enough, sometime later, I received the sad news that the building had been gutted by fire after the death of the person who was in charge.

After I migrated, I wanted to make a positive impact in the lives of the children in the neighborhood. I loved to minister to children who were not exposed to any type of religious teaching. My two-bedroom apartment became a children's church because I knew if they didn't have any spiritual teaching, they would be open to more attacks of the enemy. Sad to say, there was no father figure in their homes, and most of them had brothers and sisters. The fathers were on the run, and the government was playing their role in making those who were working pay child support. The enemy had a foothold and had entered the lives of those families.

I witnessed a particular family where the three generations were living in the same government-assisted apartment complex. The parents gave permission, and the children came to children's church. We had a small children's choir, and I miraculously learned to pick a few notes from the keyboard I had purchased. I embraced the opportunity to give religious teachings to these children; I was free in our neighborhood home church to do so. We sang together, praised God together, studied Bible stories together, colored Bible characters together, and always ended each session with snacks. I thank God the parents allowed their children to come for religious teachings.

The children were so happy, and we took the little choir to visit the nursing home in the neighborhood on special occasions, like Christmas, Easter, and Mother's Day. It was such a joy to see the faces of the elderly light up when the children went from room to room singing songs of joy. One year, we even did a simple Christmas performance. I know their parents were elated when the children would bring home cards they had prepared and colored for special occasions. I am grateful that, in the midst of the darkness in my life, the nuns had taught me religious prayers. Years later, I was thankful for the opportunity to do the same for the neighborhood kids in another country.

CHAPTER 3

The Picture-Perfect Family

May I remind you that I was born in the dark and didn't know it? We were living in the beautiful five-bedroom, two-bathroom house my deceased father had built, but without us knowing, the devil had already started casting dark shadows over us. My mother was a wonderful homemaker. I walked to and from school every day in our new neighborhood. I even came home for a hot meal at lunchtime every day because my mother cooked for us every day. I remember her cleaning and mopping her precious new kitchen every day. She would then take a power nap in her favorite chair with the front door ajar to let the fresh air in. I can still see her with her eyes shut, her head leaning against the concrete pillar, using it as a pillow.

After her power nap, she would tend to her garden and her lawn in the front yard. My father had purchased a hand mower, and she kept her lawn well attended. She fertilized it and watered it with the brand-new hose. After a while, my father purchased a sprinkler, and that made it easier. I loved to watch the pattern of the glistening drops of water as the sprinkler whirled round and round. My mother had the most beautiful flower garden in the front yard. She had canna lilies, carnations, roses, and beautiful hibiscus plants with their red flowers at Christmastime. She had gathered the stones and tilled and nurtured the soil before planting the flowers and roses. She would prune the trees, and at the right time, after the beautiful flowers had faded, she would save the seeds for planting in another season.

I accompanied her to the nursery on more than one occasion to purchase plants and fertilizers and other types of plant food. I remember her purchasing moss and coming home to tend to her precious roses. She would create new life in her hands by scraping the rosebush at a particular joint, placing the moss at that spot, then wrapping and tying it with plastic. In time, new roots would begin to sprout at that particular joint in the rose plant. She would then cut it off and place the new rose plant in its own soil. In this way, she perpetuated the life of her precious rose plants.

My favorites, though, were the yellow chrysanthemums, as they were absolutely beautiful, and people came from everywhere to purchase them by the dozens. On occasion, an Indian man would come around the neighborhood on a donkey cart loaded with bags of cow manure. My mother used to purchase the manure and dig around the trees and put some of that cow manure. Everything flourished through her hands. She kept an immaculate lawn in the front yard and had a small vegetable garden in the backyard. I remember my mother sowing the tomato seeds, the six-week ochroes seeds, and the sorrel seeds in the soil, and the soil would produce what she had sown.

From the outside, it was such a beautiful picture, especially since my father had brought his parents to live with us. I remember the day the photographer came to take snapshots of our picture-perfect family. There were three generations of us—my father, the son; his parents; and his children. Unfortunately, that family picture was destroyed years later, and I can still remember myself as a little girl with an expressionless face. There were nine of us in that family portrait. I don't remember the photographer. I don't recall his age, his height, or the clothes he wore, but I remember that day, because the lens in my photographic brain witnessed and recorded an unfortunate incident. The photographer had arrived before my brother who had stepped out of my mother's womb before me. Everyone had on their Sunday best, but he was nowhere to be found. I remember him slipping through the front gate just in the nick of time, because I was standing outside, in front of the porch.

I remember my father going into action, and the race began. I decided to call it "I dare you to catch me." My brother led my father in a chase from the front yard facing south, around my mother's beautiful flower garden, and across the well-manicured lawn, which was facing east. The race continued out of sight around the north perimeter of the house. I was riveted to the spot, but my eyes were in motion. The eyes of my photographic mind took a memorable snapshot as they came into view again after scuttling through the west side of the house, passing my mother's vegetable garden and the mango tree. In the flash of a second, my father slipped to the ground, and the race was over. My brother, the little rebellious boy, had outrun my father. I don't remember exactly what happened afterward because I was lost in my own little world of decision. Nobody told me to do it, but I was about ten years old and made a decision that day that stayed with me: "No child would ever rule me." Unfortunately, as a teacher and parent, I developed an authoritarian style of leadership, which I had to correct when I came to the light. When I came out of my reverie, my brother had changed his clothes, and the photographer positioned us and took a snapshot of our three generations.

I realize, in retrospect, that it was a seed of rebellion in my brother that had manifested that day outside the family home. We are all born with a propensity to sin, but the spirit of rebellion planted inside my brother's little soul had not been arrested and brought under the authority of God's Holy Spirit. My brother still lives in our native country, and I visit him whenever I can; however, because of the choices he made, he is living a secluded life without a postal address. Because of the fact that *the spirit of rebellion* was lurking undetected in our family home, the ultimate result of our picture-perfect family was devastating. I love my father dearly, because my heavenly Father used him to save me from my mother's womb. In my adult life, he helped me financially when I had the goal of purchasing my first car. I treasure the memory of him helping me with the down payment of my first car, because he himself had ridden a bicycle all the working days of his life. When I was physically abused by my first husband, the father of my children, my parents made room for us in the second house he had built away from the city.

The *spirit of rebellion* was lurking undetected in the shadows over my unsuspecting life, which was headed for many twists and turns of misfortune. I wish I had met someone who could have stepped into that picture and held my hand and guided me every step of the way, through different seasons and stages in my life. So many years have passed since that picture was taken, and it seems I'm looking at this little girl's life and wishing someone had come along to lead her to the right path, which is Jesus, the way, the truth, and the life. I do have a family portrait, which was taken at my parents' fiftieth wedding anniversary celebration. I still look at myself and try to imagine what was happening inside my mind then. By that time, I had accepted Jesus Christ as my personal Savior, but I remember there were so many battles I had to fight to become who I am today.

Every picture tells a unique story. Precious moments are captured, but there's always a story before the actual picture is taken; it's interesting to look back and recognize developments long after that picture was taken. Sometimes I look back over my life. I would flip through the pages of the picture album in my mind's eye and try to remember special, precious moments I can meditate and brood on. If you've experienced turmoil and devastation in the past, I'm sure if you look long and hard enough, you'll be able to salvage at least one good memory that will definitely bring a smile to your face. I've been guilty of destroying pictures in an effortless attempt to deny to myself that the place, time, and occasion of the picture didn't happen, and actually wishing it never happened. In reality, the picture was taken. I was seemingly full of expectation and excitement at the time, and that was the reason I dressed myself and smilingly allowed the picture to be taken. However, it was a reality I had to eventually face, and I had to allow Almighty God to turn it around for my good and his glory. We cannot deny our past or hide or cover it on the pretense that it never happened.

Unfortunately, some people are only left with a negative imprint about their past and always see themselves as a victim in their past life. With God's help and with time, much prayer, and determination, we can transform those negative images into fuel that will propel us forward to our future. We have to have the guts and determination to seek God's help for this transformation process to take place, because if we look at the past only through negative eyes, we will continue looking toward the future with negativity. Some people are stuck in their past and are unable to move forward. It's interesting when we think about the flow of electricity through either a series or parallel circuit. The batteries have to be lined up with the positive end of each battery connected to the negative end in order for the electricity to flow. The Bible tells us in Romans 8:28, "And we know that all things work together for good to them that love God, to them that are the called according to His purpose." Almighty God does not condone the evil devices of the devil in our lives, but he promises he'll be able to comfort us in the midst of our pain; in the process of time, He will take all the negative things that happened to us, which were at times beyond our control, and flip it around for our good.

If we allow him, God can take the painful experience of abuse and, in his perfect time, turn it around and allow you to minister to victims of abuse because you will be able to identify with their pain and suffering. When victims of abuse see you smiling and happy after your process of emotional healing, then they will be able to confide in you for a hand up to their place of victory and peace of mind. In our society, some people have experienced divorce after a seemingly happy wedding day. The wedding pictures were beautiful, but the light of love that was shining in the eyes of both bride and groom somehow, over a period, changed to darkness and gloom. Suddenly, they both decided whatever it was they had at the beginning wasn't working anymore, and they turned the final light switch off in the divorce court.

You may wish it never happened and may decide to put the entire wedding album in the trash with all those beautiful pictures, including the ones of the bridal shower and gifts. The perfect picture may be in the trash, but when pictures flash from your memory bank, you may think you must have lost your mind. Well, it's certainly time to get back every piece of your mind that you lost, by the process of forgiveness. You may have divorced your mate, but the story doesn't end there, because little versions of your hateful mate are running around in your home. How in heaven's name can you have contempt for the one who produced the seed or in whose womb your precious child was formed?

I really want to encourage you to look at some pictures of yourself at different stages of growth and development. Think about what lessons you wish you had known then and then willingly embrace the life lesson you learned in the midst of that harrowing situation. People look at pictures taken when they were in college and are either proud of what they have become or are sometimes amazed when they hear stories about their different classmates. Sometimes the ones they expected to make it didn't make it, and at times, the least-expected ones rose to the top. Think about what counsel, advice, or words of wisdom you could have benefited from at the time you were growing up but wasn't available to you then. How can we make this world a better place for the next generation? I know that times have changed, especially with all the modern technology. One thing is for certain: Pictures are being taken more than ever before. A lot of selfies are being taken by this generation. I believe if we earnestly seek God in prayer for the next generation, he will put members of the younger generation in our path so we can mentor and steer them in the right direction. This is the reason our churches have special ministry sessions for children and youths. I know for a fact that many of our churches perform yearly background checks on those who are seeking leadership positions in their congregations.

I encourage you to take a good, honest look at your family pictures, especially those that are etched in your memory bank. If you believe you were in an unfortunate situation that was beyond your control, the first thing I would like you to know is that you are not the only one this has ever happened to. I'm not attempting to minimize the impact of your traumatic situation, but do you realize the Bible is full of stories filled with family dysfunction? The reason I like to call the Bible my family album is because I can see myself in the pages. However, God always has a plan of redemption for those who have lost their way. I would like to encourage you to flip the switch of your negative memories by giving them to God and asking him to turn it around for your good and his glory. When we stay focused on our painful past and rehearse it continually, we become trapped in a vicious cycle of negativity. When I was experiencing painful situations, one day the Holy Spirit suddenly impressed upon me to flip the switch and not focus on myself. I started thinking and praying for other women who may be experiencing the trauma of abuse like me. Suddenly, I had received a key that began the process of my recovery.

Let's look at the other side of the spectrum. Think of mothers whose sons may have committed murder. We see that horrible picture flashing across the television screen or making headlines in the newspapers. Sometimes we hear that the perpetrator of the crime was a seemingly quiet individual. Have we ever stopped to think that the victim is not the only one hurting emotionally? If we take a minute to reflect, we would think of the victim's entire family. Can you imagine the mother who may be looking, with tears streaming down her face, at her child's picture with guilt and shame, wondering what she should have done differently? I'm certain the average woman doesn't decide to give birth to a callous individual who will perform hateful acts of violence and abuse. What happened to her precious little child who was smiling in that picture? He may be waiting in death row, but she has pictures etched in her memory of the day she brought him home from the hospital. She nursed him, played with him, bathed him, sang to him, and potty-trained him. She remembers his baby teeth, his first steps. She remembers his school days as he transitioned from stage to stage in his growth and development.

Yes, we can choose to think about the rapist's mother with hearts full of compassion, without understanding the facts that surrounded that situation that brought shame and disgrace to all the other family members. Pain is universal in so many different ways, and it's been said that people who are hurting end up hurting other people. So whenever we look at pictures of perfect families living in mansions, let's not think the grass may be greener on the other side of the fence, because in reality, it may not be the case. If ever we see disaster come upon a picture-perfect family, we have to stop and remember that behind the smiles, there was an invisible cloud of darkness overshadowing that picture. I dare you to really think before you take another picture and ask yourself if your smile is for real or if you are faking it, because the only way we can really deal with the turmoil of our inner emotions is to be honest with ourselves.

CHAPTER 4

Celebrating Christmas
in the Dark

I remember the first Christmas celebration in our new house. I accompanied my mother by taxi, and we traveled downtown to go shopping. Christmas spirit was in the air. Showcases were decorated with Christmas trees draped with red-and-silver tinsel. Even though it was daytime, the different-colored lights were flashing on the boughs of the trees. The nativity scene was being sold both inside and outside the stores, and even in boxes by street vendors who displayed their goods on the sidewalks or on stands. The Virgin Mary, Joseph, and Baby Jesus, with their manger animals and the three wise men, were really a popular sight to behold. My mother was on a mission at the fabric store that day, and she clutched her purse with one hand and my little hand with the other. She had already measured the windows for her brand-new home, decided what colors she wanted, and knew how much it cost because she had been paying for the fabric monthly by installments. She took out her sewing machine and stitched away when we arrived home.

The tiled floor in the living room had to be prepared, but we had no polisher. I don't remember how the polish was laid, but I remember the polisher, because I remember my two older brothers having fun with me, their baby sister. They found one of my mother's old dresses, sat me on it, and pulled me in all directions around the living room. My bottom and their little muscles caused the floor to shine that first Christmas; however, by the following year, my mother had purchased an electric polisher.

Food preparation started with the fruits being prepared for the traditional black Christmas cake. My mother had a stone jar in which she placed oranges and raisins and I don't remember what else. She did this yearly ritual months in advance to prepare her homemade wine for the cake. She also mounted the hand mixer on the countertop and minced different types of dried fruit and soaked them in Trinidad rum. The week before Christmas, she prepared the burned brown sugar on the electric stove and then put all her ingredients together and produced her delicious-tasting black fruitcake. With that aroma of spices in the air, we knew the day was drawing near. Of course, we all got a little taste of that special cake, but we had to wait until Christmas Day to get a real mouthful.

The ham and stuffed turkey were baked on Christmas Eve, before we attended midnight mass at church. I disliked turkey for decades; that is, until I came to the United States and encountered another kind of turkey. My mother purchased a turkey every year from a neighbor who lived a couple of houses around the corner in the same terrace. This retired man raised turkeys that ran around his yard all year round until he decided they were ready for slaughter. You can imagine they were anything but tender. God's provision was made, thanks to our father, and my mother never had to stand in line waiting for handouts. As the years rolled by, all the windows were washed, both inside and outside, before the new curtains were hung. Some years, we even painted the walls as we prepared for our Christmas celebration.

The Christmas tree would be decorated, but strangely enough, I don't remember much about presents. Christmas carols were heard on the radio in the Caribbean, and I can still remember singing "Frosty the Snowman" and "Jingle Bells" ("Oh what fun it is to ride in a one-horse open sleigh") even though I had never seen a flake of snow in my life and the closest thing I had to compare to the sleigh was my bicycle. We sat around the table on Christmas Day and ate and overate. We drank our traditional sorrel, which had been grown, picked, and prepared from my mother's garden. Later on, my mother would bring out the Christmas snacks and give each of us our portion. That's the only time we had apples and grapes and mixed nuts, which had been imported. We had developed the skill of stepping outside and using stones in the place of nutcrackers. We also had our traditional cake and the Christmas cookies from the beautiful tins and candies too.

Then came the fun time when we visited our friends round the corner. We went from house to house, and we had fun and ate whatever was offered and danced. I loved to dance, and I remember my brother and I were dancing the shindig, which is the name of a dance. I didn't know at that time that I was dancing for the devil and that the spirit of rebellion was brewing inside me, because I was unaware of that sinister spirit. We were having fun outwardly because dancing is a pleasurable experience, but I didn't realize there was a dark cloud hanging over our lives. Incidentally, I still dance, but I've changed dancing partners now, because I allow the precious Holy Spirit to guide me. Someone sent me an email several years ago that stated the real meaning of the word *guidance*: "God, let U and I dance."

My brother and I had been out of touch for years, and after about four years, I decided in May 2017 to visit my native country. I had prayed fervently for Almighty God to order my steps and to make sure I would be in the right place at the right time. I had heard that my brother was deceased, and I wasn't sure if this was true. I was able to locate my brother. He took my grown children and me to visit his new domain, which incidentally was located in close proximity to the first house my father had built, where the family picture was taken. My father had sold the house years ago. My brother was so happy to see his sister and nieces and nephew. He was delighted for the gift I presented to him, and he said he had a gift for me but couldn't locate it at the time.

We stepped outside his little domain and stood talking for a while about my father's other property and other family matters. He said he was writing a book. I remember my brother had been more knowledgeable than me in discussing world affairs and other matters, and I didn't doubt his sincerity about writing a book, which I believe must have been part of God's plan and purpose for his life. I reminded him about the gift he had promised me, and we both stepped inside his little domain. While he searched his stuff, I stood pleading with the blood of Jesus in my heart, because that's what I do, as I'm now living in the light. As always, the blood of Jesus reveals hidden things, and after a while, my brother found the gift he wanted to present to his sixty-six-year-old little sister.

With a pleased look on his face, he handed me a rectangular box with an electrical cord attached to it. The box was green, with a musical strip on it, a red flower, and a red stripe. I knew it was a musical Christmas box about my Jesus. I embraced this gift from my brother I lost and found.

I tested my treasure as soon as I arrived at the home where I was staying, and it played beautiful Christmas carols. I proudly showed my gift to my American husband when I returned to Texas, and our home was filled with Christmas music for about half an hour. I can enjoy Christmas at any time when I think about my brother's gift, because he knew that I did and will always love Jesus. My brother was overjoyed because his family had visited him. With mixed emotions, I said goodbye, feeling sadness and relief at the same time. I was relieved he was still alive, and I was happy that Almighty God had answered my prayer to see him again and will answer my prayer for my brother's safety and salvation for himself and his family. After our visit with my brother, I directed my daughter, and she drove around the corner to see the house where I had grown up as a child.

CHAPTER 5

Spirit of Rebellion: Tips for parents

Parental Guidance

For rebellion is as the sin of witchcraft, and
stubbornness is as iniquity and idolatry.
Because you have rejected the word of the Lord,
he has also rejected you as being king.
—1 Samuel 15:23

As a young teenager, I really enjoyed visiting with the less fortunate, and because of my faithfulness, I was promoted to the position of secretary of the Legion of Mary in the area. However, in the meantime, there were some church ordinances I tried to uphold that I was unable to uphold. This was utterly frustrating to me. Even though I knew the aforementioned prayers by heart, I was not praying daily or meditating on these prayers during the course of the day. I tried to keep the required First Fridays, but somehow I was not able to do that. I think there were about nine consecutive days, but I can't remember what they signified. If I remember clearly, I made three and broke the chain of succession. It was frustrating, so I gave up and stopped going to church. My mother never pressured me about going, because even though she was a staunch believer and a faithful churchgoer, my father never asked a question. My father was a hardworking man and provided for his family. He also did his best to protect his family. However, in retrospect, I realize that since we had no family prayer, this was an open invitation to the devil to worm his way into our lives undetected.

I would like to make an appeal to parents: if your child suddenly stops going to church with the family, that's a definite signal that indicates something is amiss. That's the time parents really need to seek God for wisdom on how to handle this matter and approach the child at the right time to discuss the matter. If this situation is handled in the right manner, without screaming and accusations, the child will open up when he or she realizes you're affording them an opportunity to share their perspective. Every single person has a desire to be heard, and we really need to listen first without pointing fingers of accusation or simply meting out stiff penalties.

We are cautioned in James 3:18, "But the wisdom that is from above is first pure, then peaceable, gentle, and easy to be entreated, full of mercy and good fruits, without partiality and without hypocrisy." In any relationship, if we approach the other person in anger and frustration, they will automatically put up a wall of defense to protect himself or herself because it will be perceived as an attack. Even if words are not spoken, facial expressions say a lot. We may even say the right words, but the actual irritated tone of voice makes a difference. I've also learned that if we approach someone with why questions like "Why do you keep doing the same thing over and over?" and "Why do you always have to do things your way?," a better approach would be "Please help me understand how that's working for you." Remember, even if you are persuaded the child or mate is wrong, the right approach at the right time with the right attitude will make a world of difference. Our family members can read us like open books simply by our actions.

Another trick children do is to use one parent against another. Our modern-day society is filled with lots of hustle and bustle away from the family home because both parents have to work. In most cases, the new role of the mother is no longer that of baby on one hip and broom and dustpan in the other, toiling all day long. Since both parents spend most of their time away from home, they really have to make a conscious effort to discuss their family affairs. If parents are not in agreement concerning situations regarding their children, this will provide an opportunity for the child or children to manipulate either one or both parents. When children are able to manipulate their parents, they lose respect for them. If this game of manipulation goes unnoticed and is not checked, it could result in an outburst from the child, and the parent may be clueless about the cause of the outburst.

We definitely want our children to understand choices and consequences. Almighty God always gives us a choice. We can choose to serve him and seek guidance in his holy Word or rebel and make decisions that are contrary to his Word. There is a classic example about how God gave the children of Israel choices in the scripture, in Deuteronomy 28:1–68. We can definitely glean the principles of what physicists call the law of cause and effect. In the first fourteen verses, we see an outline of the benefits of being obedient to God's way of doing things and the resultant blessings that will run us down and overtake us if we choose to obey. Conversely, if we choose to disobey God's principles from his holy Word, curses will definitely run us down and overtake us, according to the next fifty-four verses. Parents can sit with their children and create family rules that would enable them to receive rewards for positive behaviors displayed. These rules should also include penalties for unacceptable behavior. The penalties should be fair, taking into consideration the nature and frequency of the offence. Sometimes parents, not knowing how to deal with rebellion, may ignore issues, hoping they will mysteriously go away. When violent outbursts take place years later, they realize that the things they ignored were definitely progressive stages of rebellion.

The Bible informs us in 1 Timothy 1:9 that "the law is not made for a righteous man, but for the lawless and disobedient, for the ungodly and for sinners, for unholy and profane, for murderers of fathers and murderers of mothers, for manslayers." I believe the purpose of our judicial system is to restore law and order in the face of apparent disobedience and lawless acts of violence resulting in murders in our societies. The family is the very framework and backbone of modern civilization, and if the family is fragmented and there are unresolved issues, the resultant spillover will affect our neighborhoods. If parents do not teach their children how to exercise restraint and self-control, then unfortunately they will experience the handcuffs of restraint by law enforcement authorities. As I transitioned through each stage of the educational system, the spirit of rebellion increased gradually in my life, but I was unaware of it. I am grateful I never had to be handcuffed by police, but this spirit was leading me down a dark winding road.

Sexual Promiscuity

> *Because of the* multitude of the whoredoms *of the well-favored*
> harlot, *the mistress of* witchcrafts *that sells nations through*
> *her whoredoms and* families through her witchcraft.
> *I am against you says The Lord of Hosts, and I will*
> *discover your skirts upon your face. I will show the nations*
> *your nakedness and the kingdoms your shame.*
> —Nahum 3:4–5

Countless families, including my family, have been affected by this spirit of whoredoms, the mistress of witchcrafts. Families have been torn apart, as my family was, but because this is my story and not my parents' story, I choose to focus on how God delivered me from this evil spirit of whoredoms. I don't know my grandparents' story, but I know history tells us we are the descendants of slaves; when the Emancipation Proclamation was decreed, we were set free. Every black family who were descendants of slaves were, in fact, slaves to sin. It's a spiritual battle affecting nations and families who are still being ensnared and enslaved by sexual sin.

There was an added component that caused me to turn away from God and leave the church. I was a teenager, and members of the opposite sex had come into the picture. I was starved for love and sadly equated sex with love and allowed my body to be used. I had lost my spiritual anchor because I had stopped going to church. I had lost my spiritual compass because I had stopped praying the only prayers I knew. If I had kept meditating on what I knew, it would have helped my spiritual life tremendously; I would not have been overpowered by sin. There was a reason I had stopped going to church. After trying unsuccessfully to keep the church ordinances, I decided I would not be able to make it into heaven, and I let go of the church base and the prayers.

I also resigned as secretary from the Legion of Mary, and of course, I had stopped saying the Hail Mary and using the rosary. The rosary is comprised of a string of beads with a cross at the end. As you touch each section of the beads, you say the Our Father one time and the Hail Mary countless times. I am grateful to God for the prayers I learned as a child, but after my spiritual love awakening with Jesus, I made a decision based on the Word of God to pray only to Jesus Christ, because 1 Timothy 2:5 clearly states, "For there is one God, and one mediator between God and men, the man Christ Jesus."

Deception and Lies

Sadly, at that time, I didn't know that, according to the Word of God, "[my] body [was] the temple of the Holy Ghost" (1 Corinthians 6:19). The only thing my mother told me about sex, on one occasion, were these words: "Sex is for marriage." I don't remember exactly when she told me, but the spirit of rebellion from the devil was now pursuing me. I went to the next level of rebellion. I started deceiving my parents, as I had a partner in crime. We would get permission from our parents to attend the movies. This was a half-truth, because we didn't tell them we were going to meet our boyfriends there. We had fun times living in the dark and going to see movies like *To*

Sir, with Love; *Guess Who's Coming to Dinner*; and movies by *Elvis Presley*. By this time, we had a television set, and I enjoyed watching *Bonanza*, *Bewitched*, *The Bill Cosby Show*, and others.

So we see the progression that originated from the inappropriate touch and sexual abuse. I had stopped praying the only prayers I knew. Didn't Jesus teach us to pray in the Lord's Prayer, "And lead us not into temptation, but deliver us from evil" (Matthew 6:13)? Unknowingly and in ignorance, I had turned away from God and started pleasing myself. I had entered the world of self. So instead of letting our heavenly Father be my guide, I guided myself through my own thoughts and feelings and became a magnet for the enemy. I was looking for love in all the wrong places. In retrospect, I thank God that he had a plan but patiently waited for the right season to execute it and reveal his purpose for my life.

CHAPTER 6

Transition Due to Emotional Turmoil

By the grace of God, I successfully transitioned from elementary school to high school. I rode to school every day, because it was safe in those days. We had a bicycle shed where the students parked their bicycles. Riding prepared me for our Sports Day, as I decided to participate in the bicycle race that year. I was familiar with my instrument and knew how to position my body, whether sitting or slightly leaning forward, with my rear end lifted slightly off the seat. I knew how to pump the pedals of my cycle in a rhythmic way and build up my speed before climbing a hill. I enjoyed speeding down an incline with the breeze fanning my face, because it was hot and humid in Trinidad. I enjoyed riding my cycle because I was in control of it, and it took me to the places I needed to go.

At my high school, I appreciated the exposure to different types of sports and loved engaging in sporting activities during the year. I remember engaging in lawn tennis as an after-school activity a couple of times, but I never mastered it, even though it was fun. On our annual Sports Day, I enjoyed watching the athletes perform in their areas of expertise. The girls with winged feet would fly by, doing their fifty- and one-hundred-yard races. I would gaze in amazement at the relay races as they ran and passed the baton with such timing and finesse. The girls who did the long jump would literally build up speed like an airplane and take off into the air with their feet off the ground and land successfully at the distance they had imagined in their mind's eye.

A Thirst for Knowledge

We enjoyed a broad curriculum at school, but for some reason, I did not enjoy sciences, like physics, chemistry, or geography, which we now refer to as social studies. However, I loved English, literature, and mathematics, including algebra and geometry. I was also introduced to a bit of classical music at school but regretted not paying enough attention in our music classes, where we were taught the musical staves. I pursued the study of foreign languages French, Latin, and Spanish. I was successful in the Cambridge Ordinary Level examination and transitioned to a further two-year study at school pursuing the Advanced Level certification.

However, I was still searching for something, maybe a spiritual experience. Like my father, I had become an avid reader, and one of the girls at school introduced me to a mystical book written by Lobsang Rampa. We were fascinated by mystery, and a few of us tried to follow the suggestions in the book and meet in the spirit on one of the benches on the school compound. Of course, our attempt was futile since we were all novices, and we didn't pursue this experiment any further. But I know now that another door into a spirit realm of the unknown was opened. A book can carry us places where we've never been, depending on their author and their intent. A book can be written to captivate people's thoughts and lead them away from truth. I was able to differentiate truth from falsehood when I was exposed to God's holy Word. I remember having a scary spiritual experience one day at school during my lunch break. I don't know if it was a result of reading that ungodly book written by Lobsang Rampa. I remember suddenly falling to the ground, and even though I remained in a fixed spot, my entire body was shaking uncontrollably. After a while, the shaking subsided, and I was able to get up. But I didn't know what had happened to me that day. I know now that the mighty hand of God was upon me and that he had delivered me from some spiritual entity.

I was unaware of the fact that I was existing in the dark because I had turned away from God, but something within me was searching for satisfaction. So even though I was supposed to be a member of one religious group, I started to attend religious Anglican morning services during my high school tenure. It was refreshing to be introduced to something different, and the hymns whet my spiritual appetite for a season. I also attended religious education classes at school, and I remember the teacher's name clearly because she died of cancer before our graduation. I don't remember everything from the religious education syllabus, but this one seed was planted in my mind. I don't know why it stayed in my mind, but God knew. Even though it stayed dormant for a while and I wasn't thinking about it, my heavenly Father deposited it in a safe place, where it stayed inside me. This one seed of faith was God's promise to Abraham, which I didn't think had anything to do with me, but it was lodged in my memory bank for some reason. The promise was "I will bless you and make your name great, and in you shall families of the earth be blessed" (Genesis 12:2–3).

The Spirit of Confusion

I was now in my sixth year in high school, but I was having some internal struggles and didn't know what to do about them. I remember one evening, at about sundown, I was standing at our front gate, talking to a young man. He was a lot older than me, and we were having a simple conversation. Suddenly, my father, who is now deceased, appeared, as the watchdog, to protect his baby girl and demanded I come inside the house. In my sixteen-year-old teenage mind, I didn't think that was the right thing for him to do in his role as a father. He was angry and used words that, in my teenage mind, were inappropriate. I'm not talking about curse words, because in all my years of growing up, I never once heard either of my parents use the four-letter word. As a matter of fact, I never heard my parents argue or fight each other. But that angry spirit from my father sailed through the atmosphere and stirred up something inside me. Anger that had been churning in me overflowed through my mouth, and I yelled at him in a fit of rage. In my teenage ignorance, I won the battle of words, and it stopped my father in his tracks from pursuing the conversation. All conversations ended at that point because the young man I had been talking with had quietly slipped away. One of the first things I did when Almighty God transitioned me from darkness to light and I became born again was to ask my father's forgiveness for being rebellious. By that time, I was able to look back and see how my rebellious behavior had landed me in so much trouble. I learned later in life that the Bible gives guidelines for children-and-father relationships.

> Children obey your parents in all things: for this is well pleasing unto the Lord. Fathers provoke not your children to anger, lest they be discouraged. (Colossians 3:20–21)

You can see that if there's an absence of godly principles in families, relationships will begin to crumble.

At this point, I would like to caution parents: If your child is being rebellious and displaying fits of anger and frustration, please don't ignore it, hoping it will go away. There is a root cause of such behavior, and it will get worse if the child doesn't get the help needed. If you ignore it, hoping it will go away, the seed of rebellion will keep on growing, and the child will gravitate to his or her peers or any other person who will empathize with him or her. Our responsibility as parents is to pray for emotional healing and godly counsel for the pain our children may be experiencing. Everyone needs to be heard and given an opportunity to express their emotions, even if we are in disagreement; we need to hear what our children are thinking and create an atmosphere for discussion. It's a good thing to have a family meal at least once a week, as this will enable the parents to see their children's faces. When a parent can gaze into the eyes, which are the windows of a child's soul, they can tell when something is wrong. Through wisdom and healthy communication, the healing restorative process can begin and continue for the rest of the lifetime of that parent-child relationship.

During this time, my second sister had gone overseas to study, and my elder sister, who is now deceased, had graduated from high school and migrated to a foreign country to establish her independence. I was being compared to my older sisters because I assumed the behavior I was displaying wasn't agreeable to my parents. I remember the day the life of our family changed forever. Even though my now-deceased mother was the one who bore this burdened cross until her death, I never heard her complain or shed a tear. She was a silent sufferer, and I presume her comfort was her church and her garden. I was at home the day two strangers of another race knocked on the door of our home. My father was at home also, and he let them in, not knowing these messengers were the bearer of news that would change our family dynamics in such an unexpected way. The visitors explained that they were representatives from the Canadian embassy. They asked my parents if they had a daughter who had migrated to Canada. After giving her name, thus affirming her identity, my parents were informed she had a nervous breakdown overseas. I don't recollect the details of what happened on that day, because we never discussed this issue as a family. Heaven forbid my parents would seek thoughts and opinions about this matter from their rebellious last child. However, I remembered the day because the comparison had been made between my older sisters and me. On that day, I remember feeling I was a disappointment to my parents. Parents need to realize that each child is different, and they should treat each of their children as individuals.

False accusations continued, as after school I had ridden my bicycle to a house in the neighborhood and was seen talking to someone outside the house. It bothered me that my now-deceased father had listened to neighborhood gossip; I was accused of going to that house and smoking marijuana. My poor lost soul was hurt because my father had never asked me a question about the situation but instead believed the evil report. I sat in my high school class unable to concentrate and trying to understand what was going on in my teenage mind. My now-deceased mother was silent while my father accused me. However, I remember the day my mother broke her silence and came to my defense. It was the day of another accusation. My father had heard on the grapevine that I was skipping school and going to the beach with friends. My mother's argument was that surely she would have seen a wet bathing suit and noticed my wet hair. This, however, brought an end to my sixth year of high school, because I had an outburst of tears in class one day and was unable to concentrate on studies anymore.

Father Stepped In and Made a Difference

My father never gave up on me and was able to get me a government job. I worked in different government departments for a couple of years, and it was exciting earning and spending my own money. However, I was starved for love and was looking for it through romantic relationships with members of the opposite sex. I allowed myself to be used and dumped. I worked in different government departments until my nineteenth birthday, and then my father decided it was time for me to go to a teachers' training college. I couldn't see it at the time, but my father really wanted me to be successful in life and was trying, in his own fatherly way, to protect me from wicked men. My mother told me that, as a child, I would wave a stick and talk to the chairs at home as though I was talking to children. I'm so grateful for my parents' vigilance, because teaching is my life skill.

I had become so used to sleeping in the privacy of my own room that it was almost a shock to me, when I entered college, that I had to share a dorm with someone else—and a stranger at that. College was not such a long way from the city, but we didn't own cars. And since public transportation was not readily available, we spent most weekends on campus. However, one weekend when I was off campus, I attended a party, and someone offered me a puff of a marijuana joint. I will never forget that one puff because I started hallucinating. Thank God I was able to recover and got home safely, but one attempt was enough for me. I never had a desire to try that again, and whenever I hear reports of how some people's lives have been affected by the use of drugs, I simply have to thank God I didn't go down that pathway.

Becoming Independent, Renting My Own Place

I graduated from college by the mercies of God during the year of my twenty-first birthday. I felt I was on top of the world, as I had my teacher's diploma and had been assigned to an elementary school in a depressed neighborhood. Incidentally, I remained in this school for about seventeen years, after which I chose early retirement. Many interesting things happened to me during my tenure at that village school. I was still living at my parents' home, and after school, I would give private tutoring to some of the neighborhood children. I had developed a new relationship with a young man. We had lots of emotional disturbances, and I had decided it was time for me to end the relationship. Of course, I never discussed my relationships with anyone, especially my parents. Sad to say, because my mother had only stood up for me on one occasion, I made a vow within myself that no man was going to rule me, especially my father. I don't remember exactly when I made this vow, but I didn't realize how detrimental it was until years later.

My former boyfriend decided to visit me after school one day. I was tutoring at that time, and my father decided to exercise his parental right and asked him about his intentions toward me. I didn't even ask what his reply was, but my twenty-one-year-old mind advised me that my father had no right to confront the young man in this way without first consulting me. I was thoroughly embarrassed.

Not only did the young man leave, but he left for good, because that was the last time I saw him. I don't believe he carried out the threat to kill himself. I send the message out to young women that if a guy ever threatens to kill himself when you decide to end the relationship, please run in the opposite direction, since this is a definite attempt to control you. I decided to move out of my parents' house on that day and vowed never to return, but that was short-lived, although I didn't know it at that time.

The vice principal of the school where I was working felt sorry for me and decided to rent out the annex of her house to me. I learned some positive things from her because she was a working wife and mother, and I remembered her daily routine, which started at 4:00 a.m. every day. My mother's routine was a bit different because she was a stay-at-home mom. My landlady would prepare breakfast, cook lunch, and pack lunch bags for her husband and daughter before leaving home at 7:00 a.m. to drive us to the village school where we were both working. I developed this routine of waking at 4:00 a.m. later on in life, when I became a working mom.

I remember one of the teachers at school ate lunch at one of the neighborhood houses, and he boasted that the lunches were so delicious. As a child, I was accustomed to my mother preparing a home-cooked meal at lunchtime, so I consulted the lady, who was so loving and sweet. We agreed on a price for the lunch. It was a five-minute walk from the school where I taught, and I started this new lunchtime routine. During this time, I met the cook's granddaughter, who had been a former student at the school; she had been involved in a serious vehicular accident that had affected her for life, and she was recuperating at home. After visiting the cook's house for a while, I also met the lady's son, who lived with her. The lady, who is now deceased, also had a vacant room for lease in her house, which she offered to me, and I accepted. I moved in, and she continued preparing lunch for me on a daily basis. She was the first person who said to me the words everyone thrives on: *I love you.* This was an extremely loving family; I met her daughter who had visited from abroad, and it was evident she loved her mother.

CHAPTER 7

For Better or for Worse

I thought I had finally hit the jackpot, and when the opportunity to marry her son presented itself, I welcomed it. I was twenty-three years old and decided I would devote myself to the man who would put a ring on my finger. The key word was *marriage*, and I decided it was time to stop looking for love, as I thought I had found it right there in that house. The time to settle down and have babies had come, especially as I yearned for my own special baby to love. My parents were relieved, and my mother prepared a family lunch at the beautiful home, where all the family secrets were locked away on that day. We arrived from the courthouse and had an enjoyable time with his mother. So we honeymooned in her son's room, and it was a great beginning to my brand-new life, as I was living so close to the school where I worked. We got married without marital counseling.

I would like to strongly advise couples who are planning to get married to seek marital counseling. Some churches offer marital counseling sessions, but if you and your mate are not churchgoers, you still need to sit and have lengthy discussions about life. Some people have met on dating sites and gotten married, and it worked. However, this method of selecting your life's mate may not have worked for some others. Whether you're in the church or out of the church, you and your prospective mate should spend lots of time really getting to know each other. The conversations should include topics relating to values, religious beliefs, money management, the possibility of having children, social relationships, and living a healthy lifestyle. I believe that if these discourses are held, couples would realize whether they are compatible. Some people get married because they like the idea of marriage, but they don't really understand the importance and significance of a holy matrimony.

People fall in and out of love and have never been introduced to the biblical guide for marriage. People get married for various reasons. Some women may feel pressured because of age and, in desperation, settle for someone who they know deep within their hearts is not a good fit. Some get married for financial security, and love is not part of the equation. However, a marital blueprint can be found in the Bible, which clearly defines the roles of both the man and the woman. In Genesis 1, we see that God prepared a place for Adam called the Garden of Eden, then he created Adam before he used one of Adam's ribs to form Eve, Adam's wife. Then God gave them the assignment he wanted them to fulfill on earth in Genesis 1:27–28: "So God created man in His own image, in the image of God created he him; male and female created He them. And God blessed them and said unto them: Be fruitful and multiply, and replenish the earth, and subdue it."

God never instituted marriage with Adam and Steve. He didn't create Eve and Eva and give them the assignment to multiply. Biologically speaking and according to the course of nature, it is highly impossible and absurd for either two men or even for two women to produce life. Yet some people are simply stubborn and determined to please themselves and see and do things from their own perspectives. We are reminded in Romans 1:27–28 that Almighty God, our Creator, has given men and women the freedom of indulging in immoral practices that are contrary to his original intent. God gave them over to a reprobate mind because men and women were burning in their lustful desires and performing unmentionable practices with members of the same sex. A lot of heartache can be avoided in marriage if we seek godly counsel to determine if the couple is compatible spiritually, socially, intellectually, and emotionally. The Bible also warned us in 2 Corinthians 6:14, "Be ye not unequally yoked together with unbelievers." Seeking godly counsel will definitely lead couples along the pathway where they can explore and discover the areas where they may be incompatible and, with wisdom, prayer, and patience, work on building relationships that will withstand the vicissitudes of life.

Red Flags

Sadly enough, we stumbled into the marital experience without acquiring the tools that would make a successful relationship. We never discussed the things we valued in life or what moral standards we were upholding. My deceased husband's pride and joy was his stereo equipment, which he shined on a consistent basis, along with his speaker boxes. Before we got married, I noticed he had a small copier machine in the living room of his mother's house. I thought it strange at the time because he was working outside the home and wasn't operating his own business. I chose to ignore the machine. However, when I realized later on why the copier was in the house, I froze in amazement. I had attended high school and had been presented with my O Level Certificate, which listed all the subjects I had passed upon examination. When we met initially and had a conversation concerning our educational status, he had indicated that he had also achieved the same certification at the high school he had attended.

I didn't think at the time that I needed documented proof, but after our wedding, I asked him to show me his certificate. To my amazement, he did. He obliged by producing the document with his name on it, but as I looked closely at his document, I realized his certification had listed subjects identical to mine. Besides the basic mathematics and English language, we were allowed to choose other subjects we liked to complete the certification. I was thinking to myself that it was a strange coincidence he had chosen the same foreign languages as I had, namely French, Latin, and Spanish. However, my eyes almost popped out of their sockets when I saw the last bit of telltale information. Each school had a significant center number printed on the certificate, and my center number, which was for a girls' school, on his certificate was staring me in the face.

In haste, I fled to the room where I had secured my documents and pulled out my certificate. I hurried back to the living room and stared at both certificates in my hands. I gazed in amazement at the residue of tape that had been left on either side of my name, where he had taped his name over mine before passing it through the copier machine. I confronted him, and he acknowledged that he had falsified my certificate. It meant he had searched my belongings in my absence and hatched this plan. Upon my demand, he brought out the copies he had made, and I believe we burned them. Up to this day, I don't know if he had any other copies stashed away, but of course, he decided at this time to remove the copier from the house. I was living in darkness and didn't realize at the time that he had committed forgery. I didn't share this information with anyone; I had made a vow to make my marriage work. In retrospect, I realized the foundation of our relationship had been built on deception and lies, and I assumed I simply had to keep trying my best because I had vowed, "for better or for worse."

My now-deceased husband had erected a canopy over the bed where he slept, and this room had become the bridal chamber. He had erected a canopy that hung from the ceiling directly over the bed. I thought it was beautiful and imagined it was there as a decorative piece, until reality stepped in. One day he reached up into the canopy above the bed and pulled out a gun, which he showed me. However, in a flash, he placed it back in its hiding place, and it appeared as if nothing had happened. I remember the incident clearly. I don't know if the gun was loaded, but it scared me because I remember him saying that he had received an honorable discharge from the army. I didn't know how to label the incident. However, I didn't say anything to anyone because I was determined to make my marriage work, so we continued our married life in the dark. Strangely enough, we never had a conversation about that gun either, and somehow I knew better than to search his belongings. The thought of praying never entered my head, but Almighty God knew that someday, somehow, I would come to him.

I had decided to further my education and started attending evening classes at the local university. However, this dream was short-lived for two reasons. The main reason was that my husband was insanely jealous of the guys on campus who were part of our study group. Above everything else, I wanted to make my marriage work, so I decided to discontinue my classes. Also, at this time, I was pregnant with our first child.

His mother had to have eye surgery, and for the first time, I waited on a patient; at the time, no one in my family had ever been hospitalized. I visited her at the hospital and helped take care of her personal needs until it was safe enough for her to return home. She had to wear dark shades to protect her eyes from the sunlight. She had to stop cooking for a season as well, so I helped prepare simple meals for her. I helped take personal care of her in ways I had never done for my own mother, and that made me feel like her daughter.

There were mosquitoes in the neighborhood, and we would place lit mosquito coils all around the house to scare away the mosquitoes. I was in the kitchen that night and had placed a mosquito coil on the floor. My now-deceased mother-in-law entered the kitchen and accidentally knocked the coil over. I assumed she got burned, because a stream of venom was hurled directly at me, and it landed directly on my heart. The four-letter word shattered the love bait she had used to woo me to her house, her son, and herself.

For a moment, I stood still, like a block of ice, because everything happened so unexpectedly. I had never experienced anything like this in my life. Shock waves reverberated through my pregnant frame as I faced the reality of this nightmare. I really thought I was in a safe place, because this person was the first one in my life to speak such comforting words to me. Trust had developed when she had first said those sacred words that my thirsty soul and every other thirsty soul longed to hear: *I love you!* I didn't understand then what had just happened to me or why it happened. I had imagined she was a loving mother figure to me. But it was a defining moment, and I had to wake up from my shocked stupor and at least say or do something!

In a flash, reality kicked in, and I came to the conclusion that everything she had ever said to me was false. I realized this was no longer a safe place for me to stay. I reasoned within myself that even though I had emotional experiences with my parents, at least I had never heard the four-letter word used in their home. Her son had emerged from his room but never said anything to come to his wife's defense in any way. He didn't offer a loving embrace or say a word of comfort to me or our baby. I realized then that he didn't want to disrespect his mother by taking sides. I felt hurt and devastated, and I hastily packed my bags and fled from that scene in the twilight hour to the safety of my parents' home.

I never knew I had such a resilient spirit, but I knew I had to continue living and working, especially as I was expecting our first baby. Life was bittersweet, as I imagined my marriage had ended, but I was looking forward with joy to the birth of my first baby. My now-deceased husband pursued me and came to my parents' home to visit his wife, especially after the baby was born. But I was determined that the only time I would go back to where he lived would be to pack my remaining possessions and move out. I had remembered to pack my certificates and other personal documents the night of my flight.

I finally got my heart's desire, and our first baby was born while I was still living at my parents' house. I believe I was in the right place, because I was able to receive the support I needed from my mother, who took care of the baby while I was at work. My husband would visit to spend time with the baby.

Carnival time came along, and this was a two-day festival in our native country, which was preceded by lots of preparations for competitions and parties. Since I was in my home neighborhood again, I connected with my high school girlfriend and made plans to attend a party that Sunday night and then go directly to the Mardi Gras celebrations, which started about 4:00 a.m. that Monday morning. I don't remember much about the party, but I presumed I danced, which I loved to do, and drank my favorite rum and Coke. So we were on the streets at the start of Mardi Gras, and I realized I wasn't really enjoying myself like the other people around me, especially as my father had never allowed his girls to participate in the street aspect of the carnival. He used to purchase tickets for us to sit in the bleachers and watch the parade of bands. I suddenly felt strange because I was trying to behave like the others around me unsuccessfully, and I was also thinking about my baby daughter, who I had left at home in my mother's care.

I did what I had done previously when I was trying to follow all the church traditions from my previous religion. I had really tried, but it wasn't working for me. I felt uncomfortable because I wasn't really enjoying myself. I retraced my steps at about 4:00 a.m. that Monday morning and started walking in the opposite direction. I walked until I was able to find a taxi that was able to take me home. I didn't know it then, but that was the last carnival celebration I would ever attend. I know now that it was the mighty hand of God separating me from the things of the world. I believe God was responding to my mother's prayers, since she didn't know where I was and must have been appealing for God's intervention. There are some things I don't remember, but I clearly remember that early morning when I turned away in displeasure from that carnival cultural experience.

By this time, I began to dream about having my own place and was finally able to locate my own apartment. I furnished it and made all the arrangements to move in. However, sadly enough, I made one of the biggest mistakes of my life, as I wanted my marriage to work because I had decided I wanted to be faithful to my husband. I allowed him to move in with me without initially contributing anything to the securing of this new apartment. It seemed a good thing at the time because he had two other cousins related to his father living in separate houses within walking distance from each other. It was such a relief that one of them housed a day care where I was able to take our baby daughter. It was such a wonderful arrangement at the time, especially as it was within walking distance and we didn't have a car.

In my ignorance and lack of marital counseling, I didn't have the common sense to have an open, honest discussion about future expectations in the relationship. We reconciled without even discussing our roles and responsibilities in the relationship. I expected him to do what my father had done for my mother and be a provider for the family. I somehow imagined that, as a man, he would automatically assume responsibility when given the opportunity. By some strange coincidence, shortly after we moved into the first apartment, he lost his job. However, there was a lack of accountability in the marriage, and no realistic goals were discussed or established. Every day we both left the apartment, and I would take the baby to the sitter and then go to work. He would go back to his mother's house every day to help her, but guess who was paying the bills? I was trying my best to make my marriage work, but I really didn't know how. I tried to do things right, but somehow I was drinking from a bitter cup. I wasn't praying or seeking God, but he decided it was time I got some spiritual help; he used one of my friends to guide me along this journey called life. I had confided in my coworker that my eldest sister, who is now deceased, was having some emotional challenges, and she offered to take me to someone who would be able to help my sister.

CHAPTER 8

The Headless Family

Disintegration

But I want you to know that the head of every man is Christ,
the head of the woman is man,
and the head of Christ is God.

—1 Corinthians 11:3

Pretty Gina

I remember Gina very well, and the bits and pieces of her story will forever be etched in my memory bank. We met in the neighborhood shortly after my family had moved into our new house. We didn't attend the same elementary school, but we would meet sometimes to play. She had other siblings, but they were all different shades of brown, as her father was black. Her father was the provider for their family, and her mother stayed at home, like mine did. One can only imagine how the boys were attracted to Gina's charming smile. I must acknowledge that she had a charming personality as well. We spent those childhood days going from house to house, eating and dancing and having fun. I never understood why Gina's mother was so silent, and I didn't realize what was happening in Gina's family until my sister was brought back from overseas. She had begun to display the same silent behavior as Gina's mom. I say this with the utmost respect; my sister's silence troubled me because I wanted so very much to help her but felt powerless. I'm sure Gina and her family felt the same way about their family situation.

As the years passed, our lives took us in different directions, but we were out of touch. After I graduated from college and returned to the city, I heard Gina was on drugs, but I never did investigate the matter. There was no time to fill in the gaps in our relationship. When I remember my first experience with drugs, I just shake my head in awe and amazement at the invisible hand of God, who had been protecting me from disaster that night. I am convinced my mother had been praying that night for her child of grace, and I knew it was God who had mysteriously protected me from being raped and molested that night. That one puff had caused me to begin hallucinating so badly. I don't know how long it took me to regain some semblance of sanity, but I vowed that night that I would never put another marijuana cigarette to my lips. Sadly, Gina wasn't that fortunate. Several years later, after I had migrated, I heard Gina had passed away. I felt extremely sad when I heard her life had been short-circuited by the devil. She hadn't lived long enough to discover the plans and purpose our heavenly Father had for her life.

In light of my situation and the endless battles I had to fight to be ultimately set free from this spirit of witchcraft, I decided to really take a look at other families around me. I used the yardstick of God's truth to measure family situations. Almighty God is so orderly and structured in the way he operates, and he has set the pattern in his holy Word for our benefit. We have manuals, patterns, and architectural designs for everything man has created. Anytime I have a problem with my vehicle, I would take it to the mechanic, who would run tests to determine the root cause of the problem. After diagnosing the problem, he would consult the manual for my vehicle, taking into consideration the make, year, and model. Dr. Myles Munroe, who is now deceased, was the first preacher I heard who stated that the Bible is God's manual for his creation. Consequently, if something has gone wrong with the family, we can discover the root cause of the problem by consulting the holy Word of God.

I've encountered many different types of families in my time. Every family is precious to God. Every family has different cultural experiences, beliefs, and customs that are ingrained in their very framework. Some of these rituals, handed down through generations by ancestors, may be socially acceptable but are contrary to the standard of God's holy Word. I remember watching a movie about a young girl who had to abandon her schooling and atone for a murder that was accidentally committed by her father. She regretfully submitted to a custom that was acceptable, and she was presented to the male religious figure, who was old enough to be her grandfather. This male figure already had control of many other girls who had borne him children. I recall another movie based on a true story where a man and his daughter were living in abject poverty on the streets. After many unsuccessful efforts to feed his hungry daughter, the poor father sold his daughter to someone who had assured him of a good education and a promising future for his child. A young man came along and opened his eyes to the horrific thing he had done, because his daughter had been seduced by a gang of human traffickers.

The Bible clearly states in 1 Corinthians 11:3 that God does everything in an organized manner. He has structured the family in a way that creates protection for the family unit. God is the head of Christ, who is under God's authority and is accountable to him. Men are supposed to be operating and functioning and submitted to Christ. The apostle Paul wants every man to know that his head is Christ. Consequently, if a man doesn't have Christ as his head, that means he is a headless man. If a man has lost his head, this would result in all types of behavior that would fit the idiomatic expression "Have you lost your mind?" When I hear reports of the atrocious acts of behavior displayed by some men, I know the only reason they are performing such acts of violence is because they don't have Jesus as their head. There were no real men as father figures in their homes, and as a result, they didn't know how to function as real men.

God's original intent was for man to take the lead in being responsible. Deuteronomy 16:16–17 clearly states that "three times in a year shall all thy males appear before the Lord thy God in the place which he shall chose . . . and they shall not appear before the Lord empty." It continues to state that men were expected to bring a blessing to God in accordance with their God-given ability to produce. God kept calling men into their position of leadership. In the Old Testament, he called Abraham; then called Isaac, Abraham's son; and then called Jacob, Abraham's grandson, to be a blessing to families in every nation. In Genesis 12:1–3, Almighty God, our Creator, called Abraham and promised to make him a great nation and said that, in him, all families of the earth would be blessed. Even Jesus, when he started his ministry, called twelve disciples.

Now God also called and used women in the Old Testament in leadership positions, like Rachel, the shepherdess who kept her father's sheep, in Genesis 29:9. He also used Deborah, a judge who was also a prophetess, in Judges 4 and 5. He also used Esther, in the book of Esther, to bring deliverance to the whole nation of Jews. Why did God keep calling men primarily? In 1 Corinthians 11:3, we are informed that the head of the woman is the man. If the family structure is according to God's directive in his holy Word, then our families would be in alignment. God knows that when the man is in his rightful place, the woman will automatically submit to his authority in a way that is fit and pleasing to God. If, however, a man wants his wife to submit to anything that's contrary to God's Word, the result would be chaos in the family. Some families have been in shambles for generations, and God is looking for one person in each family to take a stand for righteousness in their individual families and to turn that sailing ship around in a completely new direction, headed toward pleasing God in all their ways.

If we are looking for answers to all the chaotic situations that are happening in families, we just need to look to the Bible, which I call the real family album. It has been said that there's nothing new under the sun, meaning there's no new sin, as somebody else did it before you or I ever thought of doing it. In the Bible, we see that our Creator always gives us the choice to do right or wrong. He also paints a picture of the benefits of doing things his way, which is right, and the sad consequences of disobeying his Word. In 1 Corinthians 11:3, we understand God is the head of everything, and we follow his directives. He is able to steer our families in the direction of righteousness.

The use of drugs is rampant in societies. I've heard of stories where the police conducted raids and arrested drug users and drug couriers. Some people don't actually use drugs but sell it to make a living. Many careers have gone down the drain and come to a sudden halt by either imprisonment or premature death. We hear reports of drivers who were intoxicated and claimed the life of innocent victims because of their intoxicated state. I've conversed with young female drug users who had a desire to change their lives. When I asked about their physical condition, they acknowledged they were pregnant. When asked who the father of their unborn child was, they would shamefacedly admit they didn't know because when they were high from the use of drugs, they had exchanges with multiple partners. Sad to say, their children will grow up without a father. They may have stepfathers or "uncles," as some would call the men in their lives, but I believe there will always be a deep hole in that child's soul at the thought of never knowing who their real father is. It will be evidenced on the birth certificate, as there will be a blank space where their father's name should be written. Sometimes I wonder where these children are, but they are present behind the scenes and planted in our classrooms. And we wonder why our children are being diagnosed with all types of learning disabilities.

Can you imagine, at school, when other children will be talking about their fathers, especially during special occasions, like their birthdays or Christmas when there are no gifts from fathers, how these fatherless children will feel? Maybe they will think, *Since I am worth nothing to my father, I am a worthless human being, and my life is a waste.* One can only imagine that the absence of a gift will be replaced by emptiness within, and over a period of years, that emptiness could become so deep that the child could become lost within. No matter how hard the mother or foster parents may be trying to please that child, the disruptive, rebellious behaviors will result from the unseen pain within. At other times, the child may have a quiet personality, and all the inner turmoil of anger and frustration of not knowing his/her true identity could result in silence and behavioral problems.

This drug demon is in operation in every facet of our society. It's in our neighborhoods, and it is also penetrating our schools and colleges; this is affecting the next generation. It has affected the medical field, because in some states, you can smoke marijuana legally. Shall I make mention of those who are addicted to prescription drugs?

Where Are the Fathers?

Some fathers here in the United States of America are on the run, and this has caused the government to step in and make them pay the penalty of monthly child support. If the father is working, that's not a problem, as the money will help the child's mother provide for that child. But even if provision is being made, there is still the problem of the absent father. The mother may do a good job at raising the children, but sometimes history repeats itself; the absent father could very well become a family tradition. According to information gleaned from the website https://www.fatherhood. org, in the article named "Fathers behind Bars: The Problem and Solution for America's Children" (infographic), *"The father absence crisis in America is real.* According to the U.S. Census Bureau, 24 million children in America—one out of three—live without their biological dad in the home" (emphasis added).

> For though you might have ten thousand instructors in Christ, *yet you do not have many fathers*; for in Christ Jesus have I begotten you through the gospel. (1 Corinthians 4:15; emphasis added)

It takes more than planting a seed in a lady's womb to be called a father. The apostle Paul is plainly stating that there is an immense difference between being an instructor in Christ and being a father. He emphasized the fact that there may be ten thousand instructors in Christ, but not everyone who is professing Christ is functioning as a "spiritual father" in Christ. We learn this from the opening scripture in 1 Corinthians 11:3, "But I would have you know, that the head of every man is Christ; and the head of the woman is the man; and the head of Christ is God." This scripture was also written by the apostle Paul, who did not walk alongside Jesus on his earthly pilgrimage. He did not know Jesus in the flesh, but he got a revelation of who Jesus is, as aforementioned, when Almighty God knocked him to the ground while his mind-set was to persecute Christians. Paul submitted to Christ Jesus, and he got the revelation of God's divine order as well. He realized he had to do more than be an instructor and stated that he had begotten the Corinthian believers through the gospel. He further stated how he had begotten these souls in Galatians 4:19 by means of the gospel of Jesus Christ when he diligently prayed for them.

Besides fathers on the run, we have fathers who may be physically present and paying the bills but, because of a breakdown of communication in the home, are not present. Besides giving their money, mothers would like fathers to give more of themselves by spending time with the family. Because of the breakdown in my family and since her now-deceased father was not available to walk her down the aisle, when my first daughter got married, I was asked to give words of encouragement. It's an oxymoron, but all I had to give was what I really hadn't experienced. I advised them to practice the three Ps, which I realized was missing from my first marriage. Every family should pray together, plan together, and play together. Effective communication is extremely important in every relationship we have, especially with our immediate family members. Families need to discuss family matters weekly and seek God's wisdom by praying for guidance in setting goals. They should then thank God for giving those divine strategies and revelation, especially through his spoken Word. Families should also plan fun times together, like walks in the park, picnics, or other outdoor activities they can all enjoy; take a drive or take an affordable vacation.

Many of our fathers are locked away in the prisons. As a matter of fact, there are generations of the male species in prison. According to information gleaned from the website https://www.fatherhood. org, the article "Fathers behind Bars: The Problem and Solution for America's Children" (infographic) further outlines these two stats:

1. There are 2.7 million children with a parent in prison or jail.
2. Ninety-two percent (92%) of parents in prison are fathers.

Who Is the Head of Your Household?

Every year, when we file our tax returns here in the US, the tax preparer asks the question "Who is head of the household?" In the traditional family, with husband and wife, the response would be the husband, the breadwinner, and family incomes would be combined. If the family hasn't paid enough taxes during the year, then the head of the family would be responsible for paying those taxes to the government entity, the IRS. If, on the other hand, enough or more taxes have been paid annually, the head of the household would get a refund on behalf of his family. In a single-parent family, the woman would be considered the head of the household.

So what can a woman do if she realizes the man she married or who fathered her children has no backbone? Colossians 2:9–10 says, "For in Him dwells all the fullness bodily. And you are complete in Him who is the head of all principality and power." The single parent is considered legal head of herself and children. She can however establish that Jesus Christ is the spiritual head of her household through prayer. She needs to understand that Christ possesses all the fullness of God in a bodily form. She also needs to understand that everything she needs will be in Christ, who makes her complete and fulfilled. Christ, the head of her life, has control over every ungodly principle that is contrary to God's holy Word. The ideal situation in every family would include a praying man and woman. If there's no praying man in the family and the woman assumes her posture of prayer, God will intervene on that family's behalf pertaining to spiritual matters. Somehow I think my mother was praying for her child of grace that night when I had started hallucinating so badly. After I took a puff of that marijuana, I knew it was God who protected me from molestation. I don't remember how long it took to regain my sanity before I was safely escorted home, but I vowed that night that I would never in my life put another marijuana joint to my lips. I believe families are sustained if there is at least one person who is praying fervently before God's throne of grace, asking for his divine intervention in circumstances that are beyond our control.

Is there hope for a single mother who has a headless family, without a man as head of the household? I remember my praying mother whose feet were directed to the neighborhood church Sunday after Sunday. My mother practiced her faith and took me to church, and for this, I am grateful. In the midst of all the painful situations in her life, I could see my mother praying for her family behind the scenes. My mother had a large picture of the Sacred Heart mounted on the walls in our home. This is a picture of Jesus with his heart pierced with sorrows. I would have imagined that every time she gazed at the Sacred Heart of Jesus, she received strength and encouragement to keep living and praying and taking care of her family the best and only way she knew. This woman made her earthly pilgrimages to Mount St. Benedict annually, and did I tell you? She always broke a piece of some plant from the garden on the mount and transplanted it in her garden at home. My now-deceased mother, this woman with her heart full of sorrows, with her eyes fixed on the mounted picture of the Sacred Heart, made her home beautiful on the inside and beautified her surroundings outside to make it look like a tiny replica of the Garden of Eden.

This was the mystery of her faith. It is said in 1 Corinthians 11:3, "But I want you to know that the head of every man is Christ, the head of the woman is man, and the head of Christ is God." My mother had made Christ the head of her household through faith and prayer. I didn't realize it then, but I understand it now. I was able to survive the vicissitudes of life. I had stopped praying the Lord's Prayer, also known as the Our Father, and had no sense of direction when I married a headless man (that's a man without Christ as his head). I was headless also when I began seeing the red flags in the midst of all the turmoil. I was living, but I knew something was missing and couldn't figure out what it was. According to the scripture, I had no prayer covering my home, and I was not receiving all the support I needed because the roles were reversed in our home. I realize now that God was mysteriously preparing me behind the scenes to "come home to the sacred heart." I never did have a picture of the Sacred Heart on the wall of my home, but in the next section, you will discover the mystery of the secret place where I hid Jesus.

CHAPTER 9

Seeing God as Our Heavenly Father

I remember in our country years ago, when I was working, there was a monthly salary deduction that was taken from our checks by the government authorities. This was classified as the widows and orphans fund. I've never heard anyone who challenged this deduction. I never stopped to think why or when it started, but after my God delivered me from manipulation through the now-deceased minister in the church where I became born again, I found this scripture: "A father of the fatherless, a defender of widows is God in His Holy habitation" (Psalm 68:5). I was able to understand that Almighty God has a father's heart and actually cares about and is willing to defend widows and orphans. I've discovered over the years that there are so many individuals, both men and women, who grew up in homes without fathers.

Then I found another gold nugget from the truth of God's holy Word in the last book of the Old Testament.

> Behold I will send you Elijah the prophet before the coming of the great and dreadful day of the Lord. And he will turn the hearts of the fathers to the

children, and the hearts of the children to their fathers. (Malachi 4:5–6)

It is evident from this scripture that God wants to heal and restore family relationships. He is looking down from his holy, heavenly habitation and seeing what is happening in every family in every nation of the entire universe. Our heavenly Father's heart is beating and vibrating with love for all the fathers who are running away from their God-given responsibility in every nation, and he can see the breaking heart of every fatherless child. God also understands that fatherless children who are raised in a home without a loving father will have a problem building a loving relationship with him and also their own children. He understands how grown fatherless children can grow up with hate in their hearts for their own fathers and become just like the fathers they hate or worse than their hateful fathers.

God is so concerned about future generations that he cautioned the children of Israel in Psalm 78. God did not want them to be repeat offenders like their fathers were, so he issued a warning in this psalm, reminding them of the expectations he had of their forefathers. However, they repeatedly broke God's heart, even though he forgave them on countless occasions. God's intention, based on the principle of his holy Word, was for fathers to show to the next generation the wonderful works of the Lord so that they would praise him for his goodness. He commanded them to make it known to each generation, who would in turn relay the good news to the next generation. God wanted each generation to set their hope in him and trust him. The reason God wanted each generation to know about him is disclosed in verse 7, "And might not be as their fathers, a stubborn and rebellious generation; a generation that set not their heart aright, and whose spirit was not steadfast with God." God didn't want them to be stubborn and rebellious like their forefathers, and in the same way, he wants us to be free from the spirit of rebellion. The psalm continues to declare how the children of Israel didn't trust in God's provision when they were in the wilderness. When they cried out to him, he remembered them and had mercy on them. In verse 37, we are told that "nevertheless, they did flatter Him with their mouth, and they lied unto Him with their tongues." God knew their hearts were not right with him. God wants us to come to him with genuine hearts. He knows when we are genuine, and it's pointless if we pretend, because we cannot fool him.

God's love is so electrifying and can be shocking also. I think about the electrical companies we pay our money to for current to flow into our homes and flood each room inside the house, along with the exterior as well. As outlined in the first chapter, we simply flip the switch automatically. About six years ago, I was driving a man who I know personally around a certain neighborhood because he was looking for a house to live in. A friend of his had offered him the opportunity of renting his abandoned home. We pulled up to this house, and to myself, I was saying, "No way, Jose!" There were overgrown bushes at the front of the house, which was facing north. The bushes were wrapped around the sides facing the east and west. So you can only imagine what was happening in the backyard, which faced south. After looking at the mess for a while, I imagined we were synchronized in our thoughts, and I was waiting for him to say, "This is not the place. Let's go!" But I looked in astonishment as he opened the door to the passenger's side in slow motion. He carefully lifted his pained knees one at a time and, on the curb, planted his cane on solid ground. His cane had become his fulcrum, and out of the corner of my eye, I watched respectfully as he strategically felt for the right spot at the correct angle. When he found the spot, he planted the cane firmly and lifted the rest of his torso out of the vehicle while maintaining his balance and bending his head so that he wouldn't knock himself on the head and fall to the ground.

Then he started walking in the slow but rhythmic manner he had grown accustomed to. I myself got out of the car, trying to figure out what he was up to. I listened in disbelief and amazement to the words that flowed from his lips: "Yes, this is the house!" I became tight-lipped, but you could imagine what I was thinking. *Do you see what I see? A dilapidated, broken-down house overgrown with weeds?*

Oh, by the way, I forgot to tell you the water had been cut off, and the lights as well. What was he doing? He was using his cane as a search agent, looking for the location of the water main.

That man had limited resources; I don't know how he did it, but he paid someone to cut down the bushes all around the house. He received favor from the owner of the property, who sent a plumber to run new pipes inside the house leading to the main. The owner also sent an electrician to rewire the house; he got connected to the electric company, and lights were turned on in the house. I know this grown man's father had been murdered when he was three years old. I also know that every day he said the prayer Jesus taught us to pray. So if you have been fatherless all your life, I plead the blood of Jesus over you as you pay attention to these scriptures from our heavenly Father.

In Matthew 6:9–15, when Jesus was asked by his disciples how to pray, he instructed them to pray in this manner: "Our Father in heaven, hallowed be your name. Your kingdom come, your will be done on earth as it is in heaven. Give us this day our daily bread. And forgive us our debts, as we forgive our debtors. And lead us not into temptation, but deliver us from evil. For yours is the kingdom and the power and the glory forever. Amen." Our heavenly Father wants us to build a relationship with him on a daily basis. Prayer is talking to God from within our heart. God wants us to get to know him as our healer because his presence is so powerful and real. God wants us to know he has a heavenly spiritual kingdom he wants to establish here on earth through our prayers. He wants us to trust him for provision of everything we need daily. He wants us to be honest with ourselves and be honest with him and confess our sins. He wants us to forgive others freely if we want him to forgive us our sins, and that means he doesn't want us to bear grudges against our offenders. Consequently, if we forgive a little, we can only receive forgiveness on a small scale. In other words, we could be polluting our own spirits with this poison called unforgiveness.

A father of the fatherless, a defender of the widows is
God in His Holy habitation. (Psalm 68:5)

Our heavenly Father understands our individual stories and really wants to spiritually adopt those who have never been fathered or will never know the whereabouts of their real father.

> When my father and my mother forsake me, then the
> Lord will take care of me. (Psalm 27:10)

It's possible at times, even though your real parents may be around, to have a feeling of hopelessness, as though no one cares. This may happen in families where parents may be busy working to provide for their family's immediate needs and may not be aware that the most important commodity they could spend with their children is time. Other times, children may be in a home without a spiritual foundation, without having a sense of purpose, and may feel lost. However, if we do feel lost at any time, our heavenly Father wants us to know he's available. We simply have to come running to him, like little children, with our arms outstretched, and he'll bend down and pick us up and cover us with his umbrella of protection called prayer. I allowed my heavenly Father to pick me up because when I left my parents' religion, they couldn't understand that God gives us free choice to follow Jesus, no matter what it may cost us. In some other parts of the world, individuals may be shunned by their families and sometimes even put to death for changing their previous religious persuasions.

> Can a woman forget her nursing child, and not
> have compassion on the son of her womb? Surely
> they may forget, yet I will not forget you. See I have
> inscribed you on the palms of my hands; your walls
> are continually before me. (Isaiah 49:15–16)

The scripture is letting us know it's possible for the most loving mother to forget her nursing child and to not have compassion for the son she birthed. There are so many situations that could cause this to happen in this world full of storms, perils, and distractions.

Our heavenly Father wants us to know that even if we feel neglected by our own mother, he would never forget us, because when he was extended on Calvary's cross, our names were tattooed on the palms of his hands. He's continually thinking about us.

> When He had been baptized, Jesus came up immediately from the water; and behold the heavens were opened to Him, and He saw the Spirit of God descending like a dove and alighting upon Him. And suddenly a voice came from heaven saying, "This is my beloved Son in whom I am well pleased." (Matthew 3:16–17)

This is stating clearly that when Jesus was completely immersed in the Jordan River and baptized by John the Baptist, a voice could be heard from heaven. It was the voice of our heavenly Father declaring that he was well pleased with Jesus, his firstborn, one and only begotten Son. Since God was pleased by Jesus's baptism, we should follow in the footsteps of Jesus and be water baptized, as this will be pleasing to our God.

> I am the way the truth and the life. No one comes to the Father except through me. (John 14:6)

Jesus is letting us know here that he is the only way to our heavenly Father. This means Jesus is the doorway that allows us access to the mansions of our heavenly Father.

> For as many as are led by the Spirit of God, these are the Sons of God. For you did not receive the spirit of bondage again to fear, but you received the spirit of adoption by whom we cry out, "Abba, Father." The spirit himself bears witness with our Spirit that we are children of God. (Romans 8:14–17)

If we allow ourselves to be led by God's Holy Spirit of truth, we will be called the spiritual sons of the Most High God. We would have new DNA because of the Blood of Jesus, which cleanses us of the very nature and propensity to sin. We will no longer have to be in bondage to our past, present, or future fears, because we will be transformed into God-fearing spiritual sons of the majestic Creator of heaven and earth. That's when our relationship changes, and we will no longer refer to our Creator as simply some unknown god or the man upstairs, but we'll have a new relationship with him and call him Abba Father.

SECTION 3

TRANSLATED FROM THE KINGDOM OF DARKNESS

Giving thanks unto the Father,
which has made us meet to be partakers of the
inheritance of the saints in light.
Who has delivered us from the power of darkness,
And has translated us into the kingdom of His dear Son;
In whom we have redemption through His
blood, even the forgiveness of sins.
—Colossians 1:12–14

CHAPTER 1

Translation from One Kingdom to Another

When I was in elementary school, we were a British colony in an island of the Caribbean. We had a local vernacular consisting of broken English, which we used at home, but at school we were taught the Queen's English. I remember my mother would admonish me at home to speak properly, and I would slip into the local vernacular for the sole purpose of offending her because I was a rebellious child. Our vernacular was not written, but I can give you some examples of the Trinidad vernacular:

- "Way yuh going?" means "Where are you going?"
- "Wah happen?" means "What has happened?"
- "Why yuh do dat?" means "Why did you do that?"
- "Way you going?" means "Where are you going?"
- "Ah dough like dat" means "I don't like that."

I can understand why my mother insisted I speak properly, because God was preparing me from childhood to speak and write in the universal English language.

So I just translated some colloquial expressions from the spoken dialect in the average Trinidad home to the English dialect, which we learned at school. Basically, the meaning was the same, but the sentence structure changed. If I translate the sentence "I am hungry" from English to Spanish, it would be this: "Tengo hambre." And in French, it would look like this: "J'ai faim." It looks different each time because the format has changed, but the meaning is the same. Now according to *Webster's New World Dictionary*, the word *translate* has the following meaning: "to change from one place, position etc. to another; transfer." Also, according to *Strong's Concordance of the Bible*, 3179 Greek word *meth-is-tan-o* means "to transfer i.e., to carry away, depose or (fig.) exchange."

I didn't know it at the time, but my heavenly Father had decided it was time to shine his light of truth and penetrate the darkness in my mind. In some mysterious way, he had been preparing me all along, because he has time and eternity in his hand. The scripture reveals that Almighty God knew everything about me and decided it was time to translate me, bring me out of the power of darkness. Let me remind you that from the very beginning, it has always been God's intent to dispel darkness and bring light (Genesis 1:3). God has a movement called the Holy Spirit that separated darkness from light, and we see in the remainder of that chapter that when God moves, he speaks; he's able to set his creation in order.

A New Testament witness is Saul, who was a citizen of the Roman Empire and had a passion for God. Because of his upbringing, he hated Christians, and according to Acts 8:3, "Saul made havoc of the church, entering into every house, and hailing men and women committed them to prison." This man was so passionate about his beliefs and doctrine that he went to the high priest for letters authorizing him to take his madness to the next level.

> And Saul yet breathing out threatenings and slaughter against the disciples of the Lord went unto the high priest, and desired of him letters to Damascus to the synagogues, that if he found any of this way, whether they were men or women, he might bring them bound unto Jerusalem. (Acts 9:1–2)

Saul, with the breath from his lips filled with anger and animosity, hurled murderous threats, and his aim was to bring his own judgment to the disciples of Christ, who had walked and talked with Jesus in the flesh. The Bible didn't say if Saul had met Jesus personally before his death, burial, and resurrection, or if he had listened to Jesus's first Sermon on the Mount. For some unknown reason, he hated all disciples of Christ; he wanted to annihilate them. He further acknowledged in Acts 26:10 that he had shut up many of the saints in prison, put many of them to death, and had spoken against them. He had punished them in every synagogue and compelled them to blaspheme because he was exceedingly mad at them.

But God, who I will refer to as Father Time, seated on his heavenly throne, looked at his clock and decided it was time to intervene in Saul's life. Almighty God, who created all flesh and who is described in 1 Timothy 1:17 as "the King, eternal, immortal, invisible, the only wise God," decided not to kill Saul because he had another plan. Saul obtained the letters he had requested and was on the road to Damascus when something extraordinary happed to him. According to the accounts in Acts 9:3–9, 22:6–11, 26:13–18, as Saul was journeying to Damascus, at midday he saw a light brighter than the sun shining around him and the men who were traveling with him. They all fell to the earth, but Saul was the only one who heard the voice, which he somehow knew was God's voice. The voice asked Saul why he was persecuting him. Saul asked him who he was, and the voice responded, "*I am Jesus of Nazareth whom you are persecuting.*" The men around him were speechless and afraid, and Saul was trembling and in a state of astonishment. Saul, who had become blind instantaneously, then asked the Lord what he wanted him to do, and God explained why he had appeared to him and explained to Saul his earthly assignment.

> For I have appeared unto you for this purpose to make you a minister and a witness both of the things which you have seen, and of the things which I will yet reveal to you. I will deliver you to the Jewish

people and from the Gentiles to whom I now send you to open their eyes, in order to turn them from darkness to light, and from the power of Satan to God, that they may receive forgiveness of sins and an inheritance among those who are sanctified by faith in me. (Acts 26:16)

So we see that our majestic God, who is rich in grace and mercy, visited Saul unexpectedly and demonstrated his power by means of a light that was brighter than the sun. Have you ever tried to look at the sun shining brightly in the sky at noon? After a second or two, it blurs the vision, and we have to turn away or wear shades to protect our eyes. God's visitation was described by Paul after his conversion as "the heavenly vision," which he felt compelled to obey because Almighty God had actually "delivered us from the power of darkness, and had translated us into the kingdom of His dear Son." (Colossians 1:13). He received forgiveness and, as a result of heaven's mandate, had also "received an inheritance among those who were sanctified by faith in Christ." Saul, who had been given earthly authority, was actually possessed with the spirit of the antichrist and was influenced deeply by satanic forces and living in a state of utter darkness spiritually. He was motivated by his natural sense of sight and did what he thought was right. However, Almighty God moved just like he did in the beginning and, in a mysterious way, with his glorious light brighter than the sun, was able to penetrate the darkness to the depths of Saul's soul and translate him from the satanic power of darkness into the kingdom of his marvelous light.

In retrospect, I understand fully what Almighty God was getting ready to do for me. God is no respecter of persons, and what he had done for Saul, whose name was changed to Paul, he was getting ready to do for me. God was about to translate me from the power of satanic influence, as I was his captive. I had the ability to see with my natural eyes and hear with my natural ears, but I was living in spiritual blindness and deafness also. Behind all the changing scenes of my life, God was orchestrating things to prepare me to become a *partaker of the inheritance of the saints in light.* My heavenly Father, who has the blueprint for my life written on the walls of eternity, was making preparations for me to receive my spiritual inheritance in spite of all the opposition from the enemy.

We all know that an inheritance is something we don't have to work for, because it is just assigned to us. According to *Webster's New World Dictionary, inherit* means "to receive (property) as an heir from a predecessor; to have certain characteristics by heredity." Before my earthly father passed away, he informed me while I was in Texas who the executors for his will were. He didn't reveal to me the contents of his will; I didn't ask him, but I wondered why he had given me that information. When he passed away, I was still in Texas, waiting on the next move of God in my life. I didn't have any money, but I asked God if he wanted me to attend my father's funeral. The ticket to my native country was provided by a kindhearted sister in Christ, and I returned unannounced. The morning after I arrived, one of my relatives gave me a box that contained my father's will and all his fixed deposit certificates. Upon reading the will, I realized all my siblings and I were about to inherit money and property, according to the contents of my father's will. I carefully placed the will and other documents back into the box and returned it to the place I thought was safe. We then visited the funeral home to view my father's body, which was being prepared for his burial. However, there was some opposition, as there were spiritual forces that wanted to hinder us from getting our full inheritance. When we returned home some hours later, the box and its contents had mysteriously disappeared. I realized the enemy was trying to steal my inheritance. After my father's funeral, we met with the executors of my father's will and explained to them the situation, and they assured us they would handle the situation. My father had a peaceful homegoing ceremony, but something was brewing behind the scenes.

My earthly father knew there might be some opposition, and he had carefully chosen the executors he wanted to carry out his last wishes on earth. The executors assured us that, in spite of the opposition, my earthly father's last wishes would be granted, because he had the wisdom to register his will with the government authorities. Even though my earthly father was dead, he, in actuality, was speaking from the grave with authority by means of his will. He had wisely chosen executors he could trust to carry out his wishes. Now this scenario happened after my mysterious conversion, which we'll discuss in the next chapter. But a new awareness seeped into my conscious mind when I completely understood what my earthly father did when he registered his will with the government authorities in our country. I realized his will was irrevocable because he had appointed two earthly executors who would do everything within their power to fight that legal battle for us to get our earthly inheritance.

I didn't know what to do to make my father's will become reality, but I understood my assignment for the first time. I realized the power of darkness was in operation then, and the part I had to play was to fast and pray, since there was a real thief working behind the scenes, trying to steal our earthly inheritance. Even though it was our earthly inheritance, I realized it was a spiritual battle I had to fight while residing in my deceased father's house. The Bible tells us in Ephesians 6:12, "For we do not wrestle against flesh and blood, but against principalities, against powers, against the rulers of the darkness of this age, against spiritual hosts of wickedness in the heavenly places." The contents of my father's will had stated specifically how his funds were to be distributed. The executors acted within their right and were able to get access to all my father's assets. After a couple of months of me fasting and praying, my deceased father's wishes became reality. The day finally came when the executors came to the house and read the full contents of the will, presented each family member with a copy of the will, and distributed checks. The two executors had completed their assignment to access all my father's assets and distribute it accordingly, as my father had stated in his will.

My deceased father's wishes became reality because he had registered it with the government and chosen executors who acted in accordance with my father's will. In the same way, the Bible tells us in Psalm 119:89, "Forever, O Lord your word is settled in heaven." That means Almighty God has the blueprint for our lives written on the walls of eternity. It is registered with the government of the kingdom of heaven and the Creator of the universe, and it is irrevocable. Jesus is the executor of our heavenly Father's will, which is recorded in "heavenly places." The following scriptures shed some light on Jesus's earthly mission and purpose, which originated from heaven.

> He who sins is of the devil, for the devil has sinned from the beginning. For this purpose the Son of God was manifested, that he might destroy the works of the devil. (1 John 3:8)

> The thief does not come except to steal, and to kill, and to destroy. I have come that they may have life, and that they may have it more abundantly. (John 10:10)

From the beginning, the devil has been stealing from humanity and empowering them to steal from and kill and destroy one another. God sent Jesus to execute his will here on earth and destroy the plans of the devil. God doesn't want us to hate and do evil things to people. That's the devil's evil, wicked plan, which God is exposing through the good news of the gospel. In God's mysterious way, God's plan is still to deliver souls from the power of darkness of evil and translate them into the kingdom of the marvelous light of his dear Son, Jesus. The opening scripture of this chapter reminds us that we have "redemption through His blood, even the forgiveness of sins." Jesus paid the price for our sins before we were born. He shed his blood on Calvary and paid the price to redeem us or buy us back from the clutches of the evil one, but we will never know about our inheritance of light with the saints unless someone tells us. With this new awareness, we will then begin to seek God's will in the Bible, his holy Word, for ourselves and our loved ones.

I will always be grateful to my earthly father for deciding of his own free will to leave an inheritance for me, his previously rebellious daughter. He didn't have to do this, and I will be forever grateful. I'm thankful he had the wisdom to choose the right executors, who carried out his last will and testament to the fullest. I expressed my gratitude the day we sat around my parents' dining room table and the executor handed me my inheritance check, which I needed to pay off some debts. But may I remind you, the executors' assignment was to act in accordance with my father's instructions; on their own, they were powerless. I thank the executors, but it wasn't their will; I think about my father, who had empowered them to carry out his will. Then I thank my heavenly Father, who used my earthly father to save me from my mother's womb. My heavenly Father is the one who motivated my earthly father to include me in his will. I think about our heavenly Father's master plan for humanity, because he sent Jesus to earth wrapped in mortal flesh to execute his spiritual plans for lost humanity.

My heavenly Father was working behind the scenes, but I didn't know it; he was about to expose me to the executor of his will here on earth. I had accepted my earthly father's inheritance at that time, so now I can use the situation that happened in the natural as an analogy for the spiritual. But the question was, how was I going to respond to my heavenly Father's will? Was I going to accept it wholeheartedly, or was I going to reject it because I couldn't see it? I invite you to step into my story and find out what Almighty God was about to do in my life. Remember, I was still operating in the kingdom of darkness, but I didn't know it.

CHAPTER 2

Born-Again Experience

Accepting Jesus Within

Jesus answered and said to him, "Most assuredly I say to you,
unless one is born again, he cannot see the kingdom of God."
Nicodemus said to Him, "How can a man be born when he is old?
Can he enter a second time into his mother's womb and be born?"
Jesus answered, "Most assuredly, I say to you, unless one is born
of water and the Spirit, he cannot enter the kingdom of God.
That which is born of the flesh is flesh, and that
which is born of the Spirit is spirit. Do not marvel
that I said to you, 'You must be born again.'"
—John 3:3–8 (NKJV)

I had been touched inappropriately as a child by another child, been molested by an older girl, and danced with the devil in and out of relationships, looking for love in all the wrong places. I had turned my back on God, stopped going to church and stopped praying, been a victim of date rape, and kept it a secret. I had been rebellious, left my father's house, and was enticed by the first woman who said the words *I love you*. Now I was trapped in a marriage with a man who had attempted to steal my identity. The thought never occurred to me to pray, because I didn't know if or how prayer worked or what its purpose was anyway. However, God had me on his mind, even though he wasn't on my mind.

On the outside, life appeared to be going well. I was respectfully married and had my own husband, not somebody else's. I was determined to be true to my wedding vows and make my marriage work, especially as we had our first baby. I was teaching at the village school, and we had our first apartment, which I had furnished. But strangely, I was paying all the bills. When I had first met my husband, he was working and living with his mother, and I was paying rent to her for an empty bedroom. I was paying her for preparing my meals. When we got married, we lived with her, and my now-deceased husband was still working. But for a mysterious reason, after I fled from her house and he started pursuing me, he lost his job. He would keep applying, get a job, and then lose it. Now we were in our first apartment, and he was not working.

For some reason, he had stopped looking, and every day he would go to his deceased mother's house to help her. I paid for childcare as well, while he helped his mother. God just decided to step right in the middle of all this turmoil around me. God was getting ready to shine his light into my dark world, just as he had done for Saul and countless other saints through the ages. The circumstances were different, but God was getting me ready to be a partaker of his heavenly inheritance, although I didn't know it at the time.

However, hovering in the background were mysterious circumstances concerning my deceased eldest sister, who had been suffering from an emotional breakdown for about ten years. My eldest sister, the one who had experienced an emotional breakdown when she had migrated, was also in my chaotic thoughts. I really wished I could help her and my mother in some way. I had watched my mother bear this burden since I was a teenager in high school, but I didn't know what to do, since my sister was physically present but seemed as though she was in another world.

I had made friends with a coworker, who is now deceased, and had confided in her about my sister. She told me she knew someone who could help my sister, and she took me to visit this elderly man at his house. I didn't think I needed help, but I was really concerned about my sister. So one day, after work, my friend took me to the house of an elderly man, who is now deceased. He was a tall black man, a little lightly colored, maybe in his early seventies. His hair was scarce, and his face and neck were wrinkled. He wore a pair of Bermuda shorts and a T-shirt. I was introduced to an older dark-skinned woman who I imagined was his housekeeper, and she wore a head covering. It was a small wooden house, nothing fancy, but kept clean and simple. After introductions were made, I was offered a seat, and I complied.

I didn't know then, but in some mysterious way, behind the scenes, Almighty God was about to use this elderly man to prepare me for the future plans he had for my life. I didn't know then that I would be making more trips to that house over the course of several years. I learned many life lessons from this man, and there were good, bad, and ugly situations. He inquired about the nature of my visit and listened carefully as I expressed concern about my sister, but the words he uttered did not help me resolve the situation with my sister at the time. He said, "You must be born again." I guess he read the expression on my face; it didn't make sense to me, since I wasn't the one who needed help—or so I thought at the time.

He spoke to my friend, who by this time had wrapped a cloth around her head as well. She took her Bible from her bag, which she always carried around. I had always wondered what was in the bag. Now I understood, as she carefully unwrapped her precious Bible, which she kept safely in another bag in her bag. This was actually the first Bible lesson I received; it was read by my friend, recommended by this man, but somehow it was orchestrated by the real teacher—God's Holy Spirit of truth. When my friend finished reading the scripture from John 3:3–8, the man explained that I needed to be born again spiritually and that I also needed to be water baptized. I explained to him that I had been baptized as a child. He then elaborated on the truth of baptism based on the scripture and referred to Jesus's baptism in the River Jordan by John the Baptist, when Jesus was completely immersed in water (Matthew 3:13–17).

I left that little cottage and ran to the day care to pick up my baby girl. I didn't get help or answers about my sister, but everything he said to me made sense. However, I had some concerns about the head covering the ladies were wearing, and I questioned my friend. In our native country, some women wore hats to church to cover their heads, but these women were wrapping their heads, which was something I had never experienced on my side of the fence.

My friend convinced me this man was different, because his church was of the apostolic faith. I should have asked her what that meant, but in retrospect, I'm not sure if she knew. I asked for the whereabouts of the church, and she told me it was in the country, about two hours' drive from the city where we lived. She seemed so knowledgeable and informative, so I accompanied her multiple times to visit this man's cottage. What drew me was the scripture about being born again. It made sense to me, and I felt it was the missing link in my life. In my head, I understood, and I realized I wanted to be born again. Then my friend explained to me also that if I got baptized, I would receive spiritual gifts. She didn't explain to me what those gifts were, and I realize in retrospect, after she died, that she didn't know either. After much reflection, I decided I wanted to do what Jesus did, because I wanted *to see the kingdom of God.*

I wanted to obey Jesus fully. He said in John 3:5, "Verily, verily, I say unto you, except a man be born of water and of the Spirit, he cannot enter into the kingdom of God." I really, really sincerely believed what Jesus was saying, and I wanted not only *to see the kingdom of God* but also *to enter the kingdom of God.* So that Easter Sunday morning in April 1975, we left early and traveled to the country, along with my baby, for me to be baptized, completely immersed in water.

Before the baptism, however, I sat on the mourners' bench with some others. This bench was placed at the front of the church, and we were given instructions in preparation for our baptism. We were instructed that baptism was a "death unto our sinful way of life, and a new birth unto righteousness" (Romans 6:3–12). I sat on that mourners' bench and thought about all the sexual sins I had committed over the years, before I was respectfully married. I thought about the rum and Coke I liked that I would have to give up, and I decided I was ready to take the next step *to enter the kingdom of God.*

I had to ignore the fact that all the women were dressed in white, with their heads wrapped in white cloths also. They reminded me of another religious sect, but they were all so kind and didn't appear to me to be evil in any way; so I pushed that thought out of my mind and focused on their instructions. I had decided to follow Jesus, and besides, I wanted to enter his kingdom and receive my spiritual gifts. This was the first step.

We were informed that the Christian pathway was not easy and that trials and tribulations would be part of our Christian heritage. As we sat on that mourners' bench, we were cautioned by another younger lady, "Rebuke not an elder, but entreat him as a father; and the younger men as brethren; the elder women as mothers; the younger as sisters, with all purity. . . . Against an elder receive not an accusation, but before two or three witnesses" (1 Timothy 5:1–2, 19). We were well indoctrinated from the Word of God about how we should treat the spiritual leaders, who were called elders.

I don't remember how many of us were baptized that Resurrection Day, which was so befitting to me. The spiritual leader and his housekeeper, along with the older women, were driven to the beach, but everyone else walked about a two-mile journey to the beach along the dusty road. Every so often, we would stand aside to let vehicles pass by on that narrow road. I could feel the gentle kiss of the morning breeze as I looked skyward, admiring the coconut trees. Their trunks were bare and rooted in the soil, but their leaves and coconuts were at the very top. This city girl had never walked so many miles before, but the ladies were singing and clapping their hands as we walked. In the distance, we could hear a strange sound, and as we drew nearer, it increased in volume slightly. In anticipation, we waited, and as we followed the downward trail, stepping carefully, it came into full view. We finally arrived at the beach just as the sun was rising, and we couldn't help but look up at the amazing blast of God's handiwork in the sky. We dropped our little bags, stuffed with our towels and change of clothes, on the sand. However, we had to shift our gaze and give attention to the voice of the person who was giving final instructions.

After the first candidate was baptized by the elder and other men who were helping him in the water, the ladies began to sing this song.

> Low in the grave he lay, Jesus my Savior!
> Waiting the coming day, Jesus my Lord!
> Up from the grave he arose!
> With a mighty triumph o'er his foes!
> He arose a victor from the dark domain,
> And he lives forever with his saints to reign.
> He arose! He arose! Hallelujah! Christ arose!

I especially love the special hymn that was also sung on my baptism day. "O happy day when Jesus washed my sins away. He taught me how to watch and pray and live rejoicing every day." I really believed on that day that all my sins were washed away, and I rose up a new person in Christ. The sun was shining brightly, and I was really so happy. I was prepared to face the trials and tribulations that were confronting me. On our trek back to the church, I was happily singing with the brethren a song entitled "It's a great change since I was born. The things I used to do, I will do them no more." I had definitely decided to change my entire lifestyle.

CHAPTER 3

Learning and Indoctrination

As the weeks progressed, godly fear was instilled in us toward church leadership as we studied the account of Korah's rebellion in Numbers 16. Korah had incited other church leaders to rise up against Moses and Aaron, the leaders who had been selected by God as his representatives. The outcome was disastrous, as the earth opened and swallowed them up, with their entire households. So I was trained never to listen to any negativity concerning the elders, and I never did, until God Almighty himself showed up in my dream about ten years later in the fullness of his time.

Then I heard the scripture from Matthew 22:37 (KJV), "Jesus said to him, 'You shall love the Lord with all your heart, with all your soul and with all your mind.'" I had to bow my head in shame, and I confessed to God that I didn't love him in that way and that, in fact, I didn't even know how to love. I whispered to God from my heart that I wanted to love him 100 percent. At that moment, my love walk with Jesus began, and I accepted Jesus in my heart and decided to give up everything and follow him. I thought following Jesus meant adapting to the religious practices of the other sisters, so I emulated them. I stopped wearing slacks and only wore dresses and skirts but said goodbye to miniskirts. I stopped wearing makeup and jewelry, and I no longer painted my fingernails. My hair was all natural now. Those around me observed the outward changes, but my religion was a secret, as I only wore the white head covering at church, never in public. My parents later found out I had left the family religion behind, and they did not approve. But I was happy because I had accepted Jesus in my heart, and that was all that really mattered to me.

The word that was whispered in my ears at baptism was "Master Jesus, save me." I was, however, warned to never share this word with anyone, because it was a secret. Stories were told about certain people who had let the secret out of the bag and lost their minds. Now the secret is out, because Master Jesus did save me, and I'm sharing the secret of my salvation with you, my readers. Since I now have the mind of Christ, I have learned to fear no man. It was a good practice that I had planted Jesus in my heart, because I used the name of Jesus to fight many, many spiritual battles. I didn't know how to seek God for myself, and I would say I remained a spiritual baby for about ten years. That one bullet in my artillery was used on countless occasions to fight my battles and defend me. Like the shepherd boy, David, I was practicing behind the scenes, but I had no clue God was preparing me to face my Goliath and bring him to the ground. In the meantime, I safely carried Baby Jesus with me in that secret place in my heart.

We had church on Sunday at the country church, but during the week, we rented the bottom floor of a facility that was closer to home. It was during these sessions that I learned Psalms 1 and 91, because they were repeated constantly. We had preaching, but what really blessed my heart were the hymns the sisters sang. These hymns, which were sung over a period of years, were a tremendous blessing to my soul, and these were the ones that brought me closer to Baby Jesus, the treasure in my heart. Some of them are "A wonderful Savior is Jesus my Lord," "All to Jesus I Surrender," "Amazing grace, how sweet the sound," "Blessed assurance, Jesus is mine," and "What a Friend We Have in Jesus." I suddenly decided to count the number of hymns I remember singing over the years that have blessed my heart, and there are about seventy of them, which is more than my children have learned over the years. I believe my soul really became anchored in Jesus, and I am truly grateful for these hymns that helped me put my trust in the Lord.

After I became born again, my spiritual eyes were open, and I began to have dreams. We had been cautioned to sleep on our right side, as this would enable us to have dreams from heaven. If we slept on the left side, we would receive a dream from hell. Our leader had the gift of interpretation of dreams, and we were supposed to tell him our dreams for him to interpret. I remember a dream I had while we were living in our first apartment. I dreamed one night that this woman was walking to and fro in our bedroom while we were sleeping. I didn't know who she was, but I felt uncomfortable, knowing that I had locked the doors but that somehow this woman had invaded the privacy of our home without my invitation. It gave me the creeps, but the leader never told me what the dream meant, because I imagined he didn't want to scare me. This woman was a mystery, and I couldn't understand why she was parading herself in my personal space during the night. I had heard spooky, scary stories before, but I had heard my father say one time that he didn't believe in evil, so I didn't believe evil really existed until other strange things started happening in my life.

Even though situations in our life were far from perfect, I decided to make the most of my marriage, and I became pregnant with our second child. It was December 1975. I was on school vacation and had traveled to the grocery store to purchase a few items, but the few somehow turned into many. There I stood in my pregnancy, holding a toddler with one hand and trying to support the grocery sacks with the other. I eventually had to place the sacks on the sidewalk until a taxi came along. I faced my reality and realized the burden was too much, and I remember vowing to myself, "Before this baby is born, I will purchase a car."

My second baby was due April, but by February of the same year, with favor from God and a loan from my father, I was able to make a down payment on my very first car, which was a brand-new Austin Mini. The only problem was, even though I had my driver's license,

I didn't have any road practice, so my now-deceased husband had to accompany me to drive it from the car lot. I got some practice, and after a while, I was confident enough to begin driving to school. Of course, I drove it over to the elder's house, and they were all happy and prayed over the car for God's protection.

My husband would ride with me to the neighborhood where his mother lived, which was very close to the school. After he alighted, my routine was to park the car under a tree on the far end of the schoolyard, closer to the church. There was no fence between the church and the schoolyard, and this was convenient, as sometimes we would take the children to the church via the schoolyard. The tree under which I parked the car was large and shady, and sometimes teachers would take their pupils outside when they wished to do oral individual work, especially reading, since we didn't have separate classrooms in those days.

After lunch one day, a child came from another class with a message from her teacher for me to come outside because, according to the report, my car was almost burned. It sounded so silly, but since the child insisted, I accompanied her outside and headed in the direction of the tree. Sure enough and to my amazement, the gas tank cover for the car was missing, and there was a lit piece of paper in its place. By the grace of God, it had burned out, and the fire had not been fully ignited. We looked everywhere for the cover to the gas tank, but we couldn't find it anywhere. On my way home, I stopped at the service station and purchased a cover with a lock. I was really grateful to God for his protection, but I found it was another strange occurrence. I remembered the counterfeit experience I had in that area, and now this attack happened in the same area. I was beginning to realize that I had a real enemy and that there was an attack launched against me. I didn't know where it originated or why I was being attacked, but God had protected me; that was all that mattered.

I thank God the Austin Mini was such a tremendous blessing to all of us—myself, my children, and my parents, as now I was able to drive my mother and elder sister around. Also, every Sunday morning, I would transport my friend's mother and another elderly lady to church, along with my children. I didn't realize I was serving God in this way, but it made me happy to be a blessing to someone else.

Then the leader suggested it was time for me to go to the upper room with some others. I remember the other secret word he whispered in my ear that I was not supposed to share. The secret word was "Comfort of the afflicted, be a comfort unto me." We would have a shut-in and were supposed to meditate on the secret word all night long and wait on God for revelation.

I cannot recall having any amazing revelation, but something quite unusual happened to another lady. That lady was my friend's sister, who had started babysitting one of my children at her home. She lived in the same area, near the village school where I was teaching, which was so convenient for me. My friend's mother and another sister had joined the church. Everyone was excited when the other sister was baptized and was also invited to the same upper room where I had been. But something went drastically wrong, because she suffered a mental breakdown as a result of her upper room experience. No one was able to explain what happened, but I believed the leader closed the doors to the upper room for quite a while. Her husband was not a happy camper, as he had to go through the ordeal of helping his wife regain her sanity. Something had gone wrong, but I was unable to prove spiritual error, as I was not knowledgeable in the Word. Besides, my friend and her mother were still attending church. However, I decided to stick to my decision to keep serving the Lord, because my mind had been made up to follow Jesus and surrender all to him.

Chapter 4

On Christ the Solid Rock

I was pregnant with my third child, and since my family was increasing in size, I decided to rent a two-bedroom house so my children would have a yard to play in. It was farther away from my job but a little closer to my parents' home. They had sold the family home in the city, and my father had built another home farther east. My father had never owned a car and couldn't drive, so it was a blessing for me to drive my mother and sister to take care of their errands.

While residing at this house, I had a dream that impacted my life. I dreamed I was in the middle of the sea, standing on a massive rock, and boisterous waves were slamming against the rock. A family member was attempting to get me off the rock, but I remained standing on that rock. Indeed, up to today, one of my favorite hymns is this:

The Solid Rock

My hope is built on nothing less than
Jesus's blood and righteousness.
I dare not trust the sweetest, but wholly lean on Jesus's name.

(Chorus)
On Christ the solid rock I stand, all other ground is sinking sand.

I believe the family member didn't realize that even though she didn't approve of the church where I heard the gospel and became born again, I now had a real relationship with my heavenly Father. That made all the difference in the world. I never did realize how many hymns I learned in those ten years while I was a member of that little country church. I started counting and realized I knew about one hundred hymns, and I was amazed. I am so glad I had a "solid rock" foundation, even though at the time I was not taught how to seek God daily in his Word. We, however, recited Psalm 1 and Psalm 91 quite often, so I learned those by heart through repetition. However, my faith in Jesus helped me overcome the following terrifying experience.

I was getting ready to give birth to my third child. I decided to have a home delivery, and incidentally, the midwife was a member of the church I was attending. One of the elderly single church mothers came to stay at the house to assist me. But something strange and mysterious was happening to my now-deceased husband about the same time I was giving birth. I had a safe delivery, but he was having a horrific experience. He claimed that everywhere he went, there was an evil smell following him, and he had this frightening experience for some weeks. So we took him to the church leader, and he was baptized in the same church. Eventually, the scent went away. It was revealed by one of the spiritual sisters that the evil spirit was sent to attack me, but instead it got hold of him. I will not comment on who the sister claimed sent the spirit, but at that time, I had no revelation. However, I was standing on Christ the solid rock, and according to Psalm 91:1, I was "dwelling in the secret place of the most high." I was divinely protected, but I had to travel a long winding road before I discovered the real entity that was fighting me. My husband, who got baptized in the same country church, wasn't really committed to the faith and wasn't standing on Christ the solid rock as I was.

I had never heard the expression *physical abuse* because I had never witnessed it between my parents. When I hear other adults talk about how they were "whooped" as children and I think about my story, I realize I never got a "whooping" from either of my parents. I never really misbehaved growing up as a child, and I had never seen my father hitting my mother. They had their arguments, but there was no yelling, screaming, or using four-letter words in our home environment. The first person who had hurled a four-letter word at me was my deceased mother-in-law at the time. Unfortunately, this experience had resulted in shock and propelled me forward in another direction.

My husband wasn't working, but every day he would go to his mother's house. One evening, I became so angry about his lack of responsibility that I threw his pillow out of the house into the backyard. What happened next was so unexpected, because at the time, I was working full-time and pregnant. I don't know which hand he used, but all I knew was that I had received one extreme blow to my right eye. Instantly, it felt so strange that I ran to the mirror. I realized I couldn't see from my right eye because it was completely swollen, and I couldn't open it. I had enough sense to know I had to go to the emergency room. By that time, he had disappeared, and it was beginning to get dark. I thank God I had accepted Jesus in my heart at that time, so I started praying as I bundled up my three other babies into the Austin Mini and drove to the neighborhood clinic for help. I was able to receive medical attention, and I knew it was nothing but the grace and mercy of God over my life that helped me on my journey of physical healing.

I believe my parents wanted me to report the matter to the police, but for some reason, I didn't do it. I believe I was still trying to make my marriage work. The church's doctrine in those days was to stick it out with your husband. However, he had fled from the house. I was scared for my life, so I decided to move in with my parents temporarily. In spite of the other occurrences, God had been good to me, and I made a down payment on a house and chose a lot and design for the construction of a two-bedroom house, which was all I could afford at the time since my husband had abandoned us. So with sadness and trepidation, I packed all my personal belongings and that of my children and moved in, along with my three girls.

Parents always make room for children who are in distress. God knows I hadn't lived with my parents for so long, as I had become an independent woman, but this was the time to eat humble pie. I ran like a prodigal child into my parents' arms.

CHAPTER 5

Mysterious Happenings
at My Parents' Home

It was a longer commute from my parents' home in the east to the village school where I taught in the west, but I soon got used to the new routine. Even though I was residing at my parents' home, I still assumed responsibility of taking care of my children. Of course, my mother helped, but I would be up about 4:00 a.m. and prepare breakfast for myself and the two girls while leaving my youngest daughter in my mother's care. It wasn't yet time for maternity leave, so I was still working; I would arrive about an hour earlier to give private tutoring to the children who needed it, as I had a class of eleven-year-olds, both girls and boys, who were preparing for an entrance examination. This was an assessment that would assist the educational department in placing the children in the secondary school system. I thoroughly enjoyed teaching, which, by the way, is my life skill. It took me about one and quarter hours in traffic before I arrived at my final destination, because I had to drop my girls off at their school in another area.

On a particular Monday, after I left home and headed for work, I noticed my indicator lights were not functioning, but I kept driving because I hated being late for work. And of course, since I was addicted to my job and doing what I loved, I drove the car all week long, back and forth, from home to work and back again, since I decided I would wait until Saturday, my day off from work, to take the car to the mechanic.

Finally, on Saturday morning, I was saying my little Jesus prayer in my heart and drove to the mechanic. This was my very first car and I was completely oblivious of car mechanics, so when the mechanic lifted the hood and was checking the engine, I was still talking to Jesus in my heart. Then the mechanic decided to open the front door and pulled out a panel inside the area where the glove compartment normally is. After pulling open the panel, he pushed his hand inside it and pulled something out. His next words, which I'll never forget as long as I live, were "Madam, I don't know how this car didn't catch on fire!" I drew closer because I couldn't understand what he was talking about. To my amazement, he had a wad of wires in his hand; some of them had been skillfully cut before the wad was put back in place and the panel was shut.

I stood with my mouth half open and with a look of disbelief on my face. I couldn't believe this was happening to me. This happened in 1979, and even as I am writing this part of my story, I am shaking my head in amazement and wonder as I look at my life then and reflect quickly on the perilous long winding road I had to travel before my deliverance came. At that time, I didn't understand what was happening in my life or why it was happening. By nature, I never liked movies with violence, I never watched a science fiction movie, and the word *espionage* was a word in the English dictionary I had knowledge about but didn't have a clue as to what it really meant. At that time, I stood in horror as I realized the Baby Jesus, who I was carrying around in my heart everywhere I went, had somehow protected me and the baby boy in my womb. Thirty-nine years ago, there were no violent movies on television, as far as I can remember, and if there were, I never watched them.

I drove home really puzzled because this was the same Austin Mini someone had crept into in the schoolyard and on whose gas tank they placed a piece of lit paper hoping it would catch on fire. I didn't grow up in a neighborhood where hate crimes were committed, so I was really naive. The first time, the person was trying to get rid of my brand-new car, but this time, it wasn't just the car but the precious cargo, which included my baby boy and me. As I am writing this chapter, I just wish I could have explained to my twenty-nine-year-old self and given her some advice, counsel, and words of wisdom. I cannot turn back the clock, but I pray my story will reach young women in the generations to come and help them find answers in the midst of their predicaments. My parents never told me that people who were kind to you would curse you like my now-deceased mother-in-law did. They didn't tell me either that people could hate you and want to destroy your life for no reason. I was trying to figure out who could have access to my car and want to kill me and my baby. After all, I was just a hardworking mom trying to make my way in this world and trying to figure out what life was all about.

I began to think about it and almost froze in my tracks when I thought of who it could possibly be. All I can do is provide pieces of evidence as I am attempting to make a thorough investigation and encourage you to read until the end, until you see the real culprit operating behind the scenes. I remembered that on the Sunday before the person tampered with my car, I had packed lunch, diaper bags, and everything we needed, and I drove by to pick up the two elderly ladies who I drove to church for years. In those days, we put babies and toddlers on laps, and the arms of the adult were like the seat belt that buckled them tight. So we had church, and we returned home safely and unpacked the car; the indicator lights were in excellent working order.

During this season of my life, the children's father would come to visit his children, and I would see him coming down the road and escape into my room and leave him to visit with his children. I wanted to stay as far away as possible from the culprit who had given me the black eye. Of course, my parents let him in to visit with his children. I don't remember how or when he started sleeping over. My older self is thinking now that if twenty-nine-year-old me had known Bishop Jakes, my life would have been different then, but I started to count on my fingers and realized he might have been about nineteen years old then. I realize now that God was still preparing him to preach "Woman, Thou Art Loosed." So he couldn't help me then, and as a matter of fact, I don't know if anyone was preaching about physical or emotional abuse at that time in the Caribbean.

So since I learned from the church, when I sat on the mourners' bench the day I was baptized, that trials and tribulations marked the Christian's pathway, my twenty-nine-year-old brain wanted to be faithful. I remembered a hymn they would sing that asked a question and gave an answer in two sentences: *"Must Jesus bear the cross alone, and all the world go free? No, there's a cross for everyone, and there's a cross for me."* So I guess I reasoned that this marriage was the cross I had to bear, and I decided to be faithful to my vows to Jesus and to my husband, even though at the time he would be hurling false accusations of me being unfaithful to him when I was carrying his child. I especially hated the times we would take our children to visit his mother; she would be pulling on the poor baby's nose to see if it had the shape of the family's nose. She wanted to make certain they were her son's children. Every time I went through the painful ordeal of having my baby's nose examined for this special vein running from the forehead to the little nose, I felt humiliated. I was the silent sufferer.

He would sleep over sometimes at my parents' home. He worked the night shift, and that Sunday evening, I had lent him the car to go to work, knowing he would bring it back in time on Monday morning for me to go to work. We all were in bed by eight o'clock, so no one was awake when he came in that night after leaving work at 11:00 p.m. So that Monday morning, the indicator lights that had been functioning when he left to go to work at 3:00 p.m. the day before were not functioning when I left for work. I didn't want my imagination to run wild, so I placed every suspicious thought out of my mind and kept living because I didn't want to be diagnosed with paranoid schizophrenia.

Finally, maternity leave had come, and I got to stay home to prepare for my son's birth. But something strange had started happening to a couple of my fingers and a few of my toes. I started to develop sores, and my mother had to help me with the children and meal preparation. I was taking medication and didn't know what was happening to me until I had this dream and woke up with goose bumps and chills. I dreamed that I was walking in front of my deceased mother-in-law's house and that a spell had been cast on me. Remember, this is the first lady who had uttered those sacred words, *I love you*. This is the same lady whose sumptuous meals I had eaten and whose son I had married. This is the same lady who had cursed me with venom to my face. I knew that somehow this was a warning and God was trying to show me something. I remember a prayer we would always pray in church, and I pray this prayer to this very day. "Lord, please warn me of my dangers and the dangers of my brethren." I realize that God was showing me bit by bit who the mystery lady was in the dream that I had when we were living in our first apartment.

Finally, one day, when I was in my mother's kitchen, my little boy gave me signs he was finally ready to make his entrance on planet Earth. I called my midwife, who worked at the hospital in the city, and told her I was on the way to pick her up, as I had planned to do a home delivery, which was quite unusual in those days, especially as we had no epidural back then. I am amazed, as I see the amount of grace and courage that Almighty God poured out on me that day. It took me about an hour and a half to get to the hospital, and as I was driving with the midwife and having a little talk with Jesus in my heart, she suddenly asked me a question. I remember the very corner we were passing by when she asked me, "Did you just have a contraction?" I replied, "Yes, how did you know?" She answered, "I saw your hands tighten on the steering wheel."

I continued driving that standard-shift car all the way to my parents' home, and we arrived about 4:30 p.m. The midwife gave my mother instructions about the preparations that needed to be made. I got myself ready, as the contractions were coming stronger as I lay on my parents' bed. About 8:30 p.m., with lots of moaning and groaning (not shouting and screaming, as some believe women do), our baby boy was born. His father arrived from work after a while to welcome his son into the world.

In spite of the marital heartache and the plan the enemy had to destroy both me and my son, there was still peace and contentment because of the fact that more of God's blessings were on the way. Then there came a bigger brand-new vehicle that God had blessed me with from the car dealership. Everyone at church was happy, especially the two elderly ladies whom I transported to church every Sunday. I would drive my family on weekends to view our new house, which was under construction, and we saw it built from the ground up, stage by stage. In spite of the traumas of life, heaven was still smiling on me, and I was able to keep my sanity up to that point.

CHAPTER 6

Jesus My Best Friend in My New Home

It took a lot of energy and time making countless trips to different offices, filling out applications, signing paperwork, and submitting required documents to get approval for an affordable loan. However, the day finally came when I was able to sign the deed of ownership for the new home for myself and the children. I will always remember my father's decision to assist me as my children and I started out in our new home. He had worked as a ledger keeper at the town hall downtown all his life. He had built his first house and sold it after a while for a whole lot more than it cost him, and he was able to build another house farther east, where my son was born. He estimated the cost and decided to pay a workman to extend the side of the house overlooking the kitchen window. I had a washing machine but no dryer, and I was able to hang my laundry outside and use it as a carport at the same time. In those days, we used cloth diapers, so I did laundry every day after school.

The church leader came, with his housekeeper and my friend, to bless the house before I moved in. Shortly after my children and I moved in, their father came knocking, and I felt sorry for him, especially as one of the church mothers had advised me that I was a youngblood and needed my husband. I remember telling her I didn't want to take the birth control pill or use any female device to prevent pregnancy. She told me to pray and the Lord would stop me. I did that but still ended up with another baby girl, who incidentally was the last child I gave birth to. God finally sent a mature sister all the way from overseas to give me some practical sense. She was a former member of the church and had migrated before I appeared on the scene. She would later play an important part in provoking me to seek God about a dream I had.

So we moved and settled into the house, and I kept living and mothering and working. Since I was a homeowner and had small children, I decided to purchase some life insurance, praying that in case anything happened to me, the Lord would send some Good Samaritan to take care of my children. You can imagine all my money went to mortgage, food, and car payments. I literally did not have money to spend on myself, and we never ate out because my morning routine was to prepare meals at 4:00 a.m., which I heated up in the evening for the children after school. Sometimes after picking up the children at school, I would get them settled in and drive around the neighborhood selling household items.

I had no inkling what was going to happen that day, and I was totally unprepared for what was about to transpire. It could have happened anywhere, but it happened right there in front of the classroom of ten- and eleven-year-olds I was responsible for educating. I am so grateful the sovereign Lord did not let it happen at home when I started my daily routine at 4:00 a.m. I performed my routine from bedroom to kitchen, where I prepared breakfast and lunch for my family. My husband had worked the night shift and was absent from home at the time. Like clockwork, I transitioned from the kitchen and started waking our four children, getting them dressed, and combing the three girls' hair. I prided myself on combing their hair every day, because one of the teachers always complimented my girls about their well-groomed appearance. She had even remarked to one of her students that she would need to send the student to our home for me to comb her hair. I remember smiling to myself, as this brought a sense of self-satisfaction.

I guess adrenaline was flowing as I performed my tasks like a religious ritual, moving from one room to the next with precision while giving orders to each child. The sound of "Mummy" would echo through the walls of our home every morning. I raced to the bathroom to have my shower, because I knew I had exactly twenty minutes before I had to drive out of the garage. On my way out to the car, I yelled roll call—by numbers, not by names. "Numbers 1, 2, 3, 4! Mummy's ready! Let's go!" The sound of little feet slapping the concrete tiles could be heard as they all came running, and the car doors were then all shut! Our dog, who was chained in the backyard, barked goodbye. We had to leave at precisely 7:00 a.m. because five or ten minutes would have made a tremendous difference in the rat race called life. I hated being late, but I am so glad the sovereign God didn't allow it to happen while I was shifting gears, traveling the freeway.

I dropped my children off at their school and arrived at my school about 8:15 a.m., as I always liked to arrive before 8:30 a.m. when the bell rang. I sat down and breathed a sigh of relief because I had arrived safely at my destination. The children lined up in class formation outside for the morning assembly, as this was the time for prayer and announcements from the principal. Assembly was dismissed, and the girls and boys entered the school building in single file. They got to their respective classrooms, separated by huge blackboards, and work began. I taught my first class, set the children to work, and sat in my chair in full view of the children. Suddenly, a feeling came over me, and I felt myself drifting. I wasn't falling asleep; it was another kind of unexplainable drifting. I was no longer aware of my surroundings, as I felt myself drifting away in such a peaceful way, but suddenly my children flashed in front of me. I started using my little Jesus prayer inside my heart. My lips were closed, and I listened to my own heart saying, "Jesus, Jesus, Jesus!" Suddenly, I snapped back to reality! I realized for the first time that I was slowly about to lose my mind! Jesus had come to my rescue! Jesus really became my best friend in my bosom. I realized the enemy was after my mind and wanted to throw me in a state of mental confusion, but the Most High God sent his angels to help me when I called on the name of Jesus.

What a friend we have in Jesus, all our sins and griefs to bear!
What a privilege to carry everything to God in prayer,
Oh what peace we often forfeit, O what needless pains we bear,
All because we do not carry everything to the Lord in prayer.
Have we trials and temptations? Is there trouble anywhere?
We should never be discouraged, take it to the Lord in prayer.
Can we find a friend so faithful who will all our sorrows share?
Jesus knows our every weakness, take it to the Lord in prayer.

I literally fell in love with the last verse, which says that if we are loaded down with cares of this world, we can find refuge in Jesus, our precious Savior. Then it counseled me that if my friends despised or rejected me, I can approach God with this concern, and he would in turn wrap his loving arms around me, because he would shield and comfort me. It thrilled my soul, and I sought refuge and protection countless times in the secret place of his presence.

I became even more aware there was a real enemy out there who was first moved by jealousy and had tried to destroy my first new car at that time. When that wasn't enough, an attempt was made to kill me and my unborn child, when the wires in the car engine had been cut. And now there had been this attack that almost made me lose my mind. I vowed that day within myself, "Oh no, the only time I am going to set foot in a mental asylum is to see a patient and not become one!" So the spiritual fight continued. I didn't know why, but I trusted Jesus because he was the only one who protected me and kept me in the midst of my trials and tribulations.

To add insult to injury, my now-deceased husband started puffing and said he wanted a car of his own. I asked, "How are we going to eat, since we have a new house and a new car?" I remember reasoning with him that he could use the new car I had purchased, and if he would buy me a used car, I wouldn't have a problem driving it. The argument stopped at that time, but I hadn't realized how determined he was until the following week, when he showed up at school and came to the door of my classroom. He had found a car and wanted me to meet him at the bank to cosign for his car loan. I didn't understand why there were so many challenges happening to me in front of the same classroom again.

In a daze, I set the children to do some work in their workbooks, and I sat down, not knowing what to do. One of the teachers must have seen the look on my face, and she came over to me and said, "There's power in the blood of Jesus." I had never received any formal teaching about the blood of Jesus. But when she mentioned Jesus's name, I remembered I had invited Jesus into my heart, and I whispered a prayer for guidance. The lunch bell rang, and I got into my car and drove all the way to the bank, praying and asking God what to do, because I wanted to be obedient to his holy Word. Ephesians 5:22 says, "Wives submit to your own husbands, as to the Lord." The question I was repeating in my mind was "Should I submit to my husband and sign for his car loan?" I had to have an answer right then because my future was hanging in the balance. Thank God I found a space in the small parking lot. I had prayed for that also, because I just had one hour for lunch. As I was getting out of the car, my pen fell to the ground, and as I bent to pick it up, the thought came to me to leave the pen in the car. I felt such a peace come over me as I mounted the steps and entered the bank. My husband came to greet me in the foyer with a spring in his step.

We were immediately ushered into the loan officer's cubicle, because evidently, my husband had made an appointment. We were offered a seat, which my husband accepted hurriedly. I sat upright because I wanted to be attentive. The loan officer asked, "What is your account number?" I was surprised because he had not interacted with me about the intended transaction. Apparently, I had just entered a previous discussion and somehow was expected to comply with the loan officer. I surprised myself with the answer that flowed out of my lips. I think now about the queen bee producing honey, and I remember the sweet smile that spread across my face as the gentle sting of my words came forth. "I believe my husband and I need to discuss this transaction some more." I felt the shock of electricity that charged the atmosphere as we both rose to our feet. My beloved never said a word, but in the lobby, his face was contorted in anger as his eyes, which were full of hate, stabbed at me. We both went our separate ways, and I am so glad for that day when the Almighty helped me fight my battle. He had met me at the point of my need and used a pen that had fallen to the ground as a stoplight of caution. I know Almighty God will always find a way to communicate with you in the midst of your situation if you allow him to do so.

I will forever be grateful to my Lord and Savior Jesus Christ because last year, when I visited my native country, I heard that the Pentecostal sister who had whispered to me about the blood of Jesus had been diagnosed with Alzheimer's. We had been out of touch for many years, but out of respect, I decided to visit her, even though she was not on my agenda. I knew she would remember me, and there she stood, on the inside of her padlocked fence, with her handbag draped over her shoulder. After her husband let me in, we hugged, and she did remember me, because only her short-term memory had been lost. The visit was short, and we talked about old times at the school. When I got up to leave, she hugged me and said I had made her day. I will eternally be grateful to God and indebted to him, because he preserved my sanity for such a time as this. That is why I have to tell my story, which is the journey of the Lord's deliverance. But I still had a lot more battles to fight ahead.

CHAPTER 7

Deliverance and an Almost Near-Fatal Car Crash

Take it away from me (2)
Anything that's not like thee, take it away from me
Take it away from me, Lord, take it away from me (2)
Anything that's not like thee, take it away from me!

This was a heart's cry of appeal to God for help, by the psalmist Shirley Caesar. The psalmist poured out her soul, asking God to deliver her from bad habits, which she herself was powerless to break. She pleaded in song with God concerning simple things she felt powerless to release. She was crying out to God, asking him to perform a deep introspection in her heart and mind, and asking that if he found anything that was preventing her from experiencing joy in her life, he would take it away. She had made a decision: She wanted to be like Jesus and was seeking help from the Most High God.

From the day I did not comply with his desire to cosign for him to get a car, there was a stony silence between us, especially as my husband was obviously going berserk with the thought of having his own car. It was an obsession, and I truly believe that if his mother had not stepped in and bought him a car, something terrible would have happened to him. In exchange, he promised to take her to her doctor's visits, which he never did. That idol was parked in the garage my father had built for me, and he never used it. He took public transportation to work. He never used it to take his children to school or to the doctor or on a family outing. That car was his idol, which he cleaned and polished and shined. The battery even died because the car was not being used, and he had to replace it. But the most painful thing for me was that my car had to be parked outside the garage and was exposed to all the external elements, like the rain and sun. I was really hurt about that, but I kept on bearing my cross. I would like to give a word of wisdom to husbands and wives. If one of you desires something that won't benefit the entire family unit, just let it go. The entire family has to benefit from each decision or purchase you make; otherwise, you would simply be satisfying your own lustful desire. So before you make a final decision about any family matter, you should ask yourselves this question: "Who will benefit if I make this decision—just me or the family?" If the answer isn't the entire family, you should release the idea, because there must be purpose in every decision.

I continued faithfully going to church and singing the hymns, which were a real comfort to me. Before long, I realized the members were providing the leader with bottles of whiskey, so you can imagine what road I started to travel. I thought to myself, if he was the leader and could do it, what about me? So I became a closet drinker at home. I labored in the kitchen early in the morning, labored at work during the day, and when I came home with the kids, I labored in the messy kitchen I had left in the morning. I wasn't getting any emotional support from my husband at that time, not during or after any of my pregnancies, and I was emotionally exhausted and found comfort in my rum and Coke. However, I did it in secret at home. It was always in the evening; I believe it was after I put the children in bed at eight o'clock. In those days, I wasn't documenting, so I don't remember how long I was a closet drinker with this dark secret. The next morning, I would awake sober and step right into my daily routine. However, God knew, and he knows how to get our attention.

One night, I dreamed I was lying on my bedroom floor, close to the door. The room was extremely dark, but I could see a crack of light from under the door, which was coming from the kitchen. I was trying my utmost to open the door so I could embrace the light, which was in another part of my house. I tried to open the door, but for some strange reason, it appeared to be stuck. I began to feel afraid and tried to exert more force, but whatever force was opposing me was stronger than me; I was unsuccessful in my attempt to open the door. I woke up from the dream, which seemed so real, but I had been sleeping on the bed, not the floor. I spent the following days pondering and reflecting on that scary dream. I was wondering about that force behind the door and trying to understand why I couldn't open the door in my own house. Then on my way to work, I began hearing a song, sung by Shirley Caesar, entitled "Take It Away from Me."

This was a situation I couldn't discuss with church leadership or any members of the church, and it made me feel so alone. I felt ashamed that I had to be in hiding, but that was my crutch; I wasn't sure if I needed to stop. But I would hear that song over and over again, until I knew it by heart, and I guess it became my heart's cry after a while. I felt better but a little strange when my husband rose up from bed one morning and declared in a daze, "Girl, you have power!" When I asked him what had happened, he said he had this dream that a woman was standing outside the house. She cast a spell, and one side of the house began falling down. He then continued that I came out of the house with the Bible open, and I was reading a scripture. Suddenly, the wall of the house went back up into place. I asked him if he knew who the woman was and what scripture I was reading, and he replied no to both questions. However, that dream had him amazed, because he declared I had power, which, I realized, came when I spoke the Word of God.

Something was happening spiritually, and I wasn't certain what it was. I continued going to church, because I didn't know what else to do, especially as I had decided to follow Jesus, with all my trials and tribulations. There are two seasons in our country: the rainy and the dry season. Part of my evening routine included washing my children's school shirts and the baby's cloth diapers, which I would hang on the clothesline until the following day, when I arrived home. One evening, I decided to multitask and give my children a treat by preparing fries and chicken. I put the skillet on the stove and poured cooking oil in it. I was outdoors hanging clothes I had taken out of the twin tub dryer, which only spin-dried after washing. When I returned to the kitchen, the skillet was on fire! Lord of mercy, I grabbed the skillet with both hands and raced through the back door, which was still open, and I dumped it in the backyard. You could imagine how afraid I was, because I didn't want the house I had labored so long and hard for to go up in flames. My heavenly Father didn't want that either and spared my life to tell the story. I held the flaming skillet in my hand, but by the mercies of God, I did not receive any burns to my body. God had a plan for my life, and I know he was with me that day.

However, since the rainy season was approaching, I knew I needed to get a clothes dryer. I checked the advertisements in the daily papers and found a used one that was reasonably priced. I was so happy with my purchase, especially since I wouldn't have to worry about towels and sheets getting wet when it was raining and I was at work. That joy was short-lived. One evening, I came home, and after doing some laundry, I realized the dryer wasn't working because my husband had cut off the electrical cord. He said he was responsible for paying the electricity bill, and using the dryer would cause the bill to escalate. I tried to explain that I would use it with discretion, but I was fighting a losing battle. The only one I could talk to was God, and since I didn't want to be a complaining wife, I continued to suffer in silence.

Then one day, my husband told me his mother wanted to see me. I had been avoiding going to visit her for obvious reasons, but after prayerful consideration, I decided to comply with her request. So after school was out one day, I drove to her house, and she greeted me in a really friendly way. She had a proposition to make. She knew I had a desire to enlarge my house, and she was offering me money to do additions with the expectation of her coming to reside with us. I told her I would think about it and would let her know. Consequently, I reasoned within myself, *Why did she think it necessary to leave her own house and come live in my house?* I didn't even ask what she planned on doing with her house. Obviously, the answer to this proposition was an emphatic no, as the idea simply didn't make sense to me. I told her I would let her know, but obviously I decided it wasn't a good idea and decided to wait on God for help.

Amid all these irregular occurrences, my dream of the enlargement of the two-bedroom house was slowly becoming a reality. I had mentioned to one of the elderly women who I transported to church regularly that I wanted to enlarge the house. She contacted her cousin, who came by and viewed the property, and I explained to him exactly what I had in mind. He gave me an estimate of how much the plan would cost, and we agreed on a payment plan. It was worth the sacrifice because I finally had the blueprint in my hand. I gazed in amazement at the architectural design in my hand, with everything in such minute detail. I had something new to concentrate on to make my dream become a reality. I filled out all the necessary paperwork in accordance with the city's ordinances so I could get the blueprint approved. Incidentally, my husband was working with the water department, so he helped in getting information for the approval of the plumbing aspect of the plan.

In spite of all the traumatic experiences, heaven was still smiling on me in the midst of all the ups and downs. The thought of not going to church never occurred to me because my heavenly Father was still good to me, and I wanted to continue faithfully following Jesus. On one particular Sunday, I awoke as usual, not suspecting that I was about to have a life-changing experience. I had no dream or premonition about what was about to occur. My children and I had breakfast. I packed their lunches, diaper bags, and snacks, of course. This was before I picked up the two older women, so I had strapped the toddler in the front seat using an old sheet for safety's sake, which I thought was common sense.

We left home, and I had been driving for about ten minutes and was approaching the roundabout that headed to the airport, when suddenly I heard within myself a voice that said, "She's praying too much. Let's get out of here!" I didn't know who was saying it, because I heard it with my spiritual ear. I knew it wasn't the Holy Spirit running from prayer, so I knew it had to be the cohorts of the devil. I don't know how many entities had been assigned to me, but I knew that I had been praying and that they had to go.

I had never entered a theological seminary, but somehow I knew my children and I could possibly be headed toward the cemetery. All our lives were hanging in the balance. I became as stiff as a statue as my hands clutched the steering wheel really hard. I am so glad Jesus was in my heart, and I breathed his name with my lips tightly shut. I was not driving an automatic car, but I knew that if I had tried to slow down or even shift my foot from gas to brakes, we would have crashed and you wouldn't be reading the account of how God delivered me again when he heard my heart's cry, calling on the name of Jesus. I continued driving along the highway, looking straight ahead, not even turning my head slightly to the left or to the right; I did not even glance at my children.

After driving for a while, I knew the devil and his cohorts had left me, and I was finally able to slow down a little and breathe a sigh of relief. Since my steering wheel was on the right, British style, I gave a quick glance to my toddler on the left to make certain she was all right. Then I swung around while my eyes made a quick inspection to see if all my other children in the back seat were safe. I was a bit shaky because I had never heard anyone tell of such a situation, so I was really perplexed by what happened to me. I continued my journey to my intended destination, praising God for his protection. I am so thankful it was Sunday morning and the road was not so busy. God had allowed me to win another round of the spiritual battle, but little did I know that God was about to continue training me in another situation. So the war was on.

CHAPTER 8

God Reveals Himself
as the Great I Am

And God said unto Moses, I AM THAT I AM: and he said,
Thus shalt thou say unto the children of Israel,
I AM hath sent me unto you.
—Exodus 3:14

We celebrated Christmas that year regular home style, with the black cake and turkey and ham, and gifts for the children. When my husband gave me a bottle of whiskey as a Christmas gift, I really got paranoid and thought he was trying to kill me. We had never discussed the problem I had. I don't know what was on his mind when he gave me that bottle of whiskey, but that was enough to sober me up. I poured the whiskey down the kitchen sink and have not touched another drink since. I had never heard about Alcoholics Anonymous, so I never signed up for any twelve-step program. The only step I made was toward Calvary's cross, and Almighty God poured out his grace to me because he had heard my plea for help. He delivered me in a supernatural way. I met someone here in the US years later who said he had cried out to God as well, for deliverance from alcohol and cigarettes without any twelve-step program, and God had also delivered him.

Around this time, one of the sisters from the country church returned home with her family. She is now deceased, but around that time, she had been living in a foreign country for a long time. When I first met her, I had no inkling how instrumental she would be in my life and the life of my children. It's still amazing how our heavenly Father caused an entire family to relocate back to their native land after more than ten years, I believe. They came with all their household furniture. She said that when she first set her eyes on me, her thought was *Look at this lady with all these children.* By that time, I had five children, and I was still waiting for God to stop me from having any more children. I had become indoctrinated in the ways of the religious organization, but my mind was closed to anyone from outside our religion, because we were taught that our church was the only true church. God knew no one outside of that denomination could help me in such practical ways, so he sent someone from way across the sea to provoke me with her love and laughter.

The sister befriended my children and me. She invited us to her home and brought out her best dishes from overseas and laid the table in such a stylish manner. I was really impressed because no one in the church had ever treated us in this way. I realize she was demonstrating real Christian love. My children loved her as well, so almost every Sunday after church, we would stop by to have a time of fellowship. Their house was being renovated, but that didn't matter because we were specially treated.

I started to pour out all my marital troubles on her shoulder, and she told me to break the wall I had built to protect myself from my husband. I had never realized my stony silence was a wall I had built to protect myself. And, of course, she would always point me back to Jesus. I had unknowingly built a wall to protect myself from my husband because I didn't trust him. He, in turn, was always accusing me of being unfaithful to him. She never did explain to me fully how to break down the wall. Sometimes I would wonder if she was on my side or on my husband's side.

I know now that there was no type of meaningful communication in the marriage. I know now that true intimacy in marriage is not sexual intercourse. The phrase I use to describe intimacy is "into me, you see." Husbands and wives should feel free to share their heart with their mate without the fear of rejection. Everyone needs a safe place, and our mate's shoulder should be available for us to lean on to pour out our feelings of fear and frustration, because everyone needs someone to listen to their voice. I've discovered over the years that many times, even if people may complain to us about a person or situation, that doesn't necessarily mean they would like us to fix the problem.

I had also been complaining to her about my deceased mother-in-law and how she had hurt and disappointed me in so many ways. I was so happy I could finally talk to someone about all my hurts and disappointments and frustrations. Every time, she would keep directing me to Jesus.

Then one night, I had another dream. We had been trained to sleep with our heads covered and to lie either on our right side or on our back. Can you imagine that I trained my body to sleep in this fashion for ten years? I knew this dream was not from the devil because I was sleeping on the right side. I dreamed I saw my mother-in-law in a gas station, and her hair was extremely unkempt, all wild and crazy. The dream puzzled me, and when I told the sister from overseas, her response puzzled me. She said Jesus loved my mother-in-law and my husband as much as he loved me. I was indignant and disappointed with God, wondering whose side he was on, especially as I was the one being wronged all the time.

I kept on running to her house and complaining because I didn't know what else to do. I had never heard about God's unconditional love. I didn't know there was nothing we could ever do to cause God to love us; neither was there anything we could do to stop God from loving us. In my mind, it didn't make sense that God would even kill his own Son; I was thinking that if I had a son, I wouldn't want to kill him. I never realized that these questions and doubts were in my mind. I didn't realize I was making the sister weary, because it seemed to her that I just wasn't getting the right understanding. Sometimes on weekdays, we would visit her simply to avoid being present in the house at the same time as my husband. She laughingly told me a dream she had about me. She said she was tired of giving me the same advice over and over, and one night she dreamed she had turned her back and was walking away from me. But the Master appeared and sternly insisted, "Go back and get her!" Can you believe Almighty God uprooted an entire family from Canada to help me? I'm not sure who else she helped, but I know my family received help.

It is still amazing and mind-boggling as I imagine how the Creator of the universe spoke to both husband and wife. They gave up their jobs and their house, withdrew their children from school, and had a family meeting. Can you imagine how their children must have felt about having to get acclimatized to the brand-new culture of their native country that had changed after all those years? They decided to leave their church family abroad, the brethren who they had prayed and fellowshipped with all these years. They packed and got information about movers who would ship all their furniture and living room, dining room, and laundry room appliances. They had to decide, after accumulating possessions all these years, what things, including books and clothes, to keep and to throw out. I still don't understand how long it took for God to get their full attention and have them all in unison with his master plan. I would imagine there were times of doubt and trepidation before they came to that point of total surrender. Can you believe that, in the midst of this entire scenario, I was on God's mind and that he was stirring a miracle for the beginning of my ultimate breakthrough? At that time, I couldn't see or imagine what it cost the family to make that great move, and little did I know that God was getting ready to do a great move in my life.

Here's another simple but profound dream God used to get my attention. Now the country church had no running water. They collected barrels with rainwater in case they had to wash dishes in the kitchen, and that was my first experience of washing dishes in this manner, as we used tap water in the city. The other thing I had grown accustomed to over the years was the outhouse, which was new to me because I had never seen one before and because we flushed our toilets in the city where I grew up. This particular night, I dreamed that the outhouse on the church property was overflowing, and I was supposed to tell those people to clean up the filth. So I went to the church leader who had the gift of dream interpretation, and I told him. He replied that it was really the condition of the outhouse located at the back of the church, and he said he would contact the sewer officials to come with their big tanker and hoses to empty the sewer. I thought my assignment was done, and I walked away.

I believe it was that same day after church that I recounted this scenario to the sister from overseas, and to my amazement, she threw back her head in one motion and began to laugh. She heartily asked, "Is that what he told you?" Her eyes were gleaming bright in some mysterious way, and that bothered me. So I went back to God and started asking him questions about the dream and what he wanted me to do. I just knew beyond the shadow of a doubt that I had to pay another visit to the elder and remind him about what God said about cleaning the filth. The following series of events happened over a certain period, but I did not keep a record of the dates of the visits. I was a baby Christian, a regular churchgoer who knew Jesus as Savior, but no one ever taught me about seeking the Lord in his Holy Bible for myself. I knew the older church mother had taught me to ask the Holy Spirit for understanding before I read the scripture, which I did.

I was stuck on the interpretation the leader had given me, and I didn't realize at the time that he was using that scripture out of context. For example, he smoked cigarettes and used the scripture from Matthew 12:20, "A bruised reed he shall not break, and the smoking flax shall he not quench," as license for smoking. It is really a serious matter when someone uses the Word of God out of context to explain their foolish behavior.

At the time, however, I believed everything the leader said, because Almighty God used him to birth me into the kingdom of God, for some strange reason. In addition to that, when we sat on the baptismal bench, we were warned about the consequences Korah reaped because he had rebelled against church authority (Numbers 16). We had been further warned in Numbers 12 about the consequences Miriam, Moses's elder sister, faced when she spoke out against Moses's choice of a wife. Miriam was the one who had placed her baby brother, Moses, in the River Nile, and maybe she thought she had a right to help him choose a wife. However, God heard, and she was struck with leprosy.

There was another factor added to this matter. There was another leader in the church who helped the main leader. Every Sunday, he would get on his knees when it was time to pray and say these exact words: "Lord, help me control my tongue for the benefit of my soul." I never figured out why he prayed like that, especially since he wasn't a busybody or gossiper. Consequently, I was trained not to discuss any of the leaders in the church because we feared God.

When the sister from overseas laughed after I told her the elder's interpretation of the dream, I realized I had to seek God for an explanation. Our heavenly Father never explained to me the mess they were supposed to clean up in the church, but my assignment was to approach the leader again in obedience. God even gave me wisdom from something practical I had in my kitchen. I had placed a bottle of Coca-Cola in the freezer, with the intention of removing it before it got too cold. It was in a glass bottle, and the next morning, when I opened the refrigerator, I saw the frozen bottle of Coke looking at me. I was afraid it would explode, and I didn't want pieces of glass flying around. I held it securely with both hands and, with my eyes fixed on the frozen bottle in my hand, walked slowly and cautiously toward the kitchen sink. I held my breath and finally breathed a sigh of relief when I placed the bottle in the sink and opened the faucet to allow water to run over it. I remember the Holy Spirit whispering gently to my spirit, "When you visit the elder, approach him with caution." I knew I had to go in obedience to issue this warning again.

Then God prepared my heart in a dream. I dreamed I was visiting the elder. He was showing me that the sole of one of his feet was sore, and I felt my soul flood with such love and compassion for him. I awoke in amazement, thinking to myself that I did not feel like that concerning this man who God was sending me to visit again with the warning from the dream. After reflecting on it, I realized God had done spiritual surgery on my heart and given me his heart of unconditional love.

I know I had to approach the elder not to *rebuke* him but *to entreat him as a father* and remind him about the dream I had received from God. I also knew I had to approach him in love, because God had removed all animosity from within me and given me a heart of compassion for him. After the sister from overseas arrived, I had begun to seek God in his Word, depending on the Holy Spirit for understanding, as one of the church mothers had told me. I remember we were trained to open the Bible using the word the leader had given us at baptism. We had been cautioned never to share the word we had received at baptism; the leader shared a story about someone who had shared the word he had whispered to her, and she had gone crazy. I can say fearlessly that the word the elder had whispered in my ear at baptism was "Master Jesus, save me." So I believed I used the word in my heart and opened the Bible on a particular morning, and the scripture I received was the opening scripture from Exodus 3:14, when God revealed himself to Moses as I Am That I Am.

The day came when I mustered enough courage to approach the leader again to remind him that I had a dream that stated, "Tell those people to clean up that mess." I remember that when I visited him the second time, he asked me, "Who sent you?" I replied to him, "I Am That I Am sent me." At the time, I didn't have a real understanding of who *I Am That I Am* was, but I simply uttered the words the Holy Spirit had given me. The reply I gave him astounded him, because his head shot up to attention. He replied in amazement, "So you know the scripture!" This leader was in ministry before I was even born. This man had knowledge and understanding about things I never knew about, but God sent me, who was one of his spiritual children, to give him a warning in a dream. I didn't realize the Holy Spirit was teaching me to grow in the faith and listen to his voice.

I remember Elder Pete would always give an account in a boastful way about a dream he had: There was a tree that was growing in the church, and it grew high up and broke through the roof of the church. In retrospect, I understand that the church represented God's building and the tree was a man, because we are like trees planted by God. The tree, figuratively speaking, grew taller and higher than the head of the church, who is Christ. That meant the elder was lifted up in pride, and God had sent that dream to warn him. I believe God may have warned him through others; he also sent me, but I wasn't well received. I continued praying for the leader. I had heard about the gift of the Holy Ghost and speaking in tongues. I asked God to bless me with the gift, and he did that at home.

I paid another visit to the elder, and this time, he was in his backyard. I don't remember how the conversation went, but I remember speaking in tongues. He replied that he had heard that language in hell. That day, I left disappointed and feeling uncertain of myself, but I continued going to church and was praying a lot more than before. I knew the elder's eyes were on me, but I took solace in God's Word, especially Psalm 91, which I had learned at church. In the meantime, an entire family who had been members before me, along with other individuals, had begun leaving the church. It was then I heard some news on the grapevine, and I pleaded with God not to allow the elder to lay hands on my baby son when it was time to offer him to the Lord. God heard my prayer, and another one of the church leaders offered up my son that day. This special hymn, which we sang at church, became so meaningful to me.

Under his wings, I'm safely abiding,
Though the night deepens and tempests are wild,
Still I can trust him, I know he will keep me.
He has redeemed me, and I am his child.

(Chorus)
Under his wings (2), who from his love can sever?
Under his wings, my soul shall abide, safely abide forever.

The hymn continues to assure us that we can find comfort, peace, and serenity if our heart desperately desires to find a place of refuge. Many times, when we're unable to find emotional healing on earth, we can be blessed by the fact that we have a safe place under Jesus's wings. This safe and secure place is an everlasting haven where we can hide until the earthly trials in life come to an end. It would give us tremendous joy knowing we'll always be protected and sheltered in a secret place where the evil one is unable to find us. Even though the hymn is written in the first person to encourage oneself, I took the liberty of including every one of us who may be looking for a place of solitude in Jesus's arms.

CHAPTER 9

The Righteous Judge Appears

But let him that glorieth, glory in this,
That he understands and knows me,
That I am the Lord which exercises loving kindness,
Judgment and righteousness, in the earth,
For in these things I delight saith the Lord.
—Jeremiah 9:24

I was beginning to grow spiritually amid all this turmoil going on around me. I accepted them as my trials and tribulations, and I was depending on God to help me. I didn't expect any of the trials to come to an end, so I accepted them as my norm and continued to live in expectancy, as the blueprint for my house expansion had been approved. The next step was to get an estimate done and submit an application for the amount of money I would need to get my loan approved. The mortgage for the house was in my name, and since I was having so much opposition from my husband, I didn't let him know how much money I was planning to borrow to make the additions to the house.

With tax returns from the previous year, I had already started breaking the dividing wall in the kitchen for the extension. I remember my deceased husband using a sledgehammer to actually break the wall, which was constructed with steel in it; as the wall crumbled, we picked up buckets filled with broken mortar mixed with steel and dump it outside the house. Besides being blessed with five adorable children, I remember this positive thing he did.

I had another dream, where a chicken had the stopper for my sink in its mouth. I was running behind it to get my stopper out of its mouth, but I couldn't catch the chicken. However, the chicken got tired of running and jumped in a box, and it changed color. At the time, I didn't know what that dream meant, but I wondered about it.

My now-deceased husband knew I had applied for the loan, and he told me that when I got the money, we would put our heads together to spend the money. I never really gave him an answer because somehow I didn't trust him. I was still trying to make my marriage work, and I was battling with the understanding of the scripture from Ephesians 5:22, "Wives submit yourselves unto your own husbands, as unto the Lord." One day, I decided to show him all the loan documents and the actual amount of money I was expecting to use to make extensions to the house. I remember arriving home and taking the documents out of the place I had hidden them and placing them on the table. However, just as I was about to open up the paperwork, he got a phone call saying that his mother had been admitted to the hospital. He rushed out of the house, and I thoughtfully put my paperwork in the secret hiding place. In some uncanny way, my plan was interrupted. I thought about that and decided I would not let him know how much money I was getting. I certainly didn't plan for us to put our heads together to spend it.

I don't recall how long his mother was in the hospital, but the inevitable happened, as one day he came home with the news that his mother had passed away. In a fit of rage, he hurled this accusation at me: "You killed my mother!" I was so flabbergasted; I didn't know what to say. I made no defense because the accusation was so ludicrous. I didn't know how to go about killing anyone. As I recalled, I was the one who had the dream about a strange woman in our apartment years ago. He had a dream a woman had cast a spell on my house; when it began to crumble, I came out reading the Bible, and the wall supernaturally went back into place. I was the one who had experienced sores on my hands and feet. I was busy trying to ward off the evil entity that had been attempting to destroy my life, because Almighty God, the righteous Judge, hates evil. I realized then that Almighty God had shown me through the dream about his now-deceased mother in the gas station and the dream where the chicken got tired and jumped into the box, which was a coffin.

I felt relieved because I had been so naive concerning evil things people do, but my heavenly Father taught me over a period of years about evil in the world. I am so glad I had learned Psalm 91:1, "He that dwells in the secret place of the Most High shall abide under the shadow of the Almighty." I can see how the sovereign hand of God had been protecting me from evil forces surrounding me.

Shortly after his mother's death, my husband went to her house and took the dining room furniture and brought it to our house. However, we were not allowed to sit at the table. We never had another conversation about my killing his mother, and I wondered about that false accusation but kept silent about it.

In the meantime, I kept going to church and continued reading my Bible during the week whenever I got the opportunity. I don't remember how I got into the book of Daniel 5, with the account of King Belshazzar, who had a feast and had taken the golden vessels, which were sacred, from the house of God and drank wine with his wives, princes, and concubines. In the midst of their merriment, the king saw a part of a hand that wrote on the wall of the palace, and it troubled him. The Bible tells us in verse 6, "Then the king's countenance was changed, and his thoughts troubled him, so that the joints of his loins were loosed, and his knees smote one against another." The story continued that he called his astrologers and his wise men to read the interpretation of the handwriting on the wall, but they were unable to do it. The queen then reminded him that in the days of his father, King Nebuchadnezzar, when his magicians, astrologers, and soothsayers were unable to interpret the king's dream, they had called Daniel, who had been able to do the interpretation.

Daniel confronted the king in Daniel 5:23, stating that he had lifted himself above the God of heaven. He pointed out that the king was serving gods of silver, gold, brass, iron, wood, and stone, which neither see nor hear nor know anything. Then Daniel gave the interpretation of the handwriting on the wall. Somehow these words and their interpretation had made an impression on my spirit, and I remembered them for some strange reason.

> And this is the writing that was written, MENE, MENE, TEKEL, and UPHARSIN. This is the interpretation of the thing: MENE God has numbered thy kingdom and finished it. TEKEL, you are weighed in the balances and are found wanting. PERES, your kingdom is divided and given to the Medes and Persians.

God had revealed himself to me, through his holy Word, as the righteous Judge.

I remembered the last visit I paid to my church leader's home. We were sitting on the front porch, and it was morning. He was talking, but I don't remember what he was saying. Suddenly, I saw three hand signals in the spirit. It was like a flash of lightning. In the same instance, I used my hands and made the same signals I had seen in the spirit. As I made the signals, the Holy Spirit gave me the interpretation. The first signal had my left palm facing upward and my right hand, which was in the form of a fist, placed in the middle of my left palm. The interpretation of that first signal was "You have been put in the balance and found wanting." The second hand signal had my left palm facing downward and my right hand vertically positioned upward with the fingers touching the middle of my left hand. The interpretation of this second signal was "Your kingdom is divided." The third signal was made using only my right palm, which was facing downward, and an imaginary horizontal line was drawn from left to the right. The interpretation of this hand signal was "Your kingdom has come to an end!"

After following the leading of the Holy Spirit of truth and pronouncing God's judgment, I rose to my feet and never returned to those premises again. I had also been praying and made a vow to God: "If you get me and my children out of this religion, I will proclaim your name from housetop to hilltop." I had served faithfully in that religious denomination for about ten years. I didn't realize I was only being fed half-truths from the Word of God. I thank God for the foundational hymns I learned that kept me anchored, as the hymn goes.

> We have an anchor that keeps the soul,
> Steadfast and sure as the billows roll,
> Fastened to the rock that cannot move,
> Grounded firm and deep in the Savior's love.

The church leader introduced me to Jesus, and I trusted him completely as my under-shepherd. However, my heavenly Father sent help all the way from Canada to alert me and awaken me to the realization that it was God speaking to me through the dream he had given me. The sister from Canada almost gave up on me, but the Master sent her back to get me and did not let her give up on me. Then finally, in God's perfect timing, he uprooted my children and me, and he planted us in another part of his vineyard in another church. I never saw that elder again because some time later, he died. I believe he may have repented, because God loved him enough to send warnings to him, and he also had me interceding for him. I have no heaven or hell to put anyone in, because it's stated in Isaiah 55:7.

> Let the wicked forsake his way,
> And the unrighteous man his thoughts:
> Let him return unto the Lord,
> And he will have mercy upon him,
> And to our God,
> For he will abundantly pardon.

However, I pray that if you or someone you know may be in a religious organization where there are possible red flags or signs of manipulation or control from the leader or someone else in authority, please cry out to Almighty God, and he will surely come to your rescue.

Prayer of Deliverance for Unsuspecting Victims
(By Mother of Nations)

Heavenly Father, Creator of the universe and everything and everyone, you are the great I Am; the all-knowing, all-seeing, all-powerful God; all-sufficient One. I enter your holiest place by the precious blood of Jesus, and I pray for your divine intervention in every nation of the earth, among every people of every kindred and tongue.

Righteous Judge, stretch forth your majestic, mighty right hand throughout the length and breadth of planet Earth—the Caribbean, Europe, Asia, Africa, America, Australia. Let there be a mighty outpouring of your Holy Spirit of truth. What is wrong, you put right. Make the crooked places straight. Set innocent victims of manipulation free in every religious organization. I cover them with the blood of Jesus. Open the spiritual eyes of every victim to see you, Jesus, and open their spiritual ears to hear the whispers of the Holy Ghost. I thank you for the renewed hope for those victims who may have given up and for making ways of escape for them in safe havens. I thank you for planting them in safe places, where they can be fed the unadulterated truth from your holy Word, where they can grow and prosper and bring forth abundant fruit of righteousness in Jesus's name. Amen!

SECTION 4

EMPOWERED TO OVERCOME DARKNESS WITHIN

The people that walked in darkness have seen a great light: they that dwell in the land of the shadow of death, upon them hath the light shined. –King James
Isaiah 9:2

CHAPTER 1

Transition

Planted in a New Church

I had vowed to the Most High God that I would proclaim his name from hilltop to housetop if he got my children and me out of that country church safely. In spite of the attacks from the altar when the shots were fired at me during preaching, the Most High protected me because I was wearing the helmet of his salvation, and after all, it was the Lord's battle, not mine. Threats were made to people who left the church, saying they would lose their minds because that was the only true church. But the almighty, omniscient God shepherded my children and me to green pastures where the Word of God was taught and true worship was taking place. This was something I had never experienced before, because I had been raised in a different denomination, left the church, went on the run, and been indoctrinated into this country church in the wilderness for about ten years.

I knew something new was on the horizon, but I didn't know what it was. I had left my friend behind, and the sister from overseas lived in the country area and was still doing what God had called her to do in that part of the vineyard. I thank God for using her to awaken me just by her laughter and cause me to come to the realization of what God was trying to show me. However, I had to move forward by faith, not knowing where I was going and simply trusting in God's mercy. I thought of God's track record in my life. He had caused me to be born again to gain entrance to his kingdom through his Son, Jesus Christ. I almost lost my mind in front of the classroom one day, but when I called on the name of Jesus, he brought my mind back to reality. I had decided to follow Jesus and had given up willingly the ways of the world, such as drinking and smoking. Even though I fell back into that alcoholic snare because of the environment in the leadership of the country church, God alerted me to that dark area in my life through a dream. I felt convicted but not condemned. I thank God for that song I heard on the radio by Shirley Caesar, "Take It Away from Me." I had learned how to cry out to God for deliverance, and he heard my cry and delivered me.

God had transported us safely out of the wilderness, but I didn't know where he was going to plant us next. I was driving to work one day, not knowing what next step to take but waiting on God. As customary, I was listening to the Christian radio station. This time, it wasn't the voice of a woman singing but the voice of a man. The voice, as I later found out, belonged to a Guyanese man called Dr. Milton Granham. I can't remember what he said at that moment, but it was so good that he got my attention. When he said he would be visiting a church in my neighborhood that I had never heard about, I wrote down the address. I visited that upstairs building that Friday night. It wasn't a church with a steeple, and I had driven past that building so many times weekly, not realizing what was taking place on the upstairs floor. I went to hear the preacher, who was the friend of the pastor, who I didn't know. I wasn't introduced to the preacher personally that night. I will always remember his message, but because of his voice on the radio, I was drawn by the Holy Spirit to this new church.

The following Sunday, I visited the new church, and I arrived on time, before the service started. There were greeters at the door, and ushers led us to a seat. Nobody had their head wrapped in white cloth, so I didn't wrap mine either. I left that behind, especially as they would have associated me with that religious sect, which people have a tendency to avoid. I didn't want to be identified with them anymore, but I didn't know who these new people were either.

The musicians were in front, and a young man led the church in song for about an hour. I later learned he was the worship leader. Then a lady with a soft, gentle voice, who I later found out was the pastor's wife, greeted the people and welcomed them into the church. Then she led a song—"Yes, I love you with the love of the Lord"— and invited the people to go around and hug and greet one another. I was a bit skeptical about this hugging and loving because of my past experience, but I allowed it for some reason.

Then the pastor, a slim dark man with a rich voice, stood before the people, called the congregation, which I didn't know at that time. The pastor, a Negro, held the microphone in his hand and, with his rich voice, declared, "This is the day that the Lord has made, and I will rejoice and be glad in it" (Psalm 118:24).

I visited this church every Sunday and allowed my spirit to be ushered into the awesome presence of God by the worship leader. We spent about an hour worshipping the Lord, and then we spent another hour listening to the pastor preach the unadulterated, uncompromising Word of God. We sang songs of praise and worship that declared the power, glory, and majesty of our King.

Majesty, worship His Majesty
Unto Jesus be all glory, power, and praise,
Majesty, kingdom authority flows from his throne
Unto his own, his anthem raise.
So exalt, lift up on high the name of Jesus.
Magnify, come glorify, Christ Jesus the King.
Majesty, worship His Majesty
Jesus, who died, now glorify King of all kings.

Here's another song that penetrated the atmosphere:

He is the King of kings! He is the Lord of lords
His name is Jesus, Jesus, Jesus, Jesus
Oh he is the King
King of kings, forever and ever
Lord of lords, forever and ever
King of kings and Lord of lords

These were all new songs based on psalms and scripture verses, and they set our souls on fire. Then we lifted our voices, singing at the top of our lungs this other psalm in song. That was my song but presented in a new way. I remember the dream I had in the stormy sea, where I was standing on the rock. Every time we sang that song, I remembered how many times Jesus delivered me, and I knew I could trust him. I found a church home and became a member of Faith Revival Ministries, and the name of my new leader was Pastor Bertril Baird.

Praise the name of Jesus (2)
He's my rock, he's my fortress
He's my deliverer
In him will I trust

The praise and worship at my new church and the word that was preached revived our souls. Then they sang another spiritual song from the Word, which remains in my soul up to today, from Galatians 2:20, "I am crucified with Christ: nevertheless I live; yet not I but Christ lives in me; and the life which I now live in the flesh, I live by faith of the Son of God, who loved me and gave himself for me." I was so happy to hear these lively songs of worship, and I became an avid worshipper in that church.

Then I was introduced for the first time to the concept of praying the Word back to God, and I later learned this was called the ministry of intercession. According to *Webster's New World*

Dictionary, to intercede is "to plead or make a request in behalf of another or others." I tuned in well to what was going on around me in the intercessory prayer meetings for souls. I heard a young male intercessor pray a scripture from Isaiah 55:11, "So shall my word be that goeth out of my mouth; it shall not return unto me void, but it shall accomplish that which I please, and it shall prosper in the thing whereto I sent it." I caught that word as it flowed out of the young man's mouth and charged the atmosphere. Another time, I heard an older man bellow in prayer from Joel 2:25, "And I will restore the years that the locust has eaten, the cankerworm, and the caterpillar, and the palmerworm, my great army which I sent among you." I didn't comprehend everything that scripture was referring to, but I knew I wanted God to restore my lost years. These intercessors were charging the atmosphere with precious promises from God's holy Word, from the Old Testament, but these truths can be applied to our present situations and circumstances, because the principles from God's holy Word do not change. The Bible tells us the Word of God is eternal and stands forever.

I also remember one of sisters praying that "Jesus spoilt principalities and powers and made a show of them openly" (Colossians 3:15). The intercessors were also praying from the scriptures Ephesians 1:17–23, Ephesians 3:14–21, and also Colossians 1:9–14, which I later adopted as my family prayer that my children and I prayed together in the morning before they left for school. I decided I wanted to learn how to pray the Word of God like the brethren, and I bought the book entitled *Prayers That Avail Much*. Before long, I, too, became an intercessor by using the powerful ammunition from God's holy Word.

Then along came the glorious experience of an international convention hosted by my new church and now-deceased Pastor Bertril Baird. I was a teacher on vacation, so I signed up to help with those who were serving food. It was all so new to me, and the guest speakers came from different parts of the Caribbean. These included Dr. Milton Granham, now-deceased Dr. Myles Munroe from the Bahamas, now-deceased Pastor Turnel Nelson, Prophet

Jefferson Edwards from Kansas City, and now-deceased Fuchsia Pickett. It was such a glorious experience, with this conglomeration of ministry giftings and anointing and intense revelations of worship and the Word; I was filled with expectation of things to come. The atmosphere was so charged with intoxicating worship and inspiring messages from the Word of God that it was really like heaven descending on earth. I think the pure worship wafted upward directly to the nostrils of the King of heaven, and he arose and graced us with his majestic presence.

CHAPTER 2

First Call to Ministry

The Spirit of the Lord is upon me,
Because He has anointed me to preach the gospel to the poor;
He has sent me to heal the broken hearted,
To preach deliverance to the captives,
And recovering of sight to the blind,
To set at liberty them that are bruised.
—Luke 4:18

I became tired of working and paying bills and not really enjoying life, so I decided to take a vacation. I took a loan from the bank and secured visas from the American Embassy for myself and three of my children, the two older ones and the baby. I was still in touch with the sister from overseas and visited her occasionally. At that time, I still wore skirts and dresses but didn't use pants, use makeup, or perm my hair. One day, when I was planning my trip, she suggested I wear jeans on my vacation. I looked at her in surprise and asked her if she was certain it would be all right, because I didn't want to adopt the ways of the world and wear pants. I trusted her judgment, and my children and I set out on vacation, pants and all. We visited my former high school friend in Canada. We went to New York to visit my sister-in-law. The children had fun in Coney Island riding the ponies. I remember that on a particular day, I was riding the train with a diaper bag filled with wipes and formula, and I was wearing a pair of jeans. Suddenly, I felt an awareness of the presence of God even though I was wearing my jeans, and I was so overjoyed that God was not angry with me and that he was still with me.

We returned from our vacation. School reopened, so I was back to the daily routine of getting up at 4:00 a.m. and preparing breakfast and lunch for my family. I would like to attribute this habit to the vice principal of the school where I worked. She and her husband had allowed me to rent their one-bedroom annex years ago just after I had left my father's home. This lady was a working wife and mother, and she had developed the discipline of that 4:00 a.m. routine of preparing and packing breakfast and lunch for her husband and only daughter. I watched her, and years later, after I got married and had children, I adopted the same routine. The only difference was that I had five children instead of one.

One evening, after work, I was cleaning up the kitchen, with all the dirty dishes and pots and pans from the morning. I suddenly felt the awesome presence of God in front of the kitchen sink, and I was riveted to the spot as I listened to the whisper of this Catholic hymn in my heart.

God's spirit is in my heart
He has called me and set me apart
This is what I have to do, what I have to do
He sent me to give the good news to the poor
Tell prisoners that they are prisoners no more
Tell blind people that they can see
And set the downtrodden free
And go tell everyone the news that the kingdom of God has come

This song ended with the reminder that in the same way God sent Jesus, our heavenly Father wants to send us as witnesses throughout the world. My spirit was awakened in a new way, and I realized, because of that hymn, that Almighty God, my Creator, was calling me to ministry. I didn't know what it meant or what part of the world he wanted to send me to. Right there, in front of my kitchen sink, I said yes without hesitation. That was no problem, because Pastor Baird was conducting a ministry training class at his church for those who felt called to the ministry. However, the class was on a Friday evening, the last day of the working week, and after dealing with my children in the morning and other children all day long, I was really exhausted by Friday. The Holy Spirit, however, said he was going to stretch me. I had developed a strange habit at home when I didn't feel like doing chores or dishes, and I began asking my heavenly Father for grace to do the things I didn't feel like doing. I knew what stretching implied in the natural sense, because I had given birth to five children, and I can still see the stretch marks on my abdomen, where my skin was stretched to accommodate the mysterious occurrences that happened in my womb. I knew it would cause my life to change in dramatic, unexpected ways, but I accepted heaven's mandate.

By God's grace, I accepted the stretching, and I started attending Friday night classes at the church. About the second or third Friday, I found a parking spot at the back of the building and raced up the stairs for class, but the door had been locked, as I was a few minutes late. I turned away dejected, thinking, *Well, I missed the calling, and that class really isn't for me.* Then on my way down the stairs, I came face-to-face with one of our teachers, our worship leader from Kansas City, who was in our country doing missionary work at our church. She asked what was wrong, and I told her I was late and had been locked out. She told me to wait a minute, and she went and spoke to the pastor. I was let in by the mercies of God and received favor, and I realize this was God's way of reaffirming that he had indeed called me to ministry.

I was never late after that, and every Friday, after picking up the children after school and feeding them, I drove to the church and pushed my tired body up that flight of stairs. Class would begin; the sister from Kansas City would start leading us in worship, and such peace and serenity would flood my soul. I love the Lord with my whole heart and soul, and that was when I truly became an avid worshipper. It was almost like going into that secret hiding place of renewal and emerging feeling refreshed in our souls as the words of each worship song swept over our souls.

I was introduced to the Word of God in a profound way. I remember Pastor Baird taking us through the book of Acts, and the phrase "signs, wonders, and miracles" was embedded in my soul. I remember him teaching us about the fivefold ministerial gifting in the body of Christ. I remember how God used him to expound the Word describing the downfall of Satan from Isaiah 14:12, 16, "How art thou fallen from heaven, O Lucifer, son of the morning! How thou art cut down to the ground, which did weaken the nations. . . . . Is this the man that made the earth to tremble, that did shake kingdoms?" He spoke with such boldness, power, and authority that certain things he said were planted in my heart without my having to memorize them. Another scripture that I believe charted the course of my destiny was the scripture he declared emphatically from Psalms 2:8, "Ask of me, and I shall give you the heathen for thy inheritance and the uttermost parts of the earth for my possession." This seed for a world vision was planted in my spirit at Faith Revival Ministries in my native land.

In addition to the Word, we studied books like *Book Titles-Management: A Biblical Approach by Myron Rush, A Tale of Three Kings by Gene Edwards, Team Ministry by Larry Gilbert, Attitude of a servant by Michael Landsman*. We were trained to be servants in the church, and we were taught that the pastor was one of the gifts from God. Pastor Baird introduced us to Ephesians 4:11, "And he gave some apostles, and some prophets, and some evangelists: and some pastors and teachers; For the perfecting of the saints, for the work of the ministry, for the edifying of the Body of Christ." I had already made my career choice as a teacher, but I knew God was now introducing me to the ministry of becoming a teacher of his holy Word. In ministry class, Pastor Baird also introduced us to the biblical apostolic church doctrines, one of which was, according to Mark 16:18, "They shall lay hands on the sick, and they shall recover." He demonstrated this biblical principle every Sunday morning, after he delivered the

Word of God, by having an altar call and laying hands on the sick and praying for them and also for the salvation of souls.

Then the Holy Spirit tested me to allow me to practice what I was learning in ministry class. I had heard the pastor preach about praying for the sick; I had seen him practice what he had preached in ministry class at the altar. Now it was my turn, even though I didn't think I was ready. My girls attended a Catholic elementary school run by some wonderful nuns, and one of the lay teachers had been in a vehicular accident and was in a coma in the hospital. Once again, I was standing in front of my kitchen sink. I don't know if it was the flowing water that calmed my soul, but it was impressed upon my heart to visit the teacher who was in a coma in the hospital. The Holy Spirit was teaching me how it was important for me to be obedient.

One evening, after ministry class was over, I went to the worship leader from Kansas City and shared with her my concern about what I thought God wanted me to do. I thought she was going to accompany me to the hospital, but she gently smiled and encouraged me to be obedient to the leading of the Holy Spirit. I had a silent argument in my heart with the Lord, trying to reason with him to see things from my perspective. I reasoned with the Lord that although Pastor Baird had been teaching us in class about signs, wonders, and miracles, and about laying hands on the sick so they would recover, I didn't think it was time for me to experiment. Even though God had been preparing me in ministry class, I hadn't begun to see myself as a minister. I even asked God if he was trying to embarrass me by sending me to do something I had never done before. Then I remembered the advice the sister from Canada had given me: "If God asks you to do anything, simply ask him for the tools to do it." I remembered also that when I accepted his call to ministry, the Lord impressed upon my spirit that he was going to stretch me. I still have stretch marks from each of my pregnancies after all these years. Every bit of muscle inside and outside the body in the area of the womb stretches and grows gradually to accommodate the fetus. My human body had accepted this stretching as something that was normal, not really understanding the full impact of all the stretching. So as I had accepted the stretching of my physical body, I said yes to God. Consequently, with this, all arguments in my mind were silenced in submission to God's will.

The next morning, after dropping off my children at school, I began to quietly sing one of the familiar spiritual songs, "To Worship You, I Live." Then it happened unexpectedly! In the midst of the traffic, like a flash of lightning, heaven touched my soul with an open vision. My spiritual eyes were now open to God's will, and I treasured and nursed this open vision in my heart. I asked God for a divine strategy to accomplish this seemingly impossible assignment. I knew I had to push past my timidity and prayed for God to endow me with his holy boldness. I decided on a partial fast and realized that, since I couldn't visit the hospital in the morning or evening after work, I had to find time somehow. I realized the only free time I had was my lunch hour, and I decided to lay my hour on the altar of sacrifice.

I never realized before how much could be accomplished in one hour. On Monday, the lunch bell rang, and I waved to the children as I sped to my car. As I drove up the hill, shifting gears to accelerate my speed, I was praying for a free parking space on the hospital compound. I breathed a sigh of relief as I pulled into the parking space, and I smiled because God had answered that prayer. With the heavenly vision in mind, I approached the information desk and heard myself say for the first time, "I am a minister, and I've come to pray for the teacher in the coma." After giving the name of the teacher, I was given directions to her room, even though visiting hours had not yet begun. I walked nervously but hurriedly along the corridor with my heart full of compassion, at the same time avoiding a near collision with a meal trolley being pushed by an orderly.

I felt like a student, since I was being taught personally by God's Holy Spirit and given directives on how to proceed with his assignment. As I stood at the door, my eyes swept the room. The woman who lay on the bed was a stranger to me but not to God. I gazed in amazement at all the tubes connected to different parts of her body, as none of my family or friends had ever been in a coma before. I know now the names of some of the pieces of medical equipment that she was surrounded by: a type of wall apparatus, an IV stand, a heart monitor, and a respirator. The nurse must have read the uncertainty in my eyes, and she beckoned for me to come closer. As I approached the bed, I remembered the open vision I had while driving of a woman who was lying on a bed but suddenly shot upright as though a bolt of lightning had hit her. I opened the small bottle of anointing oil in my hand and anointed the patient's head as I whispered seven times into her spirit through her ear gate, calling her name and declaring, "By the stripes of Jesus, you are healed!" Nothing spectacular happened, but I felt a wave of peace flooding my soul, knowing I had obeyed God.

I sacrificed my lunch hour for the next two weeks and continued my lunchtime pilgrimage to the ICU. The amazing thing was that I always got a free parking space, spent just enough time at the bedside, and returned to school in time to eat my lunch before the school bell rang. I overhead one of my coworkers, who knew the teacher and lived in the same area where she taught, saying she would be a human vegetable all her life. When I heard that, I sustained the open vision the Holy Spirit showed me of the woman sitting up in bed. Then one day, the inevitable happened, and when I arrived, the teacher's eyes were open. The heavenly vision was starting to become reality, and of course, there were a lot of other people praying for a miracle for this Roman Catholic teacher who God wanted to raise up as a living testimony of his power. I remember the last visit I paid to her bedside, along with a team of four charismatic, Holy Ghost–filled Roman Catholic believers, and we laid hands on her body in the very same areas Jesus was pierced. I laid hands on her head; there was one holding her right hand, and another holding her left hand. One held her left foot, and another held her right foot. We interceded together and touched all the points of entry Jesus experienced on the cross.

During this season in my life, I still had issues at home that I had to deal with, but I was still learning how to walk step-by-step and day by day in obedience and in accordance with God's heavenly blueprint for my life. I was released from my assignment, but I was overjoyed the day one of my daughters came home with the good news that the teacher who had been in a coma had visited the school that day. She was a walking, talking, breathing miracle. I thank God for deciding to include me in this part of his plan to perform a miracle, even in the midst of my trials and tribulations at home. I believe that because of this incident, I developed my own personal life philosophy, which is "Faith finds a way."

CHAPTER 3

Following Jesus through the Wilderness

¹ And Jesus being full of the Holy Ghost returned from Jordan,
And was led by the Spirit into the wilderness.
² Being forty days tempted of the devil.
And in those days he did eat nothing;
And when they were ended,
He afterward hungered.

—Luke 4:1–2

Verses 12 and 13 warn us that when the devil had desisted in all his attempts to distract Jesus from his earthly mission, he departed for a season. However, after Jesus was able to overcome Satan by releasing the Word of God from his mouth, he was empowered by the Holy Spirit of truth to proceed to Galilee on his heavenly mission. These verses caution us that we need to take a stand every day and receive divine enablement to overcome every temptation and attack launched by the devil, because he always departs for a season. We don't know how long each season is between the attacks he launches, so we have to be tuned into God's Spirit for him to reveal to us the devil's schemes and wicked devices.

The first church where I had been baptized was located in the country and seemingly in the wilderness, because of the long distance we had to drive back and forth weekly. When the Holy Spirit alerted me about the mess in the congregation, I started seeking God in his holy Word. The sister from Canada kept directing me to Jesus, so I started to seek Jesus. I encountered this account from Luke 4 about how Jesus was tempted by Satan in the wilderness for forty days. At that time, I had never heard anyone preach about fasting, but since I wanted to follow Jesus, I told the sister from Canada that I wanted to fast like Jesus. She assured me the Holy Spirit would lead me. Somehow I knew I should sacrifice something I loved dearly. I loved meat, especially chicken, so I decided to deny myself the pleasure of eating meat for forty days. I cooked for my family daily, stirred the meat in the pot, and by the grace of Almighty, was able to deny my flesh like Jesus did. I truly believe that because of this decision, I was graced with the anointing to approach the elder.

After God delivered my children and me, brought us out of the bondage, and let me transition to the new church, I got a better understanding of the opening scripture because of one of the visiting preachers at one of the church conferences. He pointed out that, in verse 1, after Jesus had been baptized in the River Jordan, he was full of the Holy Ghost and was led by the Holy Spirit into the wilderness to be tempted. According to *Webster's New World Dictionary*, a wilderness is "an uncultivated, uninhabited region, waste, wild, and any barren or empty or open area." The preacher drew our attention to the fact that after Jesus had endured the temptation for forty days, he "returned in the power of the Spirit into Galilee" (Luke 4:14).

When I examined the text further, I was able to understand the temptations Jesus had as the one and only begotten Son of God, who was wrapped in earthly flesh. Since Jesus did it for me as an example and was able to overcome the flesh, I decided to apply the reality of this word to my life. The devil's first temptation he hurled at Jesus in the wilderness were these words: "If thou be the Son of God command this stone that it be made bread." Jesus's response to him was "It is written that man shall not live by bread alone, but by every word of God." So when I fasted for the first time, in the midst of denying my flesh, I decided to pray this other scripture from Matthew 5:6, "Blessed are they which hunger and thirst after righteousness for they shall be filled."

When the devil tempted Jesus the second time, according to Luke 4:5–8, he offered to give Jesus all the kingdoms of the world if Jesus would bow down and worship him, Satan. The temptation is the lust of the eyes, which, unfortunately, many are struggling with today, because they fall prey to the lust of the eyes, especially through pornography in magazines, on the Internet, and even in clubs. The problem here is the eye gate. Jesus spoke the Word of God emphatically, "Get thee behind me Satan: for it is written, thou shalt worship the Lord thy God, and him only shalt thou serve." We also can overcome the lust of our eyes if we declare emphatically, like Jesus, and remind ourselves when temptation comes our way, "I will worship the Lord my God, and him only will I serve."

Every time the devil tempted Jesus, Jesus's response was from the Word of God. Jesus's first response came directly from the Pentateuch, which comprises the first five books of the Bible—Genesis, Exodus, Leviticus, Numbers, and Deuteronomy. When Jesus was tempted for the second time, he quoted the scripture from Deuteronomy 8:2–3, "And thou shall remember the way which the Lord thy God led thee these forty years in the wilderness, to humble thee and to prove thee, to know what was in thine heart . . . And He humbled thee and suffered thee to hunger, and fed thee with manna . . . that He might make you know that man does not live by bread alone, but by every word that proceeds out of the mouth of God." Jesus knew the Word of God and fought the battle in the wilderness using the Word of God, and if we also make a conscious decision to speak the Word of God in the midst of our temptation, we, too, will overcome.

However, the devil is very slick, and he realized Jesus would only respond to the Word of God. So for the third temptation, the devil quoted a scripture to tempt Jesus. They were the right words, but they were coming from the wrong vessel. Luke 4:9–11 states that he brought Jesus to Jerusalem, to the pinnacle of the temple, and told

Jesus to cast himself down. Then the devil had the audacity to quote a scripture from Psalm 91. He studied Jesus's method of response and decided that since Jesus was quoting scripture, he would quote scripture also, because the devil's intent was to beat Jesus at any cost. The devil said in Luke 4:10–11, "For it is written, He shall give his angels charge over thee to keep thee. And in their hands they shall bear thee up, lest at any time thou dash thy foot against a stone." This attack that was hurled at Jesus can be classified as *the pride of life*. "And Jesus answering said unto him, 'It is said that thou shalt not tempt the Lord thy God.'" I, however, didn't really pay close attention to verse 13, which reads, "And when the devil had ended all the temptation, he departed from him for a season." The devil left me for a season and was waiting on an opportunity to make a comeback to get me offtrack. Much to my amazement and horror, he did.

I fasted and prayed because I had developed a spiritual appetite for God's righteousness, and God continued to fill me with spiritual ammunition from his holy Word. Our heavenly Father wants us to know that, besides eating natural food daily to nourish and develop our physical bodies, we need spiritual bread daily in order to develop our spirits. Jesus entered the wilderness "full of the Holy Ghost," and he emerged from the wilderness "in the power of the spirit." He was empowered to go throughout the region teaching in the synagogues. The Son of God denied his flesh when he was tempted in the wilderness and was able to overcome every temptation. Jesus did it in his human state here on earth, and that was the reason I was able to abstain from meat and the reason my spirit was energized to approach the elder before his demise. I was also empowered to visit the teacher at the hospital who was in a coma, because I was fasting and had begun to learn and apply the Word of God in my life.

So I was inspired at my new church to pray and sing the Word of God, and that made a difference. I remember that *Larry Lee* received some powerful revelations about the Our Father, and that swept through our church and revolutionized how we actually prayed that particular prayer. I had learned Psalm 91 at the country church, but at my new church, I was taught by one of the sisters how to personalize the Word of God and make it mine. For example, Psalm 91:1, 3–4 states, "He that dwelleth in the secret place of the Most High shall abide under the shadow of the Almighty. Surely He shall deliver thee from the snare of the fowler and from the noisome pestilence. He shall cover thee with His feathers and under His wings, thou shall trust; his shield shall be thy shield and buckler." This is how I learned to personalize this scripture: "I dwell in the secret place of the Most High. I abide under the shadow of the Almighty. Surely he shall deliver me from the snare of the fowler and from the noisome pestilence."

Pastor Baird had a policy at the church that after someone had given their life to Christ, someone from the church needed to visit the new convert within twenty-four hours. I decided to serve with the team who did visitation. I was assigned a female partner, and after church on Sunday, we would get our assignment. During the course of the week, we would knock on the door of the person whose card we received and minister to the needs of the household. It was also a time when I witnessed the mature lady use her spiritual gifting and lay hands on individuals to receive the gift of the Holy Ghost with the evidence of speaking in tongues.

CHAPTER 4

God Reveals Himself as the Lord of Hosts

⁵ For thy maker is your husband, the Lord of Hosts is His name,
And thy Redeemer the Holy One of Israel,
The God of the whole earth shall he be called.
⁶ For the Lord has called thee as a woman forsaken
And grieved in spirit, and a wife of youth,
When you were refused, says your God.
⁷ For a small moment have I forsaken thee;
But with great mercies will I gather thee.
— Isaiah 54:5-7

I was becoming more confident in my faith, and my spirit was being renewed as I began to practice the presence of God in my prayers and praise and worship. My now-deceased husband had been displaying some strange behavior. Instead of buying food, he spent his money on musical things. He built large musical boxes and placed speakers inside them. He bought all the latest stereo equipment and cluttered the living room area. He never allowed the children or me to touch his stereo equipment, but he would spend time weekly dusting and shining his music boxes. He also placed a mark around each chair leg in the living room, and I was unable to move the furniture around to rearrange the living room. One day, he got really angry because I had tried to move around some item in the living room, and he broke my sewing machine and destroyed it. After that, I left him alone.

In my times of frustration, I would console myself with the story of Joseph from the Bible and remind myself that Joseph was thrown into prison through no fault of his own. My faith level would immediately rise, and I felt confident I could trust God, even though I didn't understand what he was doing. About this time, I received approval for the loan from the housing agency, and so my house renovations began. I learned from my father never to put money into a contractor's hand, so prayers ascended to God's throne of grace for him to divinely send to me the right mason, plumber, carpenter, and electrician. So while renovations were being done on the house and new rooms were added as the house was being extended, God continued his renovations in my soul.

I don't remember the day the Holy Spirit drew my attention to the scripture mentioned in the opening of this chapter. But it seemed like I was arrested by the Holy Spirit of truth. My earthly eyes were riveted to the words, and I had to pay strict attention. The spiritual eyes of my understanding became enlightened, and I began to partake of a new meal. Those words on the page became like fresh manna to my soul, and I began to mouth them; I tasted them by speaking them to myself. As I began speaking the words, I felt that some sort of connection was taking place. I realized the synapses in my brain were being connected to a new school of thought. I knew Jesus as my Savior because he had rescued my soul from that Adamic nature. I had started building my relationship with him, and I realized he was my best friend, who I could be open and honest with and who I could tell the naked truth about myself to. Then Jesus really became my Lord, as I would ask for his opinion before I made a decision.

I had transitioned from religious tradition to a loving relationship with my heavenly Father, because he sent Jesus to pay the price for my sins, and I accepted his love. Then we were courting and went everywhere together, and he protected in the midst of all those car incidents. Now Isaiah 54:5 was speaking directly to me: "For thy maker is thy husband, the Lord of Hosts is His name; and thy Redeemer the Holy One of Israel; the God of the whole earth shall He be called." I looked over my shoulder, but there was no one else in the room but me. The Word came out of my mouth, and I realized I had begun to feed my brain with some new spiritual food. "My maker is my husband; the Lord of Hosts is his name." This was spiritual meat, so I couldn't treat it like spiritual milk. I had to cut this meat into bite-size pieces and meditate on each phrase bit by bit. I began feeding myself brain food.

Normally, when we put natural meat in our mouth, we begin to chew it and masticate it with saliva and swallow. Then it goes into our digestive system, and the physical body absorbs it; we feel we have nourished our bodies. But in this instance, when I spoke the Word of God out of my mouth, it went through my spiritual ear gate and started feeding my brain. So I kept feeding my brain the Word of God concerning this new relationship I was about to have with God. It was almost like a marriage proposal, because I could have said no and instead fed my brain with words of doubt and impossibilities, negativities, and accusations. But when I thought of how much heartache I was getting from my relationship with my earthly husband, I decided I had to accept this marriage proposal from my Maker. So I said yes and gave my brain permission to accept this new school of thought. That scripture made my day. There were no bridesmaids or a matron of honor, but when I really accepted the fact that my Maker was my husband, it really made my day.

Then I put the next piece of the meat from that verse into my mouth. "Thine husband, the Lord of Hosts is His name." I had to notify my brain to slow down and chew carefully on each tidbit of the new information so the chemical substance from the neurotransmitters in my brain could process this new information. At that time, all I knew about the Lord of Hosts was that he fights our battles for us as long as we're on his side, which obviously is the winning side. Then I started repeating the new spiritual song I learned from the missionary sister from Kansas City, which was based on Exodus 15:1–3, "I will sing unto the Lord for he hath triumphed gloriously, the horse and his rider hath he thrown into the sea. The Lord is my strength and my song, and he is become my salvation: he is my God and I will prepare Him an habitation; my father's God and I will exalt Him. The Lord is a man of war; the Lord is His name." It seemed as though God was actually stretching the chambers in my mind, even as new rooms were being added to my earthly house.

One of the walls in the first bedroom had to be broken down in order to enlarge the living room area; however, we added two new bedrooms as part of the extension. God had allowed us to enlarge the house, and at the same time, he was enlarging the territory in my mind. So I chose to embrace this new school of thought as I allowed the Holy Spirit to create new pathways in my mind to accommodate this next piece of meat, *the God of the whole earth*. I think even now, as I'm completing my assignment, my mental capacity is enlarging in a way that my intellect is not able to comprehend. I just have to say yes to the expansion and allow my thoughts to escalate to the heavens. My new spiritual husband is now my Maker, whose name is *the Lord of Hosts*, and the extent of his jurisdiction is planet Earth. All my reasoning faculties cannot comprehend or explain this heavenly mystery. It is inexplicable. However, if you decide to enroll in the Holy Ghost's school of correction, demolition, and reconstruction, you will definitely become a righteous brain thinker for the rest of your life.

I am still actually amazed by verse 6, which states, "For the Lord has called thee as a woman forsaken and grieved in spirit, and a wife of youth when thou wast refused." I couldn't fathom why Almighty God, the Creator of the universe, the Lord of Hosts, could be calling me, with all my past failures, frustrations, and wrong decisions.

The electrician had come to the house, and I showed him the blueprint. He gave me a list of all the materials I would need from the hardware store, and he told me the cost. Thank God I had budgeted well; I purchased the materials, and he began wiring the rooms that were being added to the house. Some wires ran through the walls like the veins in our bodies; some ran in the ceiling overhead like the synapses in our brain. We were in the process of remodeling, but after a while, none of these wires were visible. The electrician sent the wires to the junction box that contained fuses for the different parts of the house. There were ground wires to prevent the risk of electrical shock. I trusted the electrician because he appeared to know what he was doing. He ran his test. Lights came on; there was electricity flowing throughout the entire house, and the old part of the house was connected to the new part that had been under construction. Of course, the wires were in some way connected to the outside meter, and this allowed the meter reader to enter the premises on behalf of the electric company, who billed in accordance with the amount of watts I used.

I saw it happen, but I am not able to explain exactly how electricity flows. However, I know that God, in some mysterious way, rewired my brain, as I also gave myself permission to accept this new school of thought that God was calling me to. Yes, I was a woman forsaken by her earthly husband, and I grieved in spirit. God knew I had a legal document that stated I was married. However, he knew the foundation of my first marriage was based on deception and lies. God knew I would receive attacks from the ones who were very close to me. God knew I was naive and had no one to fight for me, so he had mercy on me. God knew I never received emotional support from my deceased husband when I carried his five children, and he knew I had been physically abused that one time. God knew I was battling with this thought of submitting to my husband to make my marriage work. God knew everything—and even more than I did—about this marriage. God knew beforehand what would have happened if I had done what my husband wanted me to do when he said, "When you get the money, let's put our heads together to spend it."

God tried to show me I shouldn't trust my now-deceased husband, but I decided to put him to the test even after I saw how he had fooled his own mother. I had to run an errand, and I left money with my husband to pay the electrician. When I returned to the house, the electrician was gone, so I walked down the street to his house and asked him if he had received the money I left for him. He shook his head and smiled in an understanding way, trying to assure me it was okay. So here I was, with my cup overflowing with grief and sorrow as I walked back home with tears in my eyes. My own husband, who had caused me so much grief and heartache, had disappointed me, and I understood why God sent his messenger, the Holy Spirit, to call me to him. As the synapses in my brain began to accept the fact that God was calling me because my husband didn't want to treat me the right way, another bolt of revelation shot into my mind. It came from God's electric company on high, because he has all power in his hands. The Holy Ghost, who was my teacher, was helping me connect the dots, just like the children in kindergarten who learn to form letters of the alphabet. The teacher gives them dots to trace each letter to help develop their fine motor skills.

The Holy Ghost, whose assignment is to help us remember, did just like Jesus said he would. There was some information already stored in my memory bank, and the Holy Spirit skillfully brought Isaiah 53:3–5 to the front of my mind. "He is despised and rejected of men; a man of sorrows and acquainted with grief and we hid as it were our faces from Him; He was despised and we esteemed Him not. Surely He hath borne our griefs and carried our sorrows: yet we did esteem him smitten of God and afflicted. But he was wounded for our transgressions; he was bruised for our iniquities: the chastisement of our peace was upon Him; and with His stripes we are healed." I started to reflect on Jesus's condition, then on my condition. I looked closer at the portrait of Christ that Isaiah the prophet wrote, as he had been inspired by the breath of our holy God. I kept looking at Jesus and looking at the picture our holy, omniscient God had allowed Isaiah to paint of me as well. I wasn't trying to test a hypothesis like scientists do, but I came to a godly conclusion. Our heavenly Father, who I will call Father Time because he inhabits eternity, knew that when he gave that revelation to Isaiah about the woman forsaken, he was allowing Isaiah to paint a picture of me.

I was flabbergasted because, as I looked at myself in God's picture album, I realized I was beginning to resemble Jesus Christ, Son of the living God. I was flabbergasted as my brain performed a 180-degree revolution. My thinking had actually changed, and I was thinking what a privilege and honor it was for God to allow me to be identified with his Son as a woman of sorrows. It was like seeing the flip side of a coin, and I could see the head facing upward. I no longer felt downcast or rejected by my earthly husband; I felt the peace of Jesus as I allowed his nail-scarred hands, dripping with his precious blood, to imprint this new identity into my mental faculty.

CHAPTER 5

The Blood of Jesus Works

Because I am deeply convinced
that we Christians can never know too much
about the truth the blood proclaims.
There can be no freedom of approach to God,
Nor fellowship with Him,
Apart from the truly vital and powerful
experience of the Blood of Christ.

In the preface of his book entitled *The Blood of the Cross,* Andrew Murray stated that he was completely convinced that we as Christians would never be free to approach God or have fellowship and deep communion with him until we understand fully the wholesome truth about the shed blood of Jesus Christ. He continued to state that in order to have this extremely powerful and necessary relationship with the Lord God Almighty, our Creator, we need to be submitted to his authority. We need to be led by God's Holy Spirit of truth to Calvary's cross, with our hearts opened to him in reckless abandon. It's only when we come to Calvary's cross that Almighty God will be able to open our spiritual eyes, which will allow us to understand the hidden mysteries of the power of Jesus's shed blood. When God reveals his divine power and the implication of Jesus's blood, it will become a reality and a living witness in every area of our lives, and it will change the very foundation of false doctrine and religion.

I decided to take an early retirement on the grounds of marriage because after five pregnancies and working full-time, I was drained. I had done everything humanly possible to build a safe home environment for my family, but unfortunately, my family didn't get enough of my time. Before I retired, however, I decided to take a trip to the Bahamas to attend a conference at Myles Monroe's church. I was really inspired when he remarked that many people had died without discovering their gifts. It was definitely a defining moment for me because I knew within myself that I was feeling depleted. Teaching is my life skill, but somehow I felt I was missing something, although I was not certain what it was. I returned home and, shortly afterward, quit my job without seeking counsel or advice from anyone. I realized afterward that I had not given enough notice.

While I was still working, I was always doing something to supplement my income to make adequate provision for the family. I would pick my kids up from school, get them settled at home, and then drive through the neighborhood selling household items. After I retired, I started producing healthy snacks at home and selling them to friends. I got the assumed name for the business, but after a while, for some strange reason, I was unable to locate the paperwork I needed to take the business to the next level. Around this time, I had purchased a book on deliverance and started reading it and showed it to my husband, but for some strange reason, it mysteriously disappeared also.

In the Bahamas, I had purchased a CD set on marriage because I was really trying to make my marriage work in my own way. Marriage counseling was not an option for husbands in those days, so I decided to bring the teaching home. My husband agreed to play the CDs on his stereo set, and we invited some married couples to come to our house once a week and listen to the teaching. However, since my husband wouldn't allow me to use his stereo set in his absence, we were not able to have our sessions, and after a while, the meetings came to an end. The married couples, however, did have enjoyable times together in fellowship for a season.

Since I was home and had extra time, I started the daily practice of walking around the perimeter of the house, pleading the blood of Jesus, and declaring, "There is only one Lord operating in this house, which is Jesus Christ, the Lord." I also met a family from another church, and we would gather together at their home and have times of intercession, since prayer was the only thing that kept me going. My now-deceased husband had special plants he had around the garage area, and he would faithfully keep them well watered. I really thought he loved his shrubbery. However, it was revealed by one of the intercessors that whatever he was doing involved his plants, which he would water daily.

After a lot of hard work, countless trips to the hardware store, waiting on the mason to show up, and everything that went along with erecting a structure, the extension to the house was completed. It was really a wonderful experience visiting the hardware store to select paint colors, matching doorknobs and handles, bathroom fixtures, and all the things that go along with interior decorations. We built a sliding door instead of using shower curtains for the tub in the master bedroom. In the master bedroom, we had selected a sliding glass door, and I was beginning to see beauty around me.

I remember the Pentecostal sister who had whispered to me about power in the blood of Jesus when I was sitting in front of the class, feeling dejected. Since then, I had been experimenting with the blood of Jesus to test it and to see if it works. I started using it in practical ways to prove the validity of it, especially as the hymn states, "There is power, power, wonder, working power in the blood of the Lamb." On the night I returned from my trip to the Bahamas, I made an astounding discovery. My husband had arrived to pick me up at the airport. However, after I went through the torment of customs and immigration and finally met him and the children, he informed me he had lost the car keys. Now looking for car keys at night, in the dark, at a busy airport with lots of people bustling around as multiple flights landed, was like looking for a needle in a haystack. I didn't know what to do, so I started pleading the blood of Jesus while at the same time wondering who we could ask where the lost and found was located. I saw a security guard approaching us, and just as I was about to ask him about the lost and found section, he outstretched his hand toward us. He had a set of keys in his hand and asked us if we knew to whom they belonged. I stared in disbelief as we recognized the keys; they belonged to us. We mouthed our words of gratitude, grabbed the keys, and made our way to the car.

The blood worked that time. I thought about another blood song, and that made me have more confidence in the power of Jesus's blood.

> The blood that Jesus shed for me
> Way back on Calvary
> Oh the blood that gives me strength
> From day to day, shall never lose its power
> It reaches the highest mountain
> And flows to the lowest valley

I had another opportunity to prove that the blood of Jesus works. After I took an early retirement from teaching, I decided to homeschool my last two children. Some friends and neighbors sent their children, and my new pastor even sent his daughter, whom I enjoyed teaching, since she needed personal attention. I started in the master bedroom of our home, and when the numbers increased, the children and I prayed for more space. It was really a faith walk, and during that time, I studied the book of Nehemiah. Our favorite scripture was taken from Nehemiah 2:20, "The God of heaven, he will prosper us; therefore we his servants will arise and build." At that time, homeschooling was a new phenomenon in my native country, and I was operating by faith. The number of children grew; my eldest daughter worked in the nursery, and a young lady who wanted to become a teacher and her sister came on board as teacher trainees. We had transitioned to another three-bedroom house a short distance away from my Christian school called Back to Basics Christian Academy.

Early morning, before school started, I would walk the land in the neighborhood for about twenty minutes. Interestingly, on occasion, I would hear some strange prayers come out of my mouth, and God would answer in unexpected ways. That morning, I prayed, "Lord, I want to be a woman of strong faith." The Lord heard my prayer and acted immediately. I closed the kitchen door and walked down the driveway. I pushed the sliding wrought iron gate to the left, allowing me just enough space to slide through. Our house was fenced on all sides, as was the custom of a lot of houses in our country. I walked down our street to the main street, and when I had crossed the road to an open expanse of land, I started picking up momentum. The fresh, crisp morning air made me feel as though the Holy Spirit was gently kissing my cheeks, and I felt like I was on cloud nine.

I didn't see anything in the pathway before me, but suddenly I heard a snarling sound. Fear gripped my heart as two ferocious animals suddenly appeared before me. One was on the left, and the other was strangely on the right; so it appeared they were coming from two different directions. I had never been bitten by a dog in my entire life and still haven't up to this day. I was terrified, especially because I didn't want to take my eyes off them, and I was unable to bend down to search for a stick or stone to ward them off. By this time, I was really shaking; we had no cell phone in those days for me to call anyone, so I knew I had to stand my ground. It never occurred to me to run; instead I started screaming at the top of my lungs, above their snarls, "The blood of Jesus! The blood of Jesus! The blood of Jesus!" I could see their lips skinned back, and the teeth were exposed. Their mouths were open as they lunged forward, getting ready for the kill, ready to sink their teeth into my flesh. I don't remember how many times I screamed those words, but I know I was screaming in desperation at the top of my lungs, with boldness, since I didn't know what else to do.

Suddenly and amazingly, in unison, both dogs stopped snarling, closed their mouths, and walked away. I was shaking in the midst of that secluded open field. I had screamed so long and powerfully strong that my voice was hoarse. I changed my mind about walking that morning, and I turned around and started back home. I kept looking over my shoulder for the dogs, but they had both disappeared as quickly as they had appeared. Years later, when I relocated to Texas, I had a similar experience as I was walking on the sidewalk. Suddenly, a dog emerged through a hole in a front fence and started barking at me. I thought to myself that the same God who had shut the dogs' mouths in Trinidad was with me right there in Texas, and I started pleading the blood of Jesus. The dog responded in the same way as the other dogs did in Trinidad. So my faith in the power of Jesus's blood started increasing.

I had a dream that a lady appeared to me and told me Psalm 18 belonged to me. Psalm 18:30 states, "As for God, His way is perfect: *the Word of The Lord is tried*: he is a buckler to all those that trust in Him." Also, it states in Romans 3:24–25, "Being justified freely by His grace through the redemption that is in Christ Jesus. Whom God has set forth to be propitiation *through faith in His Blood*, to declare His righteousness for the remission of sins." So I had heard about the power of the blood of Jesus, decided to try it to prove the validity of the Word, and discovered that pleading the blood of Jesus works.

I decided that since it worked outside my house, both in the airport and the open field, it was time to bring it home. I started to plead the blood over all the items that had mysteriously disappeared in the house. I would fast occasionally, and I realized that every time I fasted, I would get a breakthrough, as the Holy Spirit would open my eyes concerning matters happening at home. One of the issues revealed by the Holy Spirit of truth was that my husband wasn't making the mortgage payments, even though he had assured me he was doing so. I had supposed he would assume responsibility of paying the bills, but I realized he never thought I would suddenly decide it was his turn to be the provider for our family. We never had a healthy discussion about it or any other family issue because we never had marriage counseling. At this juncture, I strongly advocate marriage counseling for couples who are planning to get married.

I am not a nosy person by nature, but one day, I was suddenly drawn toward the places where my documents were located. I never thought of interfering with his music boxes, because it was taboo for both me and the children. One day, however, after he left for work, I decided to spy. I had never done anything like this before, so I was feeling guilty for interfering with his personal property. I had, however, made a decision and tried to shrug off the guilt. With fear and trepidation, I crept to the kitchen and got a knife and quickly peeped through the kitchen curtains to make certain he wasn't anywhere in sight. I really didn't want him to catch me in the very act of interfering with his musical equipment. I slid quickly into the living room and pulled one of his large music boxes aside and pried open the back of the box containing the speaker. There before my eyes lay one of my documents that had mysteriously disappeared. I couldn't believe my eyes; however, with trembling hands, I removed one of my missing documents and carefully replaced the back of the speaker box, in place and intact.

I started to walk toward the master bedroom to secure the missing document I had found. I was still trembling in disbelief at my discovery and then decided on my next plan of action. However, I sped quickly to peek though the kitchen curtains again to make sure he hadn't suddenly decided to return home. I wasn't sure if the spirit he was dealing with would warn him that I was on his personal territory. I thought for a while and remembered from previous experience the gun he had threatened me with when I first got married to him, before we had any children. It seemed a fog was being lifted off my mind, so I decided to go to the first bedroom and begin searching the ceiling panels. I stood on a chair and began lifting each square panel which measured about twelve inches on each side. I was pleading the blood of Jesus during this entire ordeal. I gently lifted the panel with my left hand and searched with my right hand. Finally, I was able to locate the book about deliverance and the documentation for my business called Manna Products, which had mysteriously disappeared.

I had to find a new hiding place for my documents, but I didn't tell him I had found them. My heart was trembling after that episode. I don't recall where my children were during this ordeal, but I didn't want them to hate their father; I kept some things away from them. There was one item I couldn't locate since I had returned from the Myles Munroe conference in Nassau. This was my local passport, which I had acquired while I was a teacher. I was able to obtain a business professional visitor's visa from the United States Embassy in our country. I had a steady job as a teacher and was able to produce documentation showing that I was a property owner, so I received the visa stamp on my passport that allowed me to visit the United States.

One day, I mustered up enough courage to ask my now-deceased husband if he knew where my passport could possibly be. His response was so unexpected, and I listened in disbelief as he hurled this statement in my direction: "I tore it up and put it in the trash." I felt like exploding; I probably did, but I can't remember. I asked him what trash bag he was referring to, and he told me he had put it in the black trash bag that had been sitting outside the house, waiting for the garbage collector. I remembered afterward that, for some strange reason, my eyes had been drawn to that black trash bag, but I didn't know why. I felt disgusted and frustrated because my passport had been destroyed. I would be able to get another passport, but there was no hope of me being able to get another United States visa. I felt so alone because no one seemed to understand my plight, and I had no visible proof I was being manipulated by the father of my five children. I was unable to trust the very one who shared the same bed with me, and I felt helpless and all alone.

One day, my now-deceased husband violently accused me of having a pharaoh spirit. I made no reply and smiled secretly to myself because the Holy Spirit had already told me he was operating with a pharaoh spirit. The book of Exodus, in chapters 6–11, in the Old Testament gives a detailed account of how Almighty God heard the cries of his chosen people, who were being oppressed in the land of Egypt by Pharaoh, the king. God had appeared to Moses in the wilderness, revealed himself as I Am That I Am, and gave

Moses his assignment to approach Pharaoh and admonish him to set God's people free from this hard bondage. God knew Pharaoh had no intention of releasing his chosen people, the Jews, and he hardened Pharaoh's heart so he would not let the Israelites go to serve Almighty God. My husband did not want to let me go, but God, who is righteous and holy in all his ways, had plans to completely deliver me, although I didn't know this.

CHAPTER 6

Introduction to the Prophetic Ministry

³ And Jehoshaphat feared, and set himself to seek the Lord,
And proclaimed a fast throughout all Judea.
⁴ And Judah gathered together to ask help of The Lord:
Even out of all the cities of Judah they came to seek the Lord.
⁵ And Jehoshaphat stood in the congregation of Judah and Jerusalem
In the house of the Lord

—(2 Chronicles 20:3-5)

This scripture has remain etched in my mind and will be until eternity, because it reminds me that those in authority over me, along with the highest authority in the whole earth, feel afraid at times. So, I can learn from King Jehoshaphat by seeking complete understanding revealed by God's Holy Spirit of truth. King Jehoshaphat was afraid and acknowledged this fact to himself and to God. He became confident that the only solution he had was to seek God and proclaim a fast throughout Judea. He realized the only solution to this seemingly impossible dilemma would be by means of the supernatural right hand of our majestic God. King Jehoshaphat led his people by example, and they all came to Jerusalem from all the cities of Judah to seek the Lord God Almighty, because they were fully persuaded that somehow God would intervene and help them in their plight. I pray our heavenly Father will give us a heart to seek him daily with reckless abandon.

There was a prophet called Jefferson Edwards who would come from Kansas City to do three-day revival meetings at one of the other Christian churches in Trinidad. He was actually the pastor of the missionary who taught us in ministry class; she was an intense worshipper. She taught us the prophetic song from Exodus 15. Pastor Jefferson Edwards is the one who made us aware that the Holy Spirit is a gentleman and won't invade the privacy of our bedroom unless we allow him. However, he also informed us the Holy Spirit would be willing to help married couples in their bedroom affairs. That was really a new way of looking at our sexual intimacy with our partner, because God was the one who created the male and female species anyway. I also remember him saying that God made Adam and Eve, not Adam and Steve, partners. That was way back in the 1980s. He also made reference to the bride of Christ, and coupling that with the revelation I had, I started to call myself Mrs. Jesus Christ. I know the theologians would correct me and say Christ was not Jesus's surname, because the name Christ means the "anointed one." However, I felt a sense of intimacy when I thought of myself as Mrs. Jesus Christ.

He had also preached about the kingdom of God. It was nighttime, and I was sleepy; I don't remember a lot of what he said. However, after his prophetic teaching on the kingdom of God, I remember this nugget because he repeatedly declared it every night of the conference. These are the words he declared, which I use when I make kingdom declarations: "The kingdom of God has come; the reign of God, the rule of God, the power of God, the authority of God, let it be poured out." I believe it was the same pastor who introduced me to the scripture from Revelation 11:15, "The kingdoms of this world are become the kingdoms of Our Lord, and of His Christ; and he shall reign for ever and ever." It was revealed by the Holy Spirit of absolute truth that there were various empires set up by man, but the kingdom of Jesus alone would stand. Pastor Baird had also taken us to Daniel 2 and had painstakingly outlined the downfalls of the different kingdoms from a historical perspective. I confess that I wasn't attentive at that time, but since then, the Holy Spirit of truth has been educating me through the book of Daniel. At that time, the words of this song were added to my spiritual artillery.

Hail, Jesus, you're my King, your life leads me to sing.
Hail, Jesus, you're my Lord, I will obey your Word.
I want to see thy kingdom come, not my will but yours be done.
Glory, glory to the lamb, he'll take us into the land.
And we will conquer in his name and proclaim that Jesus reigns!
Hail! Hail! Lion of Judah! How wonderful you are!
Hail! Hail! Lion of Judah! How powerful you are!

Then around that time, another prophet, named Morris Cerullo, came to Trinidad and started having monthly Saturday morning satellite productions; he was the one who introduced us to the above scripture. This scripture shed a new light on some things, and it was interesting to read Jehoshaphat's story and allow the Holy Spirit to reveal how I could glean the scriptural principles and apply them to my life. *Jehoshaphat*, the king, received bad news; there were three sets of people gathering to come against Judah. I had been warned by Almighty God about three individuals who had been coming against me in manipulative, deceptive ways. I was innocent and naive because I was not raised with the awareness that people did evil things to one another. I was being manipulated and deceived by a spirit of witchcraft. The amazing thing was that I didn't hear it from anyone, but my heavenly Father thought it fit to alert me through dreams; for this, I will be eternally grateful, and that's why I believe I have a responsibility to pray for unsuspecting victims so that God will also alert them in whatever way he sees fit, because he is righteous in all his ways.

Jehoshaphat was honest with himself and acknowledged that he was afraid; even though he was king, he realized he did not have the ability to fight this battle on his own. He wasn't afraid to acknowledge that to the people of Judah, who were looking to him to make the right decisions. He decided to proclaim a fast throughout Judah. Everyone came from all the cities and gathered in the house of the Lord to seek God's help. Jehoshaphat stood in the presence of all the people and addressed God in this manner, and I've used this prayer format many times since: "O Lord God of our fathers, art not thou God in heaven? And rulest not thou over all the kingdoms of the heathen? In thine hand is there not power and might, so that none is able to withstand thee?"

In verse 6, we see King Jehoshaphat standing in full view of the people and addressing Almighty God, the Creator of the heavens and earth, by asking certain questions. I believe there was a reason he was asking God these questions about him. He wanted to reassure himself and all those within his hearing that our living God was in heaven ruling over all the kingdoms of the heathens. He also wanted to refresh his memory that Almighty God had all power in his hand and that no one could withstand him. Whenever I would have difficult situations confronting me, I would meditate on this scripture, and I would be filled with such confidence that I could trust God, especially when I read in that same chapter that God heard the king's prayer. The king also reminded God of his previous track record, how he had led their forefathers to the Promised Land, which they had inhabited and where they built God a sanctuary.

King Jehoshaphat was appealing to God in that very sanctuary, and he reminded God of what he had said in 2 Chronicles 20:9, "If when evil comes upon us as the sword, judgment or pestilence, or famine, we stand before this house, and in your presence, (for your name is in this house), and cry unto you in our affliction, then you will hear and help." Almighty God heard King Jehoshaphat's cry, which he poured out in the presence of all the men of Judah, who had their wives and children with them. The king confessed to God that they didn't know what to do, but their eyes were fixed on him. Almighty God heard the appeal and sent his prophetic answer through the voice of one of the Levites. Omniscient, all-knowing God assured them they shouldn't be afraid because it was his battle, and he was going to fight on their behalf since the enemy was too strong for them. He further informed them about the enemy's whereabouts and gave such specific details regarding their location and the direction they were coming from. He also instructed them what specific day they should go out to confront the enemy. This was how everyone responded after that prophetic Word, even before the battle was won: "And Jehoshaphat bowed his head with his face to the ground: and all Judah and the inhabitants of Jerusalem fell before the Lord worshipping the Lord."

Almighty God is looking for true worshippers, people who will worship him in spirit and in truth with hearts of gratitude, simply trusting him for his promises. After worshipping God with their faces bowed to the ground, according to verse 19, "they stood up to praise the Lord God of Israel with a loud voice on high." That's how I learned to worship God first and then, when he reveals the answer, praise him in advance. The story continued that they rose early in the morning and went out, just as the Lord had instructed them. King Jehoshaphat encouraged them with these words in verse 20: "Believe in the Lord your God, so shall you be established; believe His prophets so shall you prosper." He wanted the people to believe in the power of God firstly and trust in his ability to deliver them from the hands of their enemies, so that they could be established in their faith toward God Almighty. Secondly, he reminded them that if their focus was on the power of God, he would utter a prophetic word through his prophets and cause them to prosper.

We then see King Jehoshaphat's strategy in verse 21: "And when he had consulted with the people, he appointed singers unto the Lord, and that should praise the beauty of holiness, as they went out before the army, and to say, 'Praise the Lord for His mercy endures forever.'" When I heard what happened after they began to sing to the Lord in obedience to the king's decree, I asked the Lord to give me a tune to go along with those words they uttered, and I truly believed that every time I sang those prophetic words, "Praise the Lord, for his mercy endures forever," Almighty God would send reinforcements not only to surround but to protect me. I am extremely happy the Holy Spirit gave me a prophetic song based on verse 21.

This is the strategy used by the king's army when they confronted the enemy. They placed the singers in the front line and went out to battle against the enemy early in the morning. The results of the prophetic praise are recorded in verse 22, "And when they began to sing and to praise, the Lord set ambushments against the children of Ammon, Moab, and Mount Seir, which were come against Judah, and they were smitten." So Almighty God really fought their battle for them in an unexpected way, and they won the battle against their enemy, who all fled in fear, leaving everything behind.

I also remember that I had a next-door neighbor who attended the same church. She is now deceased, but we would awake early before sending our children off to school and intercede for people in different nations. I can't remember the day I found Psalm146:9, "The Lord preserves the strangers; he relieves the fatherless and widow: *but the way of the wicked he turns upside down.*" I believe my eyes almost jumped out of their sockets when I first read that Scripture. I stared in amazement as I meditated on those words and concentrated on them and repeated them. I felt such assurance that God was on my side, especially as God had revealed to me the enemy that had been plotting against me on countless occasions. Almighty God, Creator of the universe, had been divinely protecting me, and I felt a sense of security.

CHAPTER 7

Witnessing Spiritual Deliverance

For there are three that bear record in heaven,
The Father, the Word and the Holy Ghost:
And there three are one.
And there are three that bear witness in earth,
The Spirit and the water and the blood:
And these three agree in one.

—1 John 5:7–8

I had spent an entire Friday night in prayer, seeking God, and the next morning, I visited the home of one of the intercessors who lived in my neighborhood. We were in my friend's prayer room, and the three of us felt the gentle tug of the Holy Spirit and decided to answer the call to enter the presence of God. Songs of high praise and adoration were lifted before the King of kings. In obedience to the Holy Spirit, I prostrated myself before him in worship, with my face bowed to the ground. It was in the midst of the praises and intense worship that Almighty God, in his goodness, opened my spiritual eyes so I could behold heavenly visions in the process of deliverance. This was a teaching session for me, because as each vision appeared, it was the Holy Spirit who taught me how to pray and for how long to intercede. The precious Holy Spirit really helped me throughout the series of intercessions, not only with words but also with moaning and groaning in the sound of intercession. I was like a pregnant woman in travail, giving birth. There was a lot of crying, and many tears were shed in the labor room that day. I wept even more when I saw the final outcome of the process of intercession.

In the first vision, I witnessed a scene of people waist-deep in a sea of what appeared to be sinking sand. They were in this sea of muddy, murky, grimy slush, and they were not able to come out. Immediately, the burden of compassion from the Lord came upon me, and the spirit of intercession from God's holy throne caught hold of me. I knew I was on assignment from the Most High. I knew God was expecting me to pray until I got results. Although at that time I didn't know what the outcome would be, I released myself as a channel to be used by God. The Holy Spirit brought this scripture to my remembrance: "And they overcame him by the Blood of the lamb, and by the word of their testimony; and loved not their lives unto the death" (Revelation 12:11). So I started to scream "The blood of Jesus!" repeatedly, with boldness, power, and authority, because I had proved the blood many times before. It was like driving a nail into a piece of wood with all the strength I could muster.

I was not aware of the passing of time, but I continued pouring out the blood of Jesus until I saw that one person was able to get out of the miry clay. I didn't see how the person was able to get out, but in the vision, I suddenly saw the figure standing on the bank of quicksand. That day, I had a deeper revelation: wherever the blood of Jesus is applied with power, boldness, faith, authority, and persistence, deliverance will be the ultimate and only result. The miry clay represented any situation, snare, trap, or wicked device of the evil one that you may be trying to be delivered from. You may have been trying to get out but to no avail, and with every attempt you made to escape, it seemed you fell in deeper. Others may have given up on you and dumped you as hopeless, and you may even have given up on yourself. However, God hasn't given up on you. He sent Jesus to die for your freedom.

The next words that were impressed upon my spirit to pray were "A thorough purging without and within!" As before, I poured out this petition in rapid succession, especially since I was excited the person had come out of the quicksand. After a while, I saw a vision of a hand holding a water hose, which was aimed directly at the human form. I beheld a washing taking place on the outer man, as pure, clean water was flowing down his waist, meeting the slush, and washing it away. I saw the clean water flowing down to the knees and all the way down to the legs and feet until the outer form had been cleansed. I really didn't comprehend what was happening then, but in retrospect, I understand what was happening because of Ephesians 5:22–27.

> Christ is the head of the church and He is the Savior of the body . . . Christ also loved the church and gave Himself for it; that He might sanctify and cleanse it with the washing of water by the word, that He might present it to Himself a glorious church, not having spot or wrinkle, or any such thing; but that it should be holy and without blemish.

God is so amazing because, at that time, I was praying what I heard in the spirit and recording what I was seeing in the midst of the praise and worship that was surrounding me in the room. I was not even aware what the other two sisters were doing, because I was bowed, with my face to the ground. As I continued pleading 'a thorough purging without and within' from the depths of my soul, another vision flashed before me. I suddenly saw the human form bent over, and a hand began to pat the human form on the small of his back. The amazing thing was that as the hand patted, the human form began to vomit. I realized that what was happening before my eyes was the reality of the human form being thoroughly purged from within. While the human form was vomiting, I saw the appearance of a frog over his head, and I sensed in the spirit that the person was being delivered from demonic forces.

The Holy Spirit then brought to my remembrance that blood and water gushed from his side, and immediately, I started pleading the blood of Jesus again. Afterward, I looked for the reference to this verse, and it's recorded in John 19:33–34.

> But when they came to Jesus and saw that He was already dead, they broke not his feet: but one of the soldiers with a spear pierced His side and forthwith there came out blood and water.

I see now that the thorough purging of the inner man by the power of the blood would be releasing from the inner man all secret sin, including all evil thoughts, like anger, unforgiveness, bitterness, hatred, pride, jealousy, malice, greed, doubts, and fears; all manner of uncleanness; and every negative emotion that has the ability to pollute the human spirit. When we are convicted by God's Holy Spirit and decide we really want to be free from anything and everything that could contaminate our spirit, we can cry out to God like David did in Psalm 51:4–7.

> Against thee, thee only have I sinned and done this evil in thy sight. . . . behold I was shapen in iniquity and in sin did my mother conceive me. Behold thou desirest truth in the inward parts: and in the hidden part thou shall make me to know wisdom. . . . Purge me with hyssop and I shall be clean; wash me and I shall be whiter than snow.

Like David, if we are convicted and take responsibility for our actions and pour out our souls before Almighty God, he will definitely send his precious Holy Spirit to help us.

Almighty God, omniscient God, knows when we have a truly repentant heart, because the Bible tells us he searches our hearts. It was and still is truly amazing. The Holy Spirit was teaching me how to pray specifically, and as I surrendered and interceded, it was actually Almighty God who was doing the work in the spiritual realm in his mysterious way. The following words were then impressed upon my spirit: "Destroy the works of the flesh." In a flash, without any hesitation, I immediately started praying repeatedly for the destruction of the works of the flesh. After a while, I saw the entire figure of the person being set on fire. I was looking in amazement at this strange phenomenon, and then I became aware of the fact that my spiritual sense of smell had been awakened. There was an awful stench coming from the spirit of flesh being burned. While the flesh was being burned, I noticed another figure had appeared on the scene. This figure was seated on a throne and turned away, as the awful stench of the sin was offensive. I did not see the face of the figure on the throne, but immediately I started pleading the blood of Jesus again, like torrential rain, because I knew this was the only thing that would appease God, who is holy.

I continued to intercede. After a while, I realized the person who had been previously on fire was dead, and the limp form was being carried by another figure. This other figure was climbing some steps, about five or six, toward a throne. I did not see the face of the person seated on the throne, but I started praying for "a new birth unto righteousness" over and over, as the Holy Spirit gave me utterance. After a while, the man who had been previously dead was standing on his feet. Then I noticed a robe was being placed on his shoulders. The robe resembled a cape, but somehow I knew it was a robe that signified righteousness. The person's hand was now stretched forth, and I noticed a ring was being placed on his finger. After the person had received the new garment and ring, he turned and stepped down the stairs. I waited to see what would happen next, and when I saw what happened, it caused me to burst into tears, as I had just witnessed the marvelous, outstanding work of a mighty and merciful God.

I was in floods of tears and trembling in awe as I saw the individual walking down the steps. Then I saw him beckoning to a group of children who had suddenly appeared on the scene. I couldn't hear what he was saying, but apparently, he was telling them about the great and mighty deliverance that had been wrought for him by the hands of a mighty and powerful God. That day, I really understood the great significance of effectual fervent prayer led by the Holy Spirit. I was weeping and saying to myself, "My God, you are the only one who can take filth and garbage, clean it up, and then use it for your honor and glory." I then heard a voice in the spirit saying, "Many are in the valley of decision." The spirit of intercession took hold of me once again, and I started to cry out for intercessors to awake and begin crying out to God for souls to be delivered. Dear friend, my prayer is that when your deliverance is complete, in the fullness of time, you will be willing to lay your life down in prayer and fasting to deliver more souls out of the devil's clutches, knowing by faith that, beyond the shadow of a doubt, the blood of Jesus works. I'm not certain if it was before or after this series of events, but I heard myself actually praying, "God, I want to be a blood specialist!"

Chapter 8

Jesus, King of Kings
and Lord of Lords

When the Philistines took the ark of God,
they brought it into the house of Dagon, and set it by Dagon.
And when the people of Ashdod arose early in the morning,
There was Dagon fallen on its face to the earth
Before the ark of the Lord.
—1 Samuel 5:2–3 NKJV

This account of the awesome power and presence of Almighty God always has me spellbound, for want of a better expression, and I think to myself that I will always want to be on the Lord's side. God always give us a choice between choosing his way and doing good with the intent of pleasing him, or choosing the devil's way of doing evil with the intent of pleasing the devil. However, there are always consequences for whatever choices we make, because we always reap what we sow: according to the amount we sow, we will certainly reap. We can either reap the benefits of doing things God's way or face the consequences of doing things the devil's way. However, God knows whenever we make choices in ignorance, and the fullness of his tender love, grace, and compassion are expressed through the open arms of Calvary's cross.

We know as a fact from the New Testament that, in accordance with John 4:34, "God is a spirit and they that worship Him must worship Him in spirit and in truth." Your shadow is visible, but it is not really you. In the same way, everything in the Old Testament was a shadow of the reality of God's spiritual truths, which he planned to reveal in Christ in the fullness of his time. The Ark of the Covenant of the Old Testament was a symbolic representation of the power and presence of our majestic God. The Israelites had been defeated by the Philistines in the first round of battle, and they decided to carry the Ark of the Covenant into the second round of battle with them. Sadly, because of the disorderly sexual conduct of the sons of Eli the priest, Israel lost the battle against the Philistines, who captured the ark and placed it in the temple of their idol god, Dagon.

We can see from this account that the Philistines assumed they were powerful because they had captured the Israelites' God. In those days, and even today, people made all types of images from God's original creation—man, creatures from the earth and sea, and the heavenly bodies. They gave them names and made them their gods. They had decided to add the Israelites' God to their god. I would imagine they had been thinking, *The more, the merrier*, or *More gods, more power*. They felt good about their recent exploits and their latest conquest and went to sleep.

The morning after is an interesting phenomenon. Something always happens the following day. The sequence of events is always predicated on what we did the previous day. The Philistines awoke early and were in for a rude awakening because "Dagon was fallen on its face to the earth before the ark of the Lord." As I'm reading this again for the umpteenth time, I think it's rather funny—not that God was being funny, but the fact that they didn't realize what had happened to Dagon was funny. It is explicit in the book of wisdom, in Proverbs 14:19, "The evil bow before the good; and the wicked at the gates of the righteous." You and I know the evil god Dagon had to bow, with its face to the ground, before the Ark of the Covenant of the Lord of the whole earth. Keep in mind, the Ark was just a shadow of the real manifestation of the power and presence of our God.

Maybe the Philistines thought the wind had blown the god facedown. They didn't know what had moved their god from its original place. So what did they do? "So they took Dagon and set it in its place again. And when they arose early the next morning, there was Dagon, fallen on its face to the ground, before the ark of the Lord." The Bible doesn't tell us if they included any ritual with their action, but there must have been some sort of interaction among them to cause them to agree to pick Dagon up and put him back in his place. I'm trying to stretch my imagination here, thinking of the god that I serve falling down and little old me having to use my hands to pick him up and put him back in place. It is so absurd, and that's why this scenario is funny to me. The God I serve fights my battles for me. He is the one who picks me up when I fall and sets me in the right place where he wants me.

The next scene made me know that when I am walking through the dark hours of despair, there is hope for tomorrow. The Philistines performed their ritual to Dagon and went to sleep again. And this is what happened the second morning after the capture of the Ark of the Covenant:

> And when they arose early the next morning, there was Dagon, fallen on its face to the ground before the ark of the Lord. The head of Dagon and both the palms of its hands were broken off on the threshold; only Dagon's torso was left of it. (1 Samuel 5:4 NKJV)

I don't recall the first time I read about this incident, but I knew it was not by accident. This story has become imprinted in my spirit, as I remember it a lot, but every time I read it, the Holy Spirit of truth opens my spiritual eyes more and more. We see that Dagon had a head, but he couldn't think; his head was cut off. The head signifies authority, but Dagon's head was cut off because Almighty God was showing that this idol had no authority. Dagon's face was on his head. Dagon had eyes, but he couldn't see. He had ears but couldn't hear; he had a mouth but couldn't speak. In fact, according to *Webster's New*

World Dictionary, the head is described as "the seat of reason, memory and imagination; mind and intelligence." Additionally, "the palms of its hands were broken off." Every plan man has that's contrary to the will of God will be broken. Now I can sit back in my chair and smile, but I wasn't smiling then.

I was on the run from the evil that was operating in the house the Lord had blessed me with. It was frustrating because I really didn't know what else to do; people would listen, but no one seemed to understand my plight. It's impossible to prove the manifestation of evil without visible proof. Somehow I didn't feel safe in that house and was allowed to stay in the same neighborhood, in a house owned by the church. God even sent to the house a young lady who I had met years previously in the country church where I had become born again. She was sick, and the Holy Spirit allowed me to pray with her and mother her to the restoring of her soul. Even though I felt my life was torn in pieces, I knew beyond the shadow of a doubt that God loved me, and I reciprocated his love, especially as he was the only one I could really trust. He had proven himself faithful more times than I can remember, but I had decided to flee.

I was functioning but had begun to get weary in my soul. My now-deceased husband and I were not in agreement, and even though I was the one who had sacrificed to purchase a home after he had physically abused me and left me, I decided my life was worth more than a piece of property. We had been married for about twenty years at that time, but the Christian attorney convinced me I had no grounds for a divorce. No one seemed to understand that there were wicked spirits in operation in my home. I decided to sell the house and assured my husband he would receive half of the sale price after the mortgage was paid off. People started coming to view the house, but before they came, he would do things to the appearance of the house to devalue it. I don't recollect at this point exactly what he was doing at this time, because I was in a state of turmoil. I knew I couldn't give him and the evil spiritual influence the satisfaction of seeing me lose my mind, especially as I had come to the brink once before. I knew God was sustaining me, and his mighty hand was upon me. I didn't know what would happen next, but Almighty God has a time and season for everything.

I didn't know that night that I would lay my head on my pillow and experience such a life-changing dream that *put the icing on the cake* of all my previous deliverances mixed together, as this was the culmination of God's hand of deliverance for me. I thank God that in the midst of all the turmoil, I never had sleepless night. I didn't plan to dream that night, especially as my dreams are not frequent, but when they occur, they are meaningful. So I went to bed as usual with a feeling of comfort. After that dream, if I ever had any vestige of doubt about the power of God, who fights our battles, it immediately dissipated. After all these years, every time I visit that dream, I am amazed, because the revelation of that dream manifested about two weeks later.

In the dream, not only did God know the physical address of where I was located, because he was the one who opened the door for me to gain entrance to that house, but he also knew the physical address of the property I owned, as the deed of ownership bore my name. I dreamed I was in the living room of the house I had purchased. I looked up and saw an entity sitting across the room from me. The entity was sitting with its hands and legs crossed, but its eyes were fixed on me. My eyes were fixed on the entity also. I was afraid, but for some reason, I did not shift my gaze. It was eye to eye contact, as neither of us wanted to give in. No words were spoken, and I realized it was a spiritual battle. I did not know what to do, but I am so glad for the Holy Spirit of truth, who brings things to our remembrance. Revelation 12:11 came to mind: "And they overcame him by the Blood of the Lamb and by the Word of their testimony." My spirit immediately started the fight within by pleading, "The blood of Jesus! The blood of Jesus!" I had proven that the blood works on many occasions before, and I used the only real weapon I had to help me overcome this strange entity.

The entity began to levitate slowly from ground level and began moving upward. My eyes were fixed, sinking into his eyes, and I continued repeatedly pleading, "The blood of Jesus! The blood of

Jesus!" To my amazement, as the entity continued its upward rise, it changed midair into my now-deceased husband. The Holy Spirit of truth allowed me to see with my spiritual eyes what spiritual entity was controlling his operations. I was motionless but continued pleading with the blood of Jesus as the Holy Spirit helped me overcome that entity. My faith level was rising and continued to rise as I was pleading the blood of Jesus. The entity, my now-deceased husband, continued his ascent until he disappeared through the ceiling. I didn't know where he went, but somehow I felt empowered because I had used the blood of Jesus to conquer my foe.

I awoke in utter amazement, not knowing how to interpret that dream. However, I knew something unexplainable had happened that night in my house, which the Lord had blessed me with while I was on the run and sleeping in that other house. I continued living and never tried to do any research or find an interpreter for my dream. I was just satisfied I had proven the power of the blood of Jesus one more time, and I would continue running to Jesus for the rest of my life for every spiritual battle I had to fight. God himself interpreted the dream for me when I heard my first husband had packed up and left the house I had tried to sell and couldn't.

I don't remember who told me the news; it must have been one of my children. I ran to the house. The garage was empty! He never drove the car but cleaned and polished it weekly. He had never used it to go to work or to take the children to school or for a family drive. The idol was gone. His deceased mother had bought it for him, and he promised to take her to the doctor but never did. The garage looked so strange because I had grown accustomed to the car being parked there for all these years. That had been one of the things that had bothered me, because when I bought the house, my father had built the garage. Somehow the man I was married to had overpowered me, and my car had to sustain the winds and the rain while his car slept peacefully in the garage. I turned to my right, and I gazed in disbelief at the now-empty front porch! The wrought iron chairs were no longer there, but evidence had been left behind.

The cemented rings were still rooted in place, as each chair had been chained and padlocked to the rings.

I entered the house and stood in utter amazement in the living room, where the spiritual battle had been fought in my dream a couple of weeks before. I looked for his deceased mother's dining table and chairs, but they were all gone. All that remained were the marks of the living room furniture where they had been stationed; I somehow hadn't been allowed to rearrange them in the house I had sweated for and purchased with my own hands. I continued looking around, and even though I had fought the battle, it was a shock to see all his music boxes gone. He had really left the house, with all his personal belongings and everything he had forcefully taken from his mother.

I didn't try to figure out where he had gone. I wasn't certain when he had left, but I kept rehearsing that dream. I realized the influence of the entity he had surrendered his will to was no match for the power of the blood of Jesus. I remember the times I would walk around the house, making these kingdom declarations: "Jesus Christ is Lord in this house! We desire no other god but Jesus! Jesus is the King of kings and the Lord of lords!" Now Almighty God had caused that entity to bow to the Christ within me. He had purged the house from within, and that evil spirit could no longer dwell in the house. No more control! No more abuse! No more manipulation, as God was in control! I remember the times I had declared God's holy Word in the neighborhood in the house where I had set up my homeschool.

Not only did the Holy Spirit of truth reveal the source of the entity that was troubling me, but he trusted me with trouble, knowing that eventually, according to Proverbs 14:19, "the evil bow before the good; and the wicked at the gates of the righteous." Let me paint a picture of myself from the family album, the Bible, where I found myself and am still in the process of rediscovering the new me.

For the Lord has called you as a woman forsaken and grieved in spirit, like a youthful wife when you were refused. (Isaiah 54:6)

The majestic heavenly Creator had his eyes on me and was calling me to him. He knew I was grieved in my spirit in such an intimate way that I could approach him "with groanings which cannot be uttered." Furthermore, when I looked in the mirror of God's holy Word, I realized there was a semblance of his reflection in me, as I was beginning to look like him.

He is despised and rejected by men, a man of sorrows and acquainted with grief. And we hid as it were our faces from Him. (Isaiah 53:3)

When I saw the picture of Jesus painted by the Maestro of creation, inspired by the Holy Spirit, in the hands of Isaiah the prophet, whose name means "God's salvation" and who was born 765 BC, I was flabbergasted that my Creator had already chosen the broken pieces of my life and had already skillfully connected my pieces together to look like his Son. He had called me and chosen me to become like Jesus and tell his story so others could see their images in the family album also. In this era, people are born with a natural body and are free to change their images through plastic surgery with tummy tucks and other body parts. But God had spent years changing me from the inside out to become a reflection of his glory.

I didn't realize it then, but as I look back over the years and attempt to make sense of all my broken pieces and broken places, even when I broke his Ten Commandments, I can see the plan of our majestic God being fulfilled. I understand now that there was a purpose for every test, and I am so glad I was taught when I was born again that trials and tribulations were an integral part of the package deal. I will be eternally grateful to the Holy Spirit of truth, who led me to the right churches, places, and instructors. I will forever be dependent on him, as I need him to guide me to all truth.

He's still teaching me daily how to "pray effectual fervent prayers" (James 5:16) for my soul and all the souls he's entrusted to my care. I am still amazed at how almighty, omniscient God broke through my intellect and spoke to me through dreams and, at other times, gave me precise scriptures to give me understanding and to reveal his will and what he wanted me to do.

It was all about walking before him in perfect obedience, which I confess I haven't always done. At the times I went astray from his Word and will, he didn't try to stop me, but he allowed me to go my own way and knew the precise time I would come to my senses and acknowledge to him that I had taken the wrong path. In the midst of my shame and guilt, I would always go back to Calvary's cross, where I first saw the light. As I journeyed through my process of emotional healing and deliverance, he patiently waited for me to learn the lesson he was trying to teach me. At times, I was a slow spiritual learner, and I remember the senior saint God had dispatched from her comfort zone in Canada and returned to that country church in my native land where I was baptized and born again that Easter / Resurrection Day. The Holy Spirit had been using her to guide me through the rough seasons of my first marriage. I don't remember exactly what godly principle she was trying to impart to me, but I remember her telling me her dream. She said she had decided she was about to give up on me because I appeared to be stubborn, but the Master appeared to her in a dream and said in a stern voice, "Go back and get her!" Almighty God knew me and the fact that I would eventually get the revelation of what he wanted to do in me, for me, with me, and ultimately, through me.

God knew me and waited for me so patiently until I came to my senses every time to surrender to his will. His amazing love floods my soul in such a refreshing way, and consequently, I believe the Holy Spirit taught me to pray. "Lord, if someone has failed ninety-nine times, let me be the one to help pick them up that hundredth time." So if you are that one who has tried to serve the Lord but just keeps falling, I invite you to journey with him through the stages of grace until you are strengthened enough to keep from falling and are able to help a weak one stand. Please meditate with me on the words of one more foundational hymn.

Let the Lower Lights Be Burning

Brightly beams our Father's mercy
From his lighthouse evermore
But to us he gives the keeping
Of the lights along the shore

(Chorus)
Let the lower lights be burning, send a gleam across the waves
Some poor fainting struggling seaman,
you may rescue, you may save

In the last two stanzas, our awareness is heightened as sin is described as a dark night that has settled. Those trapped in the tidal waves of sin are waiting longingly for some light to penetrate their darkened souls. The writer is encouraging us to let the loving light of Jesus shine from within our hearts to allow someone who may be struggling in the midst of life's turbulent winds to see this lifeline of hope. I offer you Jesus, the Light of the World, who is willing to penetrate the darkness in and around you if you allow him to. May the supernatural power of his love, the shed blood of Calvary, and the fire of his Holy Spirit deliver you and your family and nation from the spirit of witchcraft in the same way he delivered me, because God is no respecter of persons. Somewhere along the way, when I discovered the depth of God's loving-kindness and mercy, I heard myself pray, "Father, if someone falls prey to sin ninety-nine times, let me be the one who would help pick that person up for the hundredth time." Others may give up on us; we may even give up on ourselves due to the consequences of our wrong choices. But God, our heavenly Father, Creator of the universe, is the King of nations and never gives up on us. He sent Jesus to earth to die on Calvary's cross to make a way of escape from sin by shedding his blood for people in every nation of the whole earth.

> And if it seem evil unto you to serve the Lord, Choose you this day whom you will serve; Whether the gods which your fathers served, That were on the other side of the flood, Or the gods of the Amorites, in whose land you dwell: But as for me and my house, we will serve the Lord. And the people answered and said, God forbid that we should forsake the Lord to serve other gods. (Joshua 24:15–16)

Our heavenly Father is still speaking through the book of Joshua, because he is a God who is alive; he speaks to all generations in every nation. Joshua was giving the Israelites an opportunity to choose between the living God of their forefathers or the gods of the heathen nations. Joshua had made a decision that he and his household would serve the one and only true and living God. The people responded unanimously that the only correct thing to do was to serve Almighty God. I made a decision to serve the Lord God Almighty. When I received news many years later that father of my children had passed away, I felt sad. I don't know what transpired during the remainder of the years God allowed him to spend on planet Earth. I will not allow this story to end with hearsay, because all I attempted to do was give an honest report to the best of my ability of how God delivered me from being manipulated.

Upon her father's death, one of my daughters asked me if I had forgiven her father, and I replied that I truly have. However, I would like to add that, after years of deliberation in the awesome presence of our majestic God, I have a responsibility to declare right from wrong. My heavenly Father has since given me a burden and heart of compassion for men from all walks of life and all strata of society. I have come to the realization that so many of our men have lost their way in life, just like my deceased husband. So many men were raised in homes without fathers and, consequently, are void of understanding about how they should behave as husbands and fathers. Even some married men don't understand the importance and significance of the marriage vow and do not recognize the sanctity of the marriage bed. Some of our men were never exposed to the Holy Bible and the school of Proverbs 6:32 (KJV), "But whoso committeth adultery with a woman lacketh understanding: he that doeth it destroyeth his own soul." I believe that if every single mother could rehearse the Ten Commandments to her children constantly, we would see a new breed of the next generation emerging with a high standard of morality. I believe that if every free woman really understands the profound truth of this statement, we would lift high the banner of integrity and cry out to God, asking him to restore our men to their rightful places in our society. We the mourning women are not trying to blame anyone; we are just crying out to our majestic God to give birth to a new generation of God-fearing men and women in Jesus's name.

Please email me your praise reports if this book has been a blessing to you in any way, or you may send your prayer requests or requests for additional copies to thebirthingplaceministriesint@yahoo.com.

You can also send your praise reports, prayer requests, or requests for additional copies of this book to the following address:

The Birthing Place International
PO Box 24295
Fort Worth, Texas
USA